D1570897

New Approaches to Religion and Power

Series editor
Joerg Rieger
Vanderbilt University Divinity School
Nashville
TN, USA

While the relationship of religion and power is a perennial topic, it only continues to grow in importance and scope in our increasingly globalized and diverse world. Religion, on a global scale, has openly joined power struggles, often in support of the powers that be. But at the same time, religion has made major contributions to resistance movements. In this context, current methods in the study of religion and theology have created a deeper awareness of the issue of power: Critical theory, cultural studies, postcolonial theory, subaltern studies, feminist theory, critical race theory, and working class studies are contributing to a new quality of study in the field. This series is a place for both studies of particular problems in the relation of religion and power as well as for more general interpretations of this relation. It undergirds the growing recognition that religion can no longer be studied without the study of power.

More information about this series at
http://www.springer.com/series/14754

Teresa Delgado

A Puerto Rican Decolonial Theology

Prophesy Freedom

Teresa Delgado
Iona College
New Rochelle, NY, USA

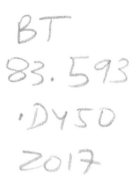

New Approaches to Religion and Power
ISBN 978-3-319-66067-7   ISBN 978-3-319-66068-4   (eBook)
DOI 10.1007/978-3-319-66068-4

Library of Congress Control Number: 2017950716

Cover credit: pictorico/Getty Images

Printed on acid-free paper

This Palgrave Macmillan imprint is published by Springer Nature
The registered company is Springer International Publishing AG
The registered company address is: Gewerbestrasse 11, 6330 Cham, Switzerland

To all Boricuas
—from every time and every place—
who, in one way or another, have inspired me by living into freedom regard-
less of political status or personal circumstances, standing with beauty and
grace when the world has said we are nothing more than colonial subjects.
This book is my love letter to you.

FOREWORD

PUERTO RICAN BACKPACKS AND LIVING ROOM DREAMS...

To be Puerto Rican is to carry a backpack. A backpack filled with your language, food, family, cuatro y timbal. A backpack held together by the flag whose cloth was woven with the memories of your ancestors: abuelas, abuelos, santeros, espiritistas, hijos, e hijas. When you open this bag the sounds of bomba, salsa, y reggaetón fill the space around it. And as you reach into the bag your hands stretch through decades of resistance and resilience. In this backpack lays the power to inspire, love, fight, and be connected to something beyond yourself. We, Puerto Ricans, carry this backpack wherever we go: from the beaches in Luquillo to la plaza en Havana to Young Lords Way in El Barrio, New York. Yet for years many have tried to take this backpack from us. Many have tried to convince us we can't open it and access its contents. Many have tried to tell us that the backpack of empire is better than our own.

A Puerto Rican Decolonial Theology: Prophesy Freedom is a testament to Puerto Rican backpacks, to the fact that they are *ours*, and to the fact that *no one* can take them from us. Yet this book simultaneously and critically asks why we as Puerto Ricans have to carry backpacks at all. Why has a colonial situation forced us to leave the physical land of our foremothers for the land of our colonizer over the last hundred years? When we arrived to New York and Orlando and Hartford and Chicago, why weren't the streets paved with gold as we were told? Why do the poverty and sexism and queerphobia that exist on the island seem only to follow us to this "promised land?" As Puerto Ricans, we've had to learn to carry our history on our backs because a debt crisis makes it economically impossible to live in our land. We've had to learn to keep our backpacks on even when an assimilationist culture in the USA wants us to trade our bags in for the "better [White-Anglo] model." And we've had to learn to tighten our straps when a family member dies on the island from a preventable illness and we can't go home to bury them. This backpack, then, is a symbol of resilience, revolt, and revolution. Yet it is also symbolic of all the broken PROMESAS[1] that continuously force us to leave nuestra tierra, sometimes never to return…

In the pages that follow, Dr. Teresa Delgado will carry the reader through an exploration of our backpacks. Using the story of Vieques as a launching pad, Delgado shows how present Puerto Rican reality is connected to decades of U.S. colonialism. In this uneven relationship, Puerto Rico has essentially been subservient to parasitic business, military, and politics stemming from the colonizer. The history of Vieques perfectly exemplifies this reality as the U.S. military used it for decades as a training site: shooting rounds, dumping chemicals, and dropping bombs on the region without regard for Puerto Ricans on that land. Yet the history of Vieques also speaks of resistance as Puerto Rican civilians, workers, and ministers stood up to empire saying *¡no más!* and brought the bombings to an end.

Such a spirit of resistance follows the book to its end as Delgado explores the great Puerto Rican writers Esmeralda Santiago, Pedro Juan

---

[1] "PROMESA" stands for the "Puerto Rico Oversight, Management, and Economic Stability Act" (Public Law 114–187) signed into law by President Barack Obama on June 30, 2016. This law imposes a financial control board on the island whose members have the power to veto or amend economic legislation offered by Puerto Rico's government as well as create new policy. Many have opposed this Act as a new form of colonialism, arguing that it further takes power away from the Puerto Rican people while instating draconian policies. Some of these include cutting funding for social services including education and slashing minimum wage from $7.25 an hour to $4.25 an hour for Puerto Rican workers 25 years of age and younger. The board's goal is to pay back Puerto Rico's creditors and, as a result, alleviate the island's debt. Yet with policies that so blatantly hurt every day Puerto Ricans one is forced to ask whether the "PROMESA" (literally meaning the "promise") is for the people of the island or for the Hedge Funds and Wall Street tycoons that fund members of the U.S. Congress.

Soto and Rosario Ferré. In their writings Delgado finds resources for that spirit of resistance and resilience that fueled protestors in Vieques and continues to fill the backpacks of Puerto Ricans today. Delgado specifically examines what these authors say about our humanity, salvation, and hope in order to drive her argument that, for Puerto Ricans, *freedom is our own*. We are whole humans even when empire demeans us. We find freedom in ourselves—in our backpacks—and no one can take that from us. And we are driven by a hope in this truth that our ancestors, community, and faith deem self-evident.

Though the Puerto Rican reality is complex and often difficult, we must find freedom in and among ourselves. So we carry our backpacks wherever we go and reach into them daily for that hope, humanity, and salvation that comes only from ourselves. Hopefully, *en lucha*, we will one day be able to take off our backpacks and set their contents in a living room, a home, of our own: but there are many parrandas to share and financial control boards to dismantle until that day. For now, we carry our backpacks, resting in the knowledge that freedom is already ours even as we keep fighting...

Jorge Juan Rodríguez V
Union Theological Seminary
New York, NY, USA

ACKNOWLEDGEMENTS

This book has been over twenty years in the making, perhaps even longer. It started as a quiet whisper in my head when, in the fall of 1991, I entered the halls of Union Theological Seminary in New York City and began reading James Cone's *Black Theology of Liberation* and Cornel West's *Prophesy Deliverance!* The whisper grew more audible as I continued to absorb the works of Ada María Isasi-Díaz, Virgilio Elizondo, Justo Gonzalez, María Pilar Aquino and many, many others. By the time I began researching and writing my dissertation in 2001, that whisper had grown to such a level that I could barely hear myself think. I felt compelled to say something meaningful about colonialism, creative freedom, literature, God and liberation—all through the lens of Puerto Rican experience. At that time, and from my social location, voices attempting to bring these elements together were few and far between.

Now over 25 years since embarking upon my journey in theological studies, this book emerges from the core thesis of my dissertation to claim that Puerto Rican writers have prophesied a new vision for understanding Puerto Rican identity, suffering and hope for our people; this vision is nothing less than a Christian promise for human flourishing. In these many years that spanned the idea from a quiet whisper to a published book, there are so many people who have provided the space for me to "fill up when empty, letting images and ideas and smells run down like water,"[2] or were just present to the emptiness until it was filled.

[2] Anne LaMott, *Bird by Bird: Some Instructions on Writing and Life* (New York: Anchor Books, 1995).

I am grateful for Mary Boys who lent me Anne LaMott's book, *Bird by Bird*, and offered me her wisdom and encouragement at a time when I was about to throw in the towel just a year before receiving my doctorate. Delores S. Williams, my doctoral advisor, believed in my ability and affirmed it without equivocation, even when I was unable to accept such affirmation. Both Ana María Díaz-Stevens and Christopher Morse took my work seriously enough to offer constructive critique out of their abundant knowledge and wisdom. David Asomaning, in the tradition of Nelle Morton, "heard me into speech," with tenderness and generosity, and helped me clear the path to give my words room to breathe and move. Joanne Rodríguez of the Hispanic Theological Initiative, and Matthew Wesley Williams of the Forum for Theological Exploration have known my passion for this project for many years and have encouraged me boundlessly.

I have often claimed that writing a book is rarely a "solo flight"; and this absolutely true in my case. As my spouse and I raised four children all of whom were born while I was engaged in doctoral work, we would not have been able to hold it all together without incredible people along the way. These include the directors of Mount Tom Day School and Camp—Jill Newhouse, Stan Friedmann, Doug Volan and Erin Barrie—who, over the last 20 years, have offered my children the incredible opportunity of spending a glorious summer at camp, and where they now work as they've grown! There were also so many mothers who, over the years, graciously invited my children to their homes so that I could have the quiet space to write, as well as the caregivers of my children when they were younger, including Maria Accocella and Teresa Rodríguez.

I would be remiss if I did not mention the Louisville Institute for the support they provided through their First Book Grant for Minority Scholars, which I was awarded in 2011–2012. Although this is not the book I had proposed at the time, I would not have been able to complete this project had it not been for the space they awarded to allow me the time to reflect and regain my bearings during a very challenging time in my family's life. The Louisville Institute grant was followed a number of years later with a sabbatical leave in 2015–16, specifically to work on this project. This sabbatical was supported by an amazing group of colleagues in the Religious Studies Department of Iona College, of which I have been blessed to be a part since 2005, and who have encouraged my intellectual aspirations throughout my tenure. During that sabbatical, I was gifted with the opportunity to work with Ulrike Guthrie; this project would not be where it is today without her tireless skill of transforming a dissertation into a book that captures my passion and love for literature and theology.

My friends in the Workgroup for Constructive Theology, including Victor Anderson, Michelle Gonzalez and the late Dale Andrews all read parts of this manuscript at different points, helping me to sharpen my analysis, all the while encouraging me to write boldly and fearlessly. The late Otto Maduro and the current director of the Hispanic Summer Program, Daisy Machado, both gave me the opportunity to teach in this transformational academic program, allowing me to be with some of the most gifted minds I've ever met as students in my classes. In many ways, these students gave me the sense of purpose I needed to overcome moments of self-doubt and apprehension.

A number of these students have journeyed with me over the last five years or so as I've served as their mentor, officially and unofficially, including Lauren Guerra, Yara González Justiniano, Elyssa Salinas, Jennifer Owens and Diana Click, to name but a few. The robust conversations I've had about theology and liberation with these remarkable young women have strengthened my conviction about the need for more voices from the margins to be central to theological discourse.

My friends and family have accompanied me, *en conjunto*, during every step of this journey, but they stepped up with incredible generosity and love to provide funding during my sabbatical year, including donors who contributed broadly to my project (C&C) and others who, anonymously and named, responded to the *GoFundMe* campaign for a graduate assistant stipend, particularly my friends from the inaugural 1987 class of Leadership America. That campaign was fully funded in less than three weeks because of this amazing group of people who, in typical humility, do not wish to be named but I am grateful for each and every one.

That graduate assistant was Jorge Juan Rodríguez V, currently a doctoral candidate in Modern Religious History at Union Theological Seminary (NYC). In addition to writing a moving Preface for this book, Jorge read the entire manuscript, offered critique and suggestions, brought information up to date, introduced new concepts and generally did anything that was needed to improve the manuscript, from the creative to the mundane. He is brilliant and he is passionate about Puerto Rico; it was a privilege to have his mind and heart so committed to this project.

My immediate family deserves particular mention; my sisters, Annette and Denise, have continued to support me—with their time, money, encouragement—that I am often speechless by their generosity. My loving parents, Mami y Papi, express their love and support in countless ways, from allowing me a "room of one's own" in their house to research and write, not to mention the chauffeuring, babysitting, cooking and innumerable acts of kindness they engage in daily for the benefit of their grandchildren, their son-in-law, and daughter. My children—Francesca, Celeste, Josiah and Xavier—are truly amazing; they have nurtured, sustained and strengthened me through this process by reflecting back to me a sense of accomplishment and pride as their mother. They have been so patient with me, especially when I've needed to retreat into a quiet space (not easy to find in our home) to work.

Finally, I am grateful beyond measure for my husband of almost thirty years, Pascal, who has been the midwife of this project for the majority of our life together. He has continued to support me in more ways than I can acknowledge in words, so that I could be filled in the midst of emptiness and despair that the dire condition of Puerto Rico has often made me feel. He is truly a remarkable human being who, in the midst of incredible hardship in his life and career, continues to persevere with determination, grit and a whole lot of humor. He finds a way to bring joy into the most desperate of circumstances, reminding me that we—as individuals and even as entire communities, including Puerto Rico—have that same capacity. This book is as much a testament of his love as it is of mine.

Mount Vernon, NY
July 2017

CONTENTS

1 Introduction: The Vieques Story and the Critical Task of a
   Puerto Rican Decolonial Theology   1

2 The Story of Puerto Rican Oppression and Resistance   21

3 Bridging the Puerto Rican Story and Christian Doctrine   61

4 The Works of Esmeralda Santiago: Puerto Rican Identity
   and Christian Anthropology   73

5 The Works of Pedro Juan Soto: Puerto Rican Suffering
   and Christian Soteriology   107

6 The Works of Rosario Ferré: Puerto Rican Hope and
   Christian Eschatology   143

7 Conclusion: The Best of Witnesses Among the Dry Bones   179

Bibliography   185

Index   201

Introduction: The Vieques Story and the Critical Task of a Puerto Rican Decolonial Theology

In May 2000, tens of thousands of people marched through the streets of the Puerto Rican capital city, San Juan, in solidarity with the people of Vieques against the US naval presence and military activity on their island. Organized primarily through the efforts of ecumenical church leaders, the movement and its peaceful activism and protest was one of extensive outreach and solidarity that focused the world's attention on a local injustice. The catalyst for this movement could not have been further from peaceful or non-violent; the implications of this movement reach far beyond what one incident could have foreshadowed.

On April 19, 1999, the small Caribbean island of Vieques, off the eastern coast of Puerto Rico,[1] entered the international stage when the US Navy mistakenly dropped two 500-pound bombs outside of the bombing zone of the island during routine military practice drills. The bombs missed their targets and killed a civilian security guard, David Sanes Rodríguez, who was stationed within the bombing zone of the eastern tip of the island. The force of the blast killed him instantly; he was 42 years old. This small territory, affectionately called "La Isla Nena," or little girl island, came to symbolize the reality of Puerto Rico since 1898: an island and a people under the jurisdiction (or some would say the heel) of the USA. Although Puerto Ricans have understood their island as nominally "autonomous," with its own insular governance structure, elections, and so forth, the aftermath of the Vieques fatality made one fact abundantly clear: that the Puerto Rican people, on the island as well as in the "outer community"[2] had little to no power to

© The Author(s) 2017
T. Delgado, *A Puerto Rican Decolonial Theology*, New Approaches to Religion and Power, DOI 10.1007/978-3-319-66068-4_1

determine the US Navy's appropriation of 70% of the land on Vieques.[3] This fact was a wake-up call to Puerto Ricans, particularly those outside the island who are not faced daily with the blatant militarism of the USA.

The story of David Sanes Rodríguez is important for this study for a number of reasons. First, a person died at the hands of the US military complex, and one person is as important as any other, or a thousand others. His life matters as his death matters. His identity as a Viequense, a native of Vieques, stood for all 9300 Vieques residents who have lived in the shadow of stealth bombers and aircraft carriers, and in earshot of deafening ammunition fire and weapons testing. His identity as a Puerto Rican killed at the hands of the US military, regardless of its accidental nature, stood for and spoke to all Puerto Ricans who continue to face indiscriminate power and its abuses. David Sanes Rodríguez' death stirred the conscience of people in Puerto Rico and beyond the island's borders because it is a classic metaphor of David and Goliath, of the confrontation between the inferior non-power–the Puerto Rican people— and the superior power–The US Navy.

WHY DID THIS HAPPEN?

The crisis around Vieques highlighted a number of things. Despite all the rhetoric of autonomy and the benefits of US status, Puerto Rico did not have the power to determine the Navy's presence on the island. Though for years its people had suffered damage to their health, that of the environment, and of the economy because of the US military presence, the Puerto Rican people were unable to secure the wider US or global public's attention and help to remove the military presence from the island until the fatal military incident of 1999.

The incident was more than an "isolated accident"; it was another in a long line of so-called "accidents" since the inauguration of this isolated base, made possible because of the unchecked authority the US military enjoyed on their prized training ground. Since 1941 when the USA "acquired" over two-thirds of the land on Vieques by strong-arming the predominantly fishermen population, the US Navy had developed a training facility that was ideal for air, land, and sea combat preparation, not least because of the optimal weather conditions. In fact, in addition to using the base themselves, the Navy advertised and sold time at the training facility to foreign nations; Vieques was a "one-stop" military facility with all the advancements and amenities of a US base. The

Defense Department profited over $80 million per year in direct revenues through the sale of training time on the Vieques compound.[4]

Since it was such an ideal training ground, the US military was adamant about maintaining this facility at all costs. Local residents tell of encounters with the military in which they felt threatened if they complained about the noise levels, the foul smell in the air from the various types of weaponry tested (including napalm), and the negative effect on the fishing of warships and submarines circumnavigating the island, among other abuses. The land utilized by the military has been stripped of its natural state; the environmental damage to both land and sea and their life forms has been severe. This has in turn affected the livelihood of the fishing community on the island—the only livelihood, aside from tourism, that the indigenous population has been able to maintain. Yet, the US Navy met these valid concerns with complete reproach; the US Navy was not about to forfeit its military readiness and national security to appease the locals.

With the death of David Sanes Rodríguez, the years of pent up frustration and anger exploded, setting off a response that rippled outward to Puerto Ricans on the main island, to those in the States, and to others in the world who watched this movement gain momentum and strength. Sanes Rodriguez's death was both the straw that broke the camel's back and what ignited resistance and courage. With the attention of the world upon them, in solidarity with many others including notable politicians, church leaders, community activists, Puerto Rican and non-Puerto Rican alike, the people of Vieques began to speak the truth of their experiences of abuse at the hands of the US military.

The protests gained such momentum that all bombing ceased temporarily in May 1999; in 2000, before leaving office, the Clinton Administration agreed to allow the residents of Vieques to decide by a vote whether they wished the military to stay. Even with this "promise" of the Navy's exit, as the residents were sure to vote them off, the movement on Vieques continued to a degree that made it virtually impossible for training to take place as usual. In a memo to the Secretary of the Navy, the Chief of Naval Operations wrote:

> [P]hysical security at Vieques is becoming ever more difficult and costly to maintain given the civil unrest which accompanies the Navy's presence on the island. We have been successful in completing our training on the island only because of extremely aggressive and costly multi-agency security actions. The level of protests, attempted incursions, and isolated successful

incursions generally remains high when Battle Group training occurs on the island. Navy has devoted significant resources to maintain range security and safety, as well as the safety of our onsite personnel. Even so, our Sailors are continually subjected to an unsatisfactory environment in Puerto Rico. The support of the local police organization has been unable to provide the kind of safety we would demand at any other site in the United States. Navy's departure from Vieques would relieve us from this burden.[5]

Not long after, prompted by the terrorist attacks of September 11, 2001, all talk about the Navy's withdrawal from Vieques ceased. Ironically, the language that the Bush Administration used to describe Al-Qaeda's activities was very similar to that which the Puerto Rican people used to describe their experience with the Navy on Vieques: not caring for the lives and well-being of the innocent, allowing their agenda to take precedence over the needs of a people, using destructive bombs in the interests of their "national security," etc. Though the training facility resumed its normal activity as a result of 9/11 and in preparation for the wars in Afghanistan and Iraq, the people protesting the situation in Vieques maintained their momentum, despite being criticized as "anti-American" and pro-terrorist.

The Bush Administration decided to carry out the "promise" of the Clinton White House and ordered the closing of the facility effective May 1, 2003. Neither Republican Party officials nor Republican legislators welcomed this decision. They felt that the President had "sold out" the national security interests and military preparedness to the Northeast Latino voting block through pressure from New York Congressional leaders such as Charles Schumer and Hillary Clinton who, at the time, were responding to the concerns of the most concentrated population of Puerto Ricans in the Diaspora community.[6]

WHERE DO WE GO FROM HERE?

The story of Vieques is the story of Puerto Rico and vice versa, a story of two islands that share the same core experience of colonial oppression and resistance. It is a story that can give hope to the Puerto Rican people for, in May 2003, the Navy withdrew. The collective efforts of a community united in solidarity attained their goal. If Vieques can achieve its freedom from the presence of the US Navy, then it is feasible for Puerto Rico to believe in the possibility of achieving freedom from the tyranny of colonialism.

Puerto Ricans, who are fiercely loyal to their land, transcended the politics of status (statehood, autonomy, independence), in light of this crisis, and came together in solidarity around this one issue regardless of their political differences. In that moment, Vieques awoke the consciousness of the Puerto Rican people, particularly of the stateside community, to the reality that despite the rhetoric of autonomy and cultural preservation under the so-called "commonwealth" status, the Unites States rules superior in all matters, military and otherwise. Vieques illustrated that the "national security" concerns of the United States override the human security concerns of the people and land of Puerto Rico.

But the struggle is far from over for the people and the island of Vieques. The US Fish and Wildlife Service, under the jurisdiction of the Department of the Interior, now administers the land that was once in the possession of the military. It has yet to be transferred back to the people of Vieques. The environmental damage to that land is so severe that the Environmental Protection Agency (EPA) has added the Vieques naval facility (Atlantic Fleet Weapons Training Area, or AFWTA) to its National Priorities List of the country's most contaminated hazardous waste sites.[7] Yet although the US Navy has committed, on paper, to the environmental cleanup that is now a crucial necessity, the transfer of the lands to the US Fish and Wildlife Service and designated as a "wildlife refuge" has proven to be a loophole so that the military could avoid the expense of the massive and extensive cleanup.[8]

The years of contamination of the land, sea, and air have had far-reaching effects on the health of the people of Vieques; rates of dental decay, epilepsy, allergic dermatitis, and abnormal heartbeat exceed those of the island of Puerto Rico by over 100%, according to the Puerto Rican Health Department.[9] Initial studies of plant life contamination, conducted by the Puerto Rican Health Department, also found "significant uranium contamination in sea grass beds from the east end firing range, all the way south past the USS Killen, and on all beaches including Esperanza."[10] In addition, concentrations of other toxic chemicals and heavy metals, such as lead, cadmium, nickel, and copper were found on Vieques in areas not isolated within the training facility and in levels significantly higher than FDA and EPA acceptable limits.[11] While Congressman Rothman (D-NJ) introduced the "Vieques Recovery and Development Act" on April 15, 2011, Viequenses have yet to see the Navy and the US government take responsibility for the environmental damage and expedite the efforts and funding for its remediation.[12]

The story of Vieques also raises serious questions about why theologians and the church in the continental United States have been so silent about the political, social, economic, and spiritual plight of Puerto Ricans. This fact cannot be ignored for three reasons: First, the resistance which has broken the silence should prompt a reexamination of the history of resistance itself, while demonstrating the collaborative efforts of religious and secular groups in strategic alliance, as well as the fierce backlash wielded against both. Second, it showcases in real life terms the struggle for self-determination that is reflected upon in the literature; it is no coincidence that Esmeralda Santiago uses Vieques as the setting for a major portion of her novel *América's Dream*. Pedro Juan Soto's novel *Usmaíl* is considered a "Vieques Classic"; and he uses the name "Nena" (little girl, reminiscent of *la isla nena*, the affectionate local name for Vieques) in his final piece, "God in Harlem," of the short story collection *Spiks*.[13] Its history of militarization and industrialization echoes themes found in the literature of the three creative writers on whom I focus in this book. Third, the recent resistance highlights the lack of a comprehensive socio-economic critique of the situation by US Latinx[14] theologians despite their emergence out of, and indebtedness to, Latin American liberation theology. While Latinx theology has claimed a liberation hermeneutic—as a voice from the margins of dominant theological discourse—as yet it has not undertaken a comprehensive critique of political and economic structures of oppression that continue to shape the consciousness of a large number of our people.

The response of the people of Vieques is a perfect example of freedom taking hold in the face of oppression, of the voices of protest rising above the imposed silence of a repressive military complex. Their response, their story, not only communicates a particular reality but also elicits in those who hear the story a desire and responsibility to initiate change toward freedom and self-determination. It prophesies a decolonial theology.

THE CRITICAL TASK OF PUERTO RICAN THEOLOGICAL DISCOURSE

To question Puerto Rico's neo-colonial status in relation to the USA, as exemplified in the Vieques story, is the theological task of Puerto Ricans. Sanes Rodríguez's death is a prophetic opportunity for the birth of a new dialogue and discourse in theology and beyond. It is not only a question of political importance, but also one of spiritual importance, for the question of colonial status is also about identity, salvation, and eschatological hope. A theological approach uniquely asks about the "spirit" of the people, which, in my view, is what is most at stake in this Vieques situation. The confrontation that has continued to escalate in relation to Vieques offers Puerto Ricans, and Puerto Rican theologians to be sure, a unique opportunity to respond in ways that move our people toward a decolonized future, unleashing the power of self-determination into all aspects of Puerto Rican life.

The emergence of a critical Puerto Rican theological voice in the USA is long overdue. In an article entitled, "Latino Theology: The Year of the 'Boom,'" "Allan Figueroa Deck outlined the emergence of a Latino/a theological voice in the USA, particularly over the past twenty years, but the particular strains of Puerto Ricans' voices are as yet barely heard in it.[15] This general Latinx theology is contextual in its location, liberative in its orientation, and practical in its application. Its sources are based on the experiences of Latinx people, its locus is evident in popular religiosity, art, literature, and collective action, and it is expressed symbolically, analogically, and emotionally. Those who "do" this theology, our Latinx theologians, are part of the community of believers; as part of such communities, they are accountable for its condition. Ada María Isasi-Díaz, Virgilio Elizondo, Justo González, Fernando Segovia, and Orlando Costas are a few of the more prominent Latinx scholars who have contributed significantly to the development of Latinx theology in the areas of ethics, pastoral theology, systematics, and biblical hermeneutics and missiology respectively.

As a Puerto Rican woman of the outer/diaspora community "doing theology" in the USA, I claim this tradition as my own. From within this new tradition of Latinx theology, I see great accomplishment and promise: the broadening of theological dialogue beyond black and white, the *mujerista* critique within and beyond Latinx theology, the critical contribution of queer Latinx perspectives, etc. Still, Puerto Ricans have yet to make heard their particular concerns, their particular voices. Of the US Latinx theology that has evolved within the last twenty years, very little has been developed from a Puerto Rican perspective.[16] Why a specifically Puerto Rican theology, why literature as a major source for its development, why decolonization as a central methodology, and why now?

Why a Puerto Rican theology? We need a distinctive Puerto Rican theological perspective within the canon of Hispanic/Latinx theology in the US. Liberal theological circles have embraced the growing contributions of Latinx/Hispanic theology, but in fact, by lumping together Mexican-Americans, Cubans, Puerto Ricans, Dominicans, we mask the fact that not all Latinxs share the same culture or the same language. For example, Cuban-Americans Ada María Isasi-Díaz and Fernando Segovia have drawn upon the experience of exile as a significant theme within their work. While exile is a relevant theme for all Latinxs living in the United States, Isasi-Díaz and Segovia describe their particular *Cuban* experience of it, and how that resonates with biblical stories of exile. Virgilio Elizondo, a Mexican-American, developed *mestizaje* as both source and locus of theological reflection in his work. *Mestizaje* is relevant to all Latinxs who must come to terms with the many combinations of cultures, races, and ethnicities residing within our very being. Yet, this theme is dominant in Elizondo's work because of the particular *Mexican-American* experience of cultural encounter at the border, of continuous boundary crossing, which resonates with the biblical experience of marginal and alienated communities.

Unless Puerto Rican theologians reflect upon their experience of God within the context of Puerto Rican life, the reality of colonization for Puerto Ricans will be slow to emerge as a relevant theme for all US Latinxs.[17] The devastating legacy of colonization—an aspect of present-day Puerto Rican experience that is a unique distinction among US Latinxs—continues to plague the US Puerto Rican community. Therefore, this theme should be a critical and central part of our developing theological discourse.

Puerto Rican pastors and scholars writing in English in the continental United States have addressed the reality of our people from a variety of perspectives and disciplines other than theology. For example, the emphasis of the pastoral/ministerial approach has been the need to address the spiritual needs of our people and minister to them. The emphasis of studies from a pedagogical perspective has been the practical application of educational methodology (i.e. testing, tutoring, mentorship programs, bilingual education) so as to reduce through education the effect of negative socio-economic conditions. Studies in Puerto Rican politics and history, while they address the colonial context through a critique of the political system, focus primarily on the question of Puerto Rico's political status and history in terms of the USA (i.e. Statehood, independence, or commonwealth [status quo]).[18] There is already an extensive body of work that examines the Puerto Rican religious experience from sociological and anthropological perspectives, such as that of Ana María Díaz-Stevens and Anthony Stevens-Arroyo, as well as the extensive repository of works held at the Center for Puerto Rican Studies at Hunter College (CUNY).[19]

It is on the foundation of their work that I build my project. I concur with such scholars that the root cause of the frustration, despair, and hopelessness in the Puerto Rican community is our lack of self-determination as a colonized people. Yet there exists in the work of Puerto Rican creative writers a prophetic vision of freedom that challenges not only the socio-political reality but also the resulting despair. Their writings have maintained the spark of hope.

Yet I quite understand the political rationale for advocating a pan-Latinx/Hispanic solidarity and for assimilating Puerto Ricans into the Latinx category at the expense of the affirming our specific cultural context. The reason lies in the strength of the numbers: by the year 2003, Latinxs/Hispanics had emerged as the largest ethnic minority in the USA. The United States Census Bureau projects that by the year 2050 Latinxs/Hispanics will be the largest ethnic group in the United States, surpassing Euro-Americans (whites).[20] So there are tremendous political, economic, and social opportunities for increasing our awareness about the issues facing Latinxs/Hispanics, an opportunity that will not want to be missed or diluted by the efforts of Puerto Ricans (or others) to demonstrate their distinctiveness. This label, Latinx, also represents a certain measure of assimilation into a new reality within the United States (i.e. Cuban becomes Latinx; Mexicans becoming Latinxs) that, perhaps, Puerto Ricans are resisting vehemently as a protest for having an identity (and US citizenship) imposed upon them as was done in 1917, just in time to draft more soldiers to fight in WWI.

Yet unique cultural groups such as Cubans and Mexicans that have taken on the identity of Latinx, I suggest, have had their opportunity to tell their story from their distinctive vantage point. For example, Virgilio Elizondo's first works were explicitly and non-apologetically Mexican-American in framework and, while they had far-reaching impact and import beyond that community, were addressed to the needs and issues of a Mexican-American audience.[21] Once that story was told, Elizondo began to do more pan-Latinx work, including through the Institute for Latino Studies at Notre Dame. The theme of exile, theologically and biblically, has been so strongly emphasized among Cuban theologians and biblical scholars (including by Segovia, Isasi-Díaz, and Espín) that, while theirs is not specifically named Cuban theology and/or hermeneutics, one cannot understand their work fully without recognizing the importance of the Cuban experience and its influence. Like Elizondo, these scholars have more freely identified themselves as Latinx, a new identity, because it does not erase the identity that has already been claimed, affirmed, and voiced. But this has yet to happen for Puerto Ricans in the USA. Now it is time to give voice to our Puerto Rican identity from a theological perspective. Otherwise, we run the risk of yet again having imposed on us an identity that is not fully our own before we have shaped our own, even if tentatively at first.

In addition, we Puerto Rican theologians must work to correct the lack of resources in theology written in English from a Puerto Rican perspective. Within the discipline of theology, the specific context of Puerto Rican lives, our story, has not been told on a grander scale or heard by a wider audience. David Traverzo's article, "Towards a Theology of Mission in the U.S. Puerto Rican Migrant Community: From Captivity to Liberation,"[22] is a good first step toward articulating a theological response to the specific reality of the Puerto Rican community in the USA. He uses sociological data to illustrate the plight of Puerto Ricans in the United States: from inferior education and housing to substance abuse and violence, the Puerto Rican community lives the evils of "neocolonial subjugation."[23] Traverzo comes closer than any other Latino theologian writing in English to address the case of Puerto Ricans; his sharp analysis of the sociopolitical and economic situation created by the capitalist imperialism of the United States informs his proposal for a faith response: the church must be the prophetic voice to denounce social injustice in the face of a corrupt secular society into which many of our people have been co-opted. Still, Traverzo's response, while pointed and accurate in relation to the church, is limited to a "pastoralist" approach to theology as opposed to a "liberationist" approach.[24] We need a broader response.

The tradition of liberation theology that has emerged since seminal works by Gustavo Gutierrez and James Cone has claimed that theology is a second act that arises out of the encounter with contradiction: one may have faith in a God of love, justice, and freedom, but in real life often one encounters only hate, injustice, and captivity. So the question becomes: How can I be a faithful Christian, believing in a God who makes a preferential option for the oppressed, and not speak a word against the oppressors/oppression of my Puerto Rican people? In order to develop a decolonial theology from a Puerto Rican perspective, I have had to wrestle with this question over and over. The question itself compels me to develop a clear understanding of what constitutes such a Puerto Rican perspective, what freedom and decoloniality mean from that distinct perspective, and how stories articulate that perspective.

Why use literature? The reasons for my use of Puerto Rican literature as a major source for the development of a Puerto Rican theology are that literature is both descriptive and prescriptive of the experiences of the Puerto Rican people. First, the literature as a deposit of culture reflects the experiences of a people on many levels: cultural, political, spiritual, psychological, etc. As stated earlier, the sources of Latinx theology are based on the everyday experiences—*lo cotidiano*—of Latinx people. For Puerto Ricans, this experience—cultural, political, spiritual, and psychological, etc.—has been circumscribed by our colonial relationship with the United States. In other words, the literature can be said to be a *descriptive* source for the development of a Puerto Rican theological perspective because it depicts the colonial reality in actuality and metaphor. As a descriptive source, the literature is an ethnographic site which provides a lens through which we can examine the culture from a variety of angles: race, color, sexuality, politics, leisure, work, marriage, migration, language, food, music, and so on.[25] From a social science perspective, literature is a source of ethnographic material, much as is true of oral history, interviews, and on-site observation.

Second, literature as a product of the imagination reflects the vision of the writer and, by extension, the community to which they are accountable. For the Puerto Rican writer, freedom and independence of thought have been constitutive elements of that vision as well as of the creative writing process itself. Puerto Rican author, playwright, and cultural critic René Marqués makes this point clearly:

> The writer has to be free to be able to struggle against that web which others fashion to impede his search for the truth. And, in effect...he knows himself to be free. This is a natural feeling, since he has the experience of creation; he knows, because he has experienced it in his own flesh and spirit, that the very act of artistic creation is an act of supreme liberty... The writer, who knows freedom not as a political concept or as a philosophical abstraction, but as a vital experience, will love liberty for himself and, by extension, for others.[26]

Therefore, the writer whose work projects a desire for freedom from the context of a condition of non-freedom (i.e. colonization) offers a prophetic vision for that which is not yet fully realized. In this way, literature is a *prescriptive* source that lends itself well to the development of a Puerto Rican theological perspective that is freedom-centered and decolonized.

I am not suggesting here that literature, in general, or the specific texts I have chosen for this study explicitly prescribe certain remedies to the current conditions in which Puerto Ricans live. I am not imposing a particular moral, ethical, or religious meaning upon the text as if to say that the author intended to articulate such meanings. On the contrary, I firmly believe that literature can make absolutely no affirmations whatsoever regarding anything remotely religious and/or theological *and still* provide us with a rich opportunity for analysis and interpretation without compromising authorial intent or textual integrity. Whether the author makes such moral, ethical, or religious claims is not my immediate focus; I am not attempting to decode the authorial intention behind the story itself. I am examining the literature from a thematic perspective, and identifying three specific themes (of identity, suffering, and hope) that are fruitful for the Puerto Rican theological enterprise. All three of the themes so prominent in the literature itself seem to be prophesying this: our Puerto Rican identity, our ability to overcome suffering and the hope to which we aspire are linked to our desire for self-determination and freedom from colonization.

Why decolonial freedom? My use of the term "decolonial freedom" is akin to the way in which the term "emancipation" has been used within theological discourse. "Emancipation" describes a rich history of many peoples and nations who have maintained a strong resistance to various forms of oppression. Emancipation, more than liberation, reflects the past condition and ongoing legacy of slavery on the island of Puerto Rico, including the relegation of black Puerto Ricans to the lowest rung of the socio-economic ladder; this racialized hierarchy was transported off the island to the continental United States in large measure during the Great Migration.[27] Emancipation is a stronger and more accurate term within a Puerto Rican context, I believe, than the appropriation of the word "liberation" which, since its inaugural usage as a new theological method/purpose, has unfortunately become so mainstream that it has lost its critical and revolutionary connotation. In addition, using an emancipatory lens positions my work in relation to

Caribbean theologians such as Carmelo Alvarez and Kortright Davis who describe their theological position via emancipation for the anti-colonial/anti-slavery history and legacy in the Caribbean.[28] While articulating a theological perspective that is informed by a North American U.S. experience, I claim the connection between this reality and that of my Puerto Rican community on the Caribbean island.

And still, "emancipation" as a contextual frame of aspiration, does not reflect accurately the real condition of Puerto Rico and Puerto Ricans. We, all Puerto Ricans, are "colonial subjects"[29]; refusing to name that existential condition—both bound by and transcending geographic location—is to mask the insidious colonial architecture that undergirds a racist and imperial project. The architecture is in place on Vieques, in Barranquitas, in Ponce, as well as Chicago, New York, and Orlando.

In claiming the island community and Diaspora community as my own, I offer a corrective to the conflict between the Puerto Rican voice from the island (Spanish) and state side (English). The distinctive voice of Puerto Ricans in the USA comes into conflict in another arena in addition to resisting the Latinx group-speak within theological circles: that is, the Spanish-speaking island Puerto Rican theology versus the English-oriented stateside Puerto Rican theology. While the anti-colonial discussion has taken place for a long time in theological circles and in churches in Puerto Rico, much of that conversation is inaccessible and/or unavailable to the English-oriented Puerto Rican like me as a result of the forces of assimilation at work in the United States. Thus, not speaking Spanish has been equated, from the Puerto Rican island perspective, with an abandonment of culture, because the preservation of Puerto Rican culture has been intimately connected with the preservation of Spanish. Iris Zavala speaks of this when she states, "Opposition in the cultural sector has been difficult, because the cultural aspect forms an integral part of the unsheathed weapons of domination. The invaders have tried to stop the development of culture, which always brings a consciousness of one's own capacity for freedom. The most celebrated triumph of the *Indice* generation was in the realm of language: in 1905, English was made compulsory in the Island's schools and did not cease to be so until 1948, although it has not been eliminated completely."[30]

The barriers of language imposed by the socio-historical reality of migration and survival in a colonial context have therefore created a contentious relationship, and sometimes animosity, between theological conversations, which only further silences the English-oriented voice that is seen as a "sell-out" and a less than legitimate voice to speak, theologically or otherwise, on issues of Puerto Rican freedom and power. It is like saying that one can only affirm one's "Puerto Ricanness" if one speaks Spanish. This notion fails to acknowledge the fact that Spanish was once the language of the colonizer and that even those who spoke Spanish fluently were able to maintain fervor for independence from Spain. With such a critique waged against the English-oriented audience, in addition to the racial and ethnic discrimination faced in the USA, it is not difficult to imagine why a more prominent voice in theology from a Puerto Rican stateside perspective has not been heard.

The classic "divide and conquer" tactic of coloniality has had the upper hand in the case of the Puerto Rican island and stateside communities. This tactic has also succeeded, to some extent, in masking the history of Puerto Rican oppression and resistance from our own people. Much of the historical information I present in the next chapter was unknown to me, even as a well-educated Puerto Rican woman, until I began researching for this book. While some might wonder why I would include this sociohistorical section, I believe it is critical to ground a decolonial theological discourse within the particular context of Puerto Rican history because the colonial project as it has been played out has erased that history from our collective consciousness. So many of our young Puerto Rican people (who I consider my community of accountability) have no sense of that history, for reasons I will outline throughout the book. While this information may not be necessary for the contextual theologian or scholar of diaspora studies, it is absolutely necessary for a people whose coloniality has meant a forced amnesia. This amnesia was awakened with Vieques, bringing us back together in solidarity with our dispersed people and our disappeared history. The use and affirmation of the term "decolonial" could not be any more timely.

Why address this now? We are witnessing a critical moment in the history of Puerto Ricans in relation to the USA. All social indicators of the last six decades of census data point to the decreasing standard of living among Puerto Ricans, the lowest among the larger US Latinx groups; I will illustrate this data in more detail in the next chapter. This continues to be the case despite the predominance of English as the primary language among the children of those Puerto Ricans from the Great Migration period (1946–1964). In spite of the demoralizing conditions in which the majority of Puerto Rican people live within the United States, there remains still the seduction of the "American Dream," a vision of the good life in the country that has promised development, advancement, and improvement to our people (e.g. through targeted initiatives such as Operation Bootstrap as well as through the generalized language of the culture).[31] As a result of being situated in the midst of a US society that markets the myth of social mobility, Puerto Ricans in the USA have become complacent, in my opinion, and have not taken seriously enough the colonial relationship that still exists; this is certainly the case within the US theological arena. Moreover, we have allowed that complacency to dull our critique of the colonial relationship as a factor in the socioeconomic condition of our people.

Our creative writers, on the other hand, have used their stories to point to the "writing on the wall," even when the walls surrounding Puerto Ricans in the USA are more likely to be those of prisons, barrios, crack houses, teen pregnancy wards, drug rehab facilities, welfare offices, and juvenile detention centers. As our writers have, any Puerto Rican theologian, like myself, must respond to this crisis by reflecting upon whether the God in whom our people believe is a God who works also through our Puerto Rican history to bring love, justice, and freedom into our lives.

The recent situation on the island of Vieques presents another occasion for serious reflection on the history of Puerto Ricans in the USA. Vieques presents a microcosm of the contradiction and ambiguity that is experienced in Puerto Rican life. Though the US government has pledged its stewardship over the island of Vieques, it has done everything *but* take care of its environment, much less the people who live there. While life in the United States purports to enhance one's quality of life and access to opportunity, the census data confirms the opposite for Puerto Ricans living here.

The journey to freedom from bondage, of which colonial status has been representative, has not been any easy road. It has met with a great deal of backlash, as witnessed by the most recent failure of the Vieques Recovery and Development Act of 2011. On paper, it seems as if the effort can never lead to the result of freedom. But Vieques has shown us that the miraculous is within our reach. In the wake of that and other international events which have cast a spotlight on the imperialistic tactics of occupation that world powers use, I believe it is an opportune moment to ask this question in relation to Puerto Rico: Is it possible for Puerto Ricans to transcend a colonial imaginary of dependence and docility while living within and maintaining a neo-colonial relationship? Stated differently, is it possible for the Puerto Rican spirit to be free when the body is bound? I am suggesting here that the subtitle *Prophesy Freedom* delves deeper than proclaiming a particular political status. I am exploring here whether the theological question of identity in relation to God can be reconciled with the political question of Puerto Rican identity in relation to the United States. I am exploring whether the theological question of salvation in Christ can be reconciled with the socio-economic reality of Puerto Rican suffering in a poverty-stricken environment. Finally, I am exploring whether the theological question of eschatological hope can be reconciled with the overwhelming sense of despair in the Puerto Rican community. As I pose these questions, I am presupposing that in relation to God, all are free; yet that in relation to the USA at this moment in history, all Puerto Ricans are not free. But, as the title also suggests, freedom prophesied is freedom claimed in the here and now. No one else can bestow it upon us and no one can take it away. It is a freedom of our own design and definition; it is our story. We belong to it and it belongs to us.

NOTES

1. Puerto Rico is an archipelago consisting of three main islands which, in descending order of size, are Puerto Rico, Vieques, and Culebra.
2. Maria Teresa Babín in Arturo Morales Carrión, ed. *Puerto Rico: A Political and Cultural History* (New York, NY: W. W. Norton and Company, Inc., 1983), 344–352. Some have also referred to Puerto Ricans living outside of Puerto Rico as the "diaspora community."
3. The official political terminology for Puerto Rico is *estado libre asociado* or free associated state, which was decreed in 1952 under Public Law 600; the term "commonwealth" is often used interchangeably with Free Associated State. This term, however, is problematic for a number of reasons, not the least of which is the choice of words themselves, since Puerto Rico is neither free (the U.S. government maintains ultimate decision-making power over it), nor associated (since association implies equal power, which is not the case here), nor state (since Puerto Rico is not a state of the union or a sovereign state); see Arturo Morales Carrión, *Puerto Rico: A Political and Cultural History* (New York, NY: W.W. Norton and Company, Inc., 1983), 256–307, for a PPD-friendly perspective on the events leading to the institution of Free Associated State status and its immediate implications.
4. Even after the death of David Sanes Rodríquez, an advertisement for the Vieques facility was found on the Navy's website that boasted of the

base's multi-dimensional capabilities for live weapons training and war simulation. It was immediately pulled from the site. Various news reports also began to research numerous other "accidents" that had occurred on Vieques since the Navy's occupation, reports that were subsequently denied; see both *The Vieques Times* and www.viequeslibre.com.

5. Letter from Admiral V.E. Clark, Chief of Naval Operations, to Gordon England, Secretary of the Navy, on 10 December 2002. This memo was attached to a letter sent to the Speaker of the House of Representatives, Dennis Hastert, on 10 January 2003, as well as to the President. In addition to the reason given for the cessation of training at the Vieques facility, Admiral Clark claimed that Vieques had become less suitable for preparing for "the challenges of armed conflict in the 21st century;" from www.viequeslibre.com.

6. In 2000, four of the five counties with the largest Puerto Rican population in the continental United States were in New York State; see Pew Research Center, "Puerto Rican Population By County," August 11, 2014, http://www.pewhispanic.org/2014/08/11/puerto-rican-population-by-county/.

7. *The Vieques Times*, Vol. 152 (Summer 2004): 9.

8. Kathleen McCaffrey states, "Legally, cleanup of unexploded ordinance and other military waste is determined by projected land use. Land designated for "conservation use" requires only a superficial cleanup, since presumably no humans will inhabit it. The wilderness designation to the live-impact range, bombed 60 years, has less to do with maintaining the quality of the ecosystem than with evading responsibility for environmental remediation. Land inhabited by pelicans and sea turtles, simply put, is not a national priority for cleanup." Cited in "Clearing Out without Cleaning Up: The U.S. and Vieques Island," by Josue Melendez, Council on Hemispheric Affairs (COHA) Forum, May 19, 2011.

9. This information was reported in *The Vieques Times* (Vol. 152, Summer 2004), which cited its source as the 7 May 2004 report released by the Puerto Rican Health Department. Other startling health statistics include impaired vision (82% higher than Puerto Rico), anemia (64% higher), and headache (60% higher). Health Secretary Johnny Rullán declared Vieques an "emergency medical situation," as the rate of cancer is 27% higher than that of the rest of Puerto Rico.

10. *The Vieques Times*, Vol. 152 (Summer 2004): 3.

11. Studies conducted by CasaPUEBLO, an independent community organization, and reported on the website www.viequeslibre.com in Spring 2002: "The most affected [plant] species were those with shallow root systems, such as chili peppers, pigeon peas, pasture grass and squash, while the trees of guamá and mango were less contaminated. This is consistent with the thesis that heavy metals are deposited in the civilian area

through air dispersion by windblown dust from the bombing zone." The studies from a variety of different and unrelated sources confirm these findings; they are too numerous to cite in this work. The www.vieques-libre.com website is an excellent starting point for articles gathered from Puerto Rican, U.S., and international new sources on the various aspects of the Vieques environmental and health impact. Most sinister is the press release from the former Head of the Pentagon's Depleted Uranium Project (dated 9 February 2000); Dr. Rokke acknowledges the Navy's willful violation of regulations regarding the use of depleted uranium munitions on Vieques. The Navy's disregard for the welfare of the people and environment of Vieques is both criminal and reprehensible. The numerous photos of the waste products from years of unchecked damage speak for themselves.

12. H.R. 1645 Vieques Recovery and Development Act of 2011 was introduced by Congressman Steve Rothman (D-NJ); "Vieques Recovery and Development Act of 2011—Directs the President to acquire or convert real property located within the Municipality of Vieques, Puerto Rico, for the purpose of constructing: (1) a specialty hospital that provides treatment for the sick and injured; and (2) a toxins research center that studies the existence, prevalence, and impact of toxins in Vieques, provides recommendations regarding the prevention of exposure to harmful levels of such toxins, and shares findings with medical personnel at such hospital. Requires the President to: (1) operate and maintain the quality of the hospital and research center; (2) develop an interagency plan to ensure that such residents benefit from improved access to federal programs, federal discretionary funding sources, and federal agency technical assistance; and (3) appoint a federal ombudsman for Vieques, who shall monitor the development and implementation of such plan. Prohibits the President from carrying out this Act until the administrative claims filed on May 18, 2009, by the Mayor of Vieques for money damages against the Department of the Navy have been settled or compromised. Authorizes a $10,000 award for settlement of any personal injury claim filed before enactment of this Act by an individual who was a resident of Vieques during or after the Navy's use of chemical weapons, toxic chemicals, and heavy metals for military training operations on the island, including for illness or death arising from such use. Increases awards for individuals who submit medical documentation of contracting a disease that is life-threatening, chronic, or related to heavy metals toxicity. Deems any award payment to be full settlement of the claim and a complete release by the individual of such claim against the United States or its employees" https://www.congress.gov/bill/112th-congress/house-bill/1645.

13. Pedro Juan Soto, *Usmaíl* (San Juan, PR: Editorial Cultural, 1959). This novel presents the "horror and fear of life on Vieques,...which was in the past a peaceful agricultural [and fishing] community but is now a United States naval base where military maneuvers are carelessly and tragically carried out and the local population is left to fend for itself." Victoria Ortiz, "Introduction" to *Spiks* by Pedro Juan Soto (New York, NY: Monthly Review Press, 1973), 17.

14. I use the term "latinx" as a recognition that the binary linguistic structure of the Spanish language—with the masculine "o" and feminine "a"—does not reflect adequately the broader gender identities and realities of queer identified folk; the term "Latinx" is an effort to challenge that binary and recognize the multi-gendered identities of our people.

15. Allan Fiqueroa Deck, "Latino Theology: The Year of the 'Boom,'" *Journal of Hispanic/Latino Theology* 1.2: 51–63.

16. There have been a few articles and essays in selected journals and/or edited volumes, such as David Traverzo's "Towards a Theology of Mission in the U.S. Puerto Rican Migrant Community: from Captivity to Liberation." *Apuntes* 9.3: 51–59; Juan A. Carmona, *The Liberation of Puerto Rico: A Theological Perspective*. D. Min. thesis. Rochester, NY: Colgate-Rochester Divinity School/Crozer Theological Seminary, 1982 (although this has not been published beyond the thesis level); and Caleb Rosado. "Thoughts on a Puerto Rican Theology of Community." *Apuntes* 9.1: 10–12; but nothing approaching the volume of writing being generated from other U.S. Hispanic/Latino(a) theologians from a Mexican-American and Cuban-American perspective, or Puerto Rican theologians in Puerto Rico.

17. Again, I am referring here to the limited voice of Puerto Rican theologians in the continental United States, as opposed to the Puerto Rican theologians in Puerto Rico, writing in Spanish.

18. Catherine E. Walsh, *Pedagogy and the Struggle for Voice: Issues of Language, Power and Schooling for Puerto Ricans* (New York, NY: Bergin and Garvey, 1991).

19. The tremendous production of the Program for the Analysis of Religion among Latinos (PARAL) has been a critical contribution to the area of Puerto Rican religion in the U.S.; see http://centropr.hunter.cuny.edu/ and bibliography for more titles in the field.

20. Roberto Ramirez and G. Patricia de la Cruz, *The Hispanic Population in the United States: March 2002* (Washington, D.C.: Current Population Reports U.S. Census Bureau, 2002).

21. See Elizondo, *Galilean Journey: The Mexican-American Promise* (Maryknoll, NY: Orbis Books, 1983); *Guadalupe, Mother of the New Creation* (Maryknoll, NY: Orbis Books, 1997).

22. Traverzo, "Towards a Theology of Mission in the U.S. Puerto Rican Migrant Community," 51–59.
23. Ibid., 51.
24. This distinction is made by Antonio M. Stevens-Arroyo and cited as footnote (11) in Allan Figueroa Deck's article, "Latino Theology," 56.
25. The concept of social/cultural formation and its use of story as a social scientific device is being utilized within interdisciplinary religious studies, such as the model of the *African Americans and the Bible* project spearheaded by Vincent Wimbush.
26. René Marqués, "The Function of the Puerto Rican Writer Today," in *The Docile Puerto Rican* (Philadelphia, PA: Temple University Press, 1976), 115.
27. See Ana María Díaz-Stevens, *Oxcart Catholicism on Fifth Avenue: The Impact of the Puerto Rican Migration upon the Archdiocese of New York* (Notre Dame, IN: University of Notre Dame Press, 1993), 12–15, for a complete description of this migration and its years of concentration.
28. Alvarez, Carmelo. "Theology from the Margins: A Caribbean Response…" in *Theology: Expanding the Borders*. María Pilar Aquino and Roberto S. Goizueta, eds. (Mystic, CT: Twenty-third Publications, 1998); Davis Kortright, *Emancipation Still Comin': Explorations in Caribbean Emancipatory Theology* (Maryknoll, NY: Orbis Books, 1990).
29. Ramón Grosfoguel, *Colonial Subjects: Puerto Ricans in Global Perspective* (Berkeley, CA: University of California Press, 2003). In this critical work, Grosfoguel asserts that the perspective he articulates therein, a "Puerto Rican subaltern perspective" does not "essentialize or…pretend to represent the voices of Puerto Rican. Instead [he] take[s] as a point of departure some voices and expressions of Puerto Rican subaltern thinking" (p. 1–2). In this book, I employ the same starting point.
30. Iris M. Zavala, "Introduction," *The Intellectual Roots of Independence: An Anthology of Puerto Rican Political Essays*, Iris M. Zavala and Rafael Rodríguez, eds. (New York, NY and London, UK: Monthly Review Press, 1980), 35.
31. Ibid., 12–15. Operation Bootstrap was an economic development plan conceived and imposed by the United States in the 1940s to hasten the pace of "industrialization" on the island of Puerto Rico; it was a major catalyst for the massive migration from the island to the continental United States.

CHAPTER 2

The Story of Puerto Rican Oppression and Resistance

The tradition of liberation theology has taught us that all theology is contextual and emerges from the experience of a specific community. Theology, as Gustavo Gutiérrez has asserted, is the second step; the first is one's life experience and praxis. The story of oppression and resistance of Puerto Rican people must be understood in the context of our sociohistorical experience of colonization, both on the island and in the continental US, as the foundation upon which a decolonial theology can be constructed. This chapter provides the backdrop, but it does so in a particular way: with the lens of history focused squarely on the relationship between Puerto Rico and the USA, a relationship of colonized and colonizer, of oppressed and oppressor, of non-power and super-power, of those silenced and those who speak.

In order to resist the silence itself and to legitimize the larger story, my own family/community story serves as a personal illustration of the communal context. Just as a story moves from particular terms to greater commonality as it progresses, so too will I delve more deeply into the lives of the particular people, including myself, as part of the overall process of breaking the silence, with freedom as its goal. I engage in this reflective and revealing process because all theology is both contextual and personal; the personal is political; and the political is communal/relational if it is to be authentically Puerto Rican.

I believe that the story of our people has a profound effect on our ability to do justice in the world. By telling our story, we realize our freedom and power that is part of the freedom and power of God within us.

© The Author(s) 2017
T. Delgado, *A Puerto Rican Decolonial Theology*, New Approaches to Religion and Power, DOI 10.1007/978-3-319-66068-4_2

This power frees and empowers us even more to tell the story and to hear the stories of others, which, in turn, unleashes the power of others and moves them into freedom through solidarity. The stories themselves confirm this same movement: in the face of oppression, captivity, and powerlessness, the whisper of freedom and power can be heard. Both story content and storytelling process illustrate our collective struggle against oppression, captivity, and powerlessness and lead us toward freedom and power, confirming a belief that freedom and power cannot be denied the Puerto Rican people, now or ever, because they reside within and are God-given.

The Puerto Rican, in relation to the United States,[1] constantly wrestles with forces of assimilation while maintaining a distinctive voice and perspective. This conflict, which manifests itself internally and externally, highlights the underlying issue at stake: How do we make peace with and create balance among the intertwined relationships that we Puerto Ricans embody so that we can live in freedom? The "triple consciousness"[2] as noted by Eldin Villafañe demonstrates that no matter what tactics are used to silence a segment of the Puerto Rican population, the desire to be heard is stronger than the effort imposed by those who benefit from our voicelessness.

I believe that Puerto Ricans will not be content with our story being ignored; the writers who address these conflicts in their stories affirm this.[3] As part of the larger story, I now turn to the shadows of my own family and community story, reversing the hands of time to the bucolic hills of Puerto Rico when a world was turned upside down at the speed of a Pan Am flight, and the vibrant island green faded to a steely asphalt gray.

MY COMMUNITY/FAMILY STORY[4]

The story of my Puerto Rican community begins with my Puerto Rican family, which is extensive and diverse. My mother, Ana Julia Rodríguez, the sixth of eight children, came to New York City in the early 1950s at the age of ten or so. She, along with her younger siblings, Elsa and Gilberto, plus two older sisters to help care for them, Carmen Lucía and Ana Marta, had been living in their small mountain town of Barranquitas in central Puerto Rico with their father, Severiano Rodríguez. Their mother, Francisca Santos, along with two older sisters, Carmen Mónica and Rosa, had migrated to New York a few years earlier to find work and save enough money to send for the others. They found piecework in Manhattan's garment district. In order to make more money, they would take home some of the pieces and work well into the night on their own sewing machines, only to return the completed pieces to the factory the next day.

My grandfather Severiano stayed behind in Puerto Rico performing odd carpentry jobs to support the children in his care. For more than three generations, his family had owned a large coffee plantation in the hills of Barranquitas but was forced to sell the majority of the land to a large and powerful US company after they were squeezed out of the coffee export market in the 1930s. Unable to work the land for sustenance, Severiano and his siblings, who had also sold their land holdings, were faced with the choice of moving out of the *campo* to live in either San Juan, the coastal capital city, or New York. Either way, they were forced to decide between finding sustainable work and leaving their home or remaining in place and starving.[5]

The Rodríguez family was finally reunited and settled in New York City in the early 1950s; at age ten, my mother and her siblings (at least the ones who were not working in the factory) entered the New York City school system without understanding or speaking much, if any, English. A shy, mild-mannered child, my mother was so devastated by the mocking and teasing she endured not only from the other children but also from the teacher as she attempted to speak English that for a year she became completely silent outside the home. She did not speak at all in the classroom until she had acquired enough English skills to escape the ridicule. But this period of having no voice, of being silenced, would be an experience that would remain with her for a very long time.

On my father's side of the family, another version of a similar story was taking place. On the southern part of the island, my grandmother, Monserrate Pagán, was preparing to leave San German and move to New York. It was the early 1930s and, as an unmarried woman in her late twenties, my grandmother was doing what few Puerto Rican women did at that time: make an independent move to live an independent life. But her motives went beyond feminist ideals; she was leaving the island, in part, to escape the racial discrimination that she encountered every day. While her older brother was lighter in complexion, defying their definite African ancestry, my grandmother's darker complexion and African features did not allow her to "pass." When this same brother married into the prominent Lugo family, Monserrate felt that she was not welcome.

She left so as not to make life more difficult for her brother, hoping to leave the racial oppression behind as well.

When she arrived in New York, she too found work in the garment factories and supported herself financially. She also met and fell in love with a man, Gregorio "Gollo" Delgado. It was only after she became pregnant in 1937 that she discovered the man she loved was actually married; his wife was waiting in Puerto Rico for her ticket to join him in New York. Now, as a single woman with a child out of wedlock, my grandmother was forced to leave her job,[6] collect public assistance monies, and seek out the help of her younger unmarried brother and other relatives who had also relocated to New York. Her pride and determination compelled her to carve out the best life she could for her son who, despite her anger, hurt, and betrayal, she named after his father. She would never marry nor have any children other than my father. And for the rest of her life, she would never speak another word to the father of her child, even though they lived within a city block of each other, even though she lived in an apartment above his sister's flower shop, and even though she watched her son play with his five half-siblings. That silence would be carried over to the next generation for whom the unspoken rule was clear: No one was to talk about my grandfather, know his whereabouts, or care about his life. His presence was erased from the picture; he was no longer part of the official family story.

100 YEARS OF SOLITUDE: THE STORY OF PUERTO RICAN OPPRESSION AND RESISTANCE

Prelude: A Snapshot of Puerto Rican Life Before 1898

The complex phenomena of religious, political, and economic experience in Puerto Rico is a necessary prelude to the story of US involvement in Puerto Rico because it forms at least part of the backdrop for the storytelling of Puerto Rican creative writers Esmeralda Santiago (1948–), Pedro Juan Soto (1928–2002), and Rosario Ferré (1938–2016), as well as the contextual foundation of their literature for theological development.

The specifics of Puerto Rican religious identity are an intricate mixture of Taíno and African spiritual/cosmological belief systems as well as Catholic Christianity of medieval Iberia.[7] The spirituality of the people whom the conquistadors encountered on the island of Boriquen (Land of the Brave Lord)—Puerto Rico's indigenous name prior to Spanish colonization[8]—was a spirituality of the cosmos in which all the cycles of nature were woven into the everyday lives of the people.[9]

The impact of the Spanish colonial conquest on this cosmological order was immense. Forceful conversion became necessary in order for the Taínos to accept a civilized and cultured life necessary for true Christian existence, marked by Catholic theology and economic prosperity.[10] Those who were responsible for imposing this new order of church/state were burdened by the following theo-political questions on the nature of humanity relevant for Puerto Ricans today:

> Is humanity one or diverse? Are some human beings superior in intelligence and prudence, and do they therefore have a right to special privileges and unique responsibilities? Is the domination of some nations by others justified because of natural or historical inequalities? Do valuable mineral resources belong to the inhabitants of the territory where they are, or to whoever can invest in their development?[11]

At the time of the conquest and immediately following it, a clear link between the evangelization of the native population and the capital enrichment of the Spaniards existed. Rivera-Pagán outlines these events in detail and comes to the conclusion that some, such as Bartolome de las Casas, were forging a theology of liberation and regarded as sinful the conquistadors' violent attempts to evangelize the native people.[12] Despite such prophetic voices against the inhumane powers of church and state in the sixteenth through the nineteenth centuries, four hundred years of exclusive Iberian Catholicism endured, shaped by the actions of the conquistadors.

The Spanish missionary clergy molded this exclusive Iberian Catholicism, but their presence did not sustain the faith of the populace. In fact, the distance of the Catholic Church, geographically and otherwise, and the absence of permanent clergy in the central rural areas of Puerto Rico's mountain interior, "led to the evolution of an unorthodox, Creole Catholicism,"[13] characterized by popular religious devotion to the saints, recitation of the rosary, an oral tradition of the biblical stories, as well as an integration with and interdependence upon the cycles of the natural world in an agriculturally based social system. Still, the influence of the Spanish Catholic Church in shaping Puerto Rican society cannot be underestimated. With little, if any, competition from outside cultural or intellectual influences, the Catholic Church in Puerto Rico molded both social institutions and popular attitudes, characterized by a complete deference to a "fundamentally authoritative society,"[14] sheltered from the exterior world by an insular colonial government; and sheltered from the interior by a lack of access, infrastructure, and communication among the populace, particularly the peasants living in the mountainous interior of the island.[15]

The agricultural system sustained by these peasants of the interior was the basis for the Puerto Rican economy during the period of Spanish colonization. As a Spanish colonial outpost, Puerto Rico's economy was in an unhealthy state by the early 1800s given the numerous trade restrictions imposed upon it by Spain that limited any production that would compete with products from Spain itself. Prohibitions and heavy taxes were levied on both land and production, further limiting the economy's growth. In fact, the island was seen primarily as a strategic geographic location and a provider of certain export commodities, namely sugar and coffee. Very little, if any, profit was reinvested in the island, except in areas where it bolstered the domestic market supply of goods necessary for the production of the export industries. After over 250 years of Spanish rule, the island had no real infrastructure or industry. Besides, Spain had larger and more profitable ventures elsewhere such as in South America, Mexico, and Cuba.[16] From an economic perspective, Puerto Rico cost Spain more than it produced in goods and services.[17]

However, Spain was not about to relinquish its hold on Puerto Rico so easily, for what it lacked in economic value it made up by being a strategic military gateway to Central and South America as well as the Gulf region, indeed to the entire Caribbean basin.[18] Puerto Rico was for Spain, "a strategic outpost of empire—the cockpit...of the Hispanic Caribbean defense system—so that its civilian aspect was altogether subordinated to its military significance."[19]

Four main factors mitigated the emergence of a national movement for sovereignty as had begun in other Spanish colonies. First, the majority of the elite of the island, in professional and administrative positions, remained loyal to the Spanish monarchy. Those of the elite class who were willing to entertain the possibility of independence were aware that they had to mobilize the masses for a successful campaign. The apathy of the masses toward the political status of the island, combined with the fear instilled in the elite class by exiled elites from other French and

Spanish colonies that had experienced violent rebellion, was yet a second factor against the effort to break from Spain. The formidable presence of Spanish troops on the island was a third factor in deterring an independence movement. While the military had maintained a presence in Puerto Rico since the beginning of the colonial period, it increased dramatically after 1810 with their defeat on the mainland colonies; they were redeployed in greater numbers on the island as an effort to maintain a stronghold after numerous failures. The increased presence of the military served to tighten the colonial noose around the island; for if Spain were to loosen its ties in San Juan and Havana, it would in a sense be admitting that it was no longer a great empire with an even greater spirit and vocation for colonization.[20] Finally, the elite class was reluctant to begin a radical movement toward sovereignty since Spain was gesturing toward greater autonomy for the island in the form of increased participation in the island's governance structure as well as in the Spanish Cortes, the legislative assembly of Spain at the time. The elite were not willing to jeopardize their potential to be more heavily involved in the colony's political future.[21]

The authorities of the Catholic Church in Puerto Rico were also unwilling to jeopardize their standing by promoting any dissent among the masses against the Spanish crown, upon which it was financially dependent. While there were a small number of priests who tried to bring the concerns of the Puerto Rican people to the island administrators, the Catholic Church as an institution was less concerned with the needs of the people and more focused on maintaining its position of power and privilege. The economic and political security of the Spanish bishops, then, required an unwavering loyalty to the monarchy. To this end, the bishops propagated a message of passivity and silent acceptance of Spanish rule, bolstered by a doctrine of God's providence for the Puerto Rican people.

Despite the unchanged status of the Catholic Church on the island, many other changes were occurring in the three latter decades of the nineteenth century, clearing the path for heightened United States' interest in Puerto Rico and its eventual occupation in 1898. First, the Puerto Rican economy was shifting from subsistence crops to more commercial crops concentrated on coffee, sugar, and tobacco, in this order of importance. Puerto Rico's agricultural economy had improved somewhat as a result of eased restrictions from Spain; it still consisted mainly of small farming of minor, yet diversified, crops.[22] In contrast to the larger plantations of Cuba, these farms cultivated vegetables, particularly root vegetables, and kept livestock including cattle, horses, pigs, fowl, sheep, and goats.[23] Despite such expansion, only twenty-one percent of the arable land of the island was being cultivated by the year 1898, the consequent mass poverty a fact not lost on the American invaders.

Second, with economic growth, albeit modest, came an increase in the level of discontent with the colonial status of Puerto Rico among the intellectual and professional elite. Because they witnessed the actual improvement of quality of life on the island through increased trade with countries other than Spain, including the USA, these elites realized that their colonial overlord was stifling the island's potential for greater growth and progress. Murmurs of political autonomy began to be heard, particularly among those who would benefit economically from severed ties, including the industrial and entrepreneurial classes. By contrast, those in positions made more secure by Spanish monarchical rule, including political officials, military, and clergy, opposed any change to the island's colonial status. Spaniards themselves usually held these positions, not Puerto Rican-born *criollos*.[24]

Luís Muñoz Rivera and José Celso Barbosa were two such proponents of Puerto Rican autonomy from Spain. Autonomy, in their view, did not mean complete severance from Spain; in an autonomous relationship, Puerto Rico would be granted greater powers of self-governance in the administration of the island, and participation in the Spanish Cortes. There were contemporaries of Rivera and Barbosa for whom autonomy served only as a gateway to complete independence; Román Baldorioty de Castro, Rosendo Matienzo Cintrón, and José de Diego represented such a perspective.[25] For others, such as Eugenio Maria de Hostos and Ramón Emeterio Betances,[26] complete and immediate independence was the only viable option for Puerto Rico.

Betances was a key figure in the independence movement though he had been expelled from the island as a result of his anti-slavery and pro-independence stance. While exiled in New York, Santo Domingo, and St. Thomas, he organized the Puerto Rican Revolutionary Committee, gathering like-minded persons to the cause of Puerto Rican sovereignty. With the help of others including military personnel and small farmers, he succeeded in organizing a group of several hundred men who successfully occupied the town of Lares on September 23, 1868. The revolutionaries declared the Republic of Puerto Rico on that site and established a temporary system of self-government. However, as units pushed forward to gain more control, the Spanish military squelched the resistance. Known as *El Grito de Lares*, and considered by some as "the most serious challenge to Spanish domination in Puerto Rico,"[27] this event came to symbolize both the seemingly insurmountable power of colonialism as well as the indomitable spirit of Puerto Rican resistance and self-determination. While some historians have termed Lares "an amateur-like skirmish" without lasting consequence,[28] it has become for many Puerto Ricans more than a symbol of "the continuing struggle for Puerto Rican self-determination, identity, and nationalism."[29]

It is important to note that the slave population in the other Spanish colonies of Cuba and Santo Domingo connected the gain of independence and sovereignty with the struggle for emancipation, as with the revolutionaries in Puerto Rico such as Betances. The abolition of slavery and the rhetoric of independence went hand in hand given the large African slave populations on these islands, which were heavy sugar and cotton producing economies. Such was not the case in Puerto Rico; in fact, slaves represented only 5% of the total population in 1872. This relatively small population faced the presence of a substantial military, which had relocated to Puerto Rico after its numerous defeats in other Spanish territories; such a presence would have made insurrection by a small number of slaves virtually impossible. In addition, the island's economy did not necessitate the importation of more slaves since an abundance of free non-black labor already existed on the island. After making the case to the Spanish monarchy, which had by this time witnessed the violent insurrections in Cuba and Santo Domingo and feared the same in Puerto Rico, the island succeeded in abolishing slavery in 1873, not by having to fight for it but by decree.[30]

It was also by decree that Puerto Ricans gained a modicum of autonomy from Spain in 1897; this charter granted (1) political and civil rights to Spanish citizens on the island; (2) an electoral system, allowing for self-government on the island and representation in the Spanish Cortes; and (3) an autonomous regime which would lead to complete sovereignty.[31] There were some among the Puerto Rican liberal elite who anticipated complete independence as the next logical step in the autonomic governmental experiment; given the fact that Spain was in the midst of a major war effort, many believed that such sovereignty would be granted in the face of more pressing conflicts. What the Puerto Ricans did not anticipate was the complete overruling of all that had been gained when General Sampson and his troops marched onto the island's shore on that fateful July day in 1898.

ACT I: UNITED STATES POLITICAL AND ECONOMIC HEGEMONY CIRCA 1898

The year 1898 marked a major turning point for the Puerto Rican people who had, by this time, made Catholicism their own by imbuing it with Taíno and African influences and those of the natural world around them. The invasion of the USA at the end of the Spanish–American War gave Puerto Rico a new colonial overlord replacing Catholic Spain. But while Spain saw no conflict of interest in a Catholic state, and indeed had strongly underlined it, the United States was vehemently opposed, at least outwardly, to such religious collusion, except when it applied to US Protestant denominations. Catholic missionaries, priests, and religious were forced to leave, and Catholic hospitals, schools, etc., were taken over by US authorities.[32]

Protestant denominations saw the acquisition of Puerto Rico as a prime opportunity to move into a territory that had been inaccessible for four hundred years. Missionary accounts of the time speak of the US entry into the island as a "saving grace," an opportunity for the Protestant denominations to bring the true gospel to a people for whom religion was dead.[33] To these missionaries, the Catholic Church under the Spanish crown had done a great spiritual disservice to the people, depriving them of knowledge of the Gospel through the Bible and tolerating superstitions. Therefore, the missionaries and church leaders did not admonish the United States' political and economic actions as oppressive. On the contrary, they heralded them for allowing an opportunity to bring more into the Christian fold and educate Puerto Ricans with the true Christianity as opposed to the "obscurantist" nature of Catholicism to which they had been exclusively exposed.

The Christian mosaic on the island of Puerto Rico was further elaborated by the introduction of the Pentecostal missionary movement. It was the only missionary effort that was initiated indigenously; that is, a native Puerto Rican migrant worker Juan L. Lugo, converted in 1912 on the island of Hawaii where he had migrated for agricultural work, brought it to Puerto Rico. Lugo came to Puerto Rico as an ordained minister of the Assemblies of God and began his ministry in Ponce in

1916. However, Catholic and Protestant officials alike attacked this new "spirit filled" ministry as a threat to Catholic ecclesial authority and Protestant biblical tradition.[34] Yet, the predominantly poor Puerto Ricans who were attracted to Pentecostalism brought with them Puerto Rican spiritism and African traditional religion which continued to exist in its own right as an undercurrent within and despite Catholic and Protestant missionary efforts.[35]

The invasion of Puerto Rico by the USA in 1898 dealt a serious economic blow to the island as well. The USA was quick to establish complete and absolute control, militarily and economically. While super-ficially economic conditions seemed to improve, in fact the new eco-nomic and political policies fostered growing dependence on the United States and less self-sufficiency for the island. The doctrine of "manifest destiny" coupled with the Monroe Doctrine had dire consequences for the economic condition of the island.[36] The agricultural economy shifted from subsistence to commercial farming with the large plantation model as central. Sugar became the monopoly crop with United States multi-nationals maintaining majority ownership of sugar plantations. Because land that had previously been used for subsistence crops was now used for sugar production, the island began to import more and export fewer subsistence goods, and this increase in imports and therefore US tariffs drained the island financially.[37] Those who had previously owned their own land for subsistence farming were forced to sell it and become wage laborers; there was more land available than people to work the land.

The production of coffee suffered greatly at the hands of the USA as well. After 1898, the lucrative export of Puerto Rican coffee to Spain and Portugal was severed. Without a market in which to sell their crop, coffee growers began to lose money. The Puerto Rican monetary unit was devalued at the same time, making it difficult for coffee growers to secure any financial assistance (loans) to tide them over. This situation forced them to buy into a "deal" to sell off their land and/or switch to sugar cane production, which had a great market for export in the United States. One cannot tell the story of the emergence of sugar on the island without telling the parallel story of the decline of coffee.[38]

While the Depression of the 1930s had a tremendous impact on the native inhabitants of the island with unemployment at 60%,[39] the United States (via corporations or government) controlled 44% of all cultivated land, 60% of all banks and 100% of the sea lines/waterway access by 1930.[40] By the year 1940, the majority of the land on the island was owned or managed by absentee landlords who reaped the profits but did not reinvest in the island, except for what was absolutely necessary for the continuation of profitability. The island's infrastructure began to improve to support the commercial farming efforts, leading to more roads built and utilities available even in remote locations. Whereas in 1898 the United States described Puerto Rico as underdeveloped and backward, it has been described, after four decades of US economic intervention, as "mis-developed and stagnant."[41]

The US invasion of Puerto Rico had a significant impact on the political landscape of the island. In the years leading up to the Spanish–American War, the island's advocates for independence had secured an audience in the Spanish monarchy, namely through Sagasta who, after the assassination of Prime Minister Cánovas del Castillo, became the leading political figure in Spain and one who had the power to grant Puerto Rico its autonomy, which he did in 1897.[42] Once the island became a possession of the United States, however, all former agreements/treaties with Spain were deemed null and void. Those who had fought so hard for the ultimate goal of independence saw their efforts come to naught.[43]

The imposition of colonial rule was solidified by the United States through the enactment of two significant pieces of legislation, which continue to affect political policy in Puerto Rico to this day. The Foracker Act of 1900 granted the residents of Puerto Rico subordination to the rule of the US military and resident governor, all appointed by the executive branch of the US government.[44] The Jones–Shaforth Act of 1917 granted the residents official US citizenship; yet this citizenship does not include representation in the Congress nor does it permit Puerto Ricans to vote in the general election for President of the USA—though it did allow the US government to draft Puerto Ricans to fight under the US flag during World War I. The role of the governor was a new appointment under the US regime and one assigned by the president. The governor, at this early stage of the colony, was not a native son or daughter.[45] In addition, English was instituted as the official language of the island as well as the primary medium of instruction in all schools.[46]

The US invasion of Puerto Rico had a significant impact on the social fabric of the island. With the commencement of large capital business ventures, many Puerto Ricans who were accustomed to working only for subsistence and necessity were required to work for excess and profit in order to be considered a "good worker." Thus, the system of capitalism instituted on the island brought with it a moral judgment about labor: If you work only for what you need, you are considered lazy and lacking in initiative; if you work for more than what is needed, you are considered entrepreneurial, the latter being more desirable.[47] Since many families were forced to sell their land holdings, the concentration of jobs shifted from the rural to the urban areas, usually in the coastal region. Families were either separated in order to find work, or were relocated altogether. In both cases, this led to a breakdown in the communal bonds of the rural community.[48]

Resisting US Hegemony: 1898–1945

The period following the US invasion of Puerto Rico was met with resistance commensurate with the levels of political, economic, social, and religious upheaval. Pedro Albizu Campos, a Harvard educated lawyer who became the President of the Nationalist Party of Puerto Rico in 1930, was a significant figure in this period; he became increasingly insistent upon sovereignty as time progressed.[49] His contemporary and friend, José de Diego, was also a strong nationalist whose poetry reflected his unbending vision of independence for Puerto Rico. Both were radicals in the political sense, yet coupled with a conservative Catholicism that lent itself to a strong anti-American sentiment.[50] De Diego's poetry, for example, is laden with religious motifs that graphically invoke the death and resurrection of Jesus.[51]

The quest for sovereignty and self-determination, although thwarted at the onset of US occupation, did not falter or despair. Resistance took on a number of different shapes, some subtle and others overt. In their unique way, the *jíbaros* of the interior resisted a change in their way of life and community customs by refusing to sell and/or leave their land until it was absolutely necessary.[52] While "English" was the language required in the schools, Spanish was maintained in all other matters and certainly within the home.[53]

The decade of the 1930s witnessed the pinnacle of violent opposition to the colonial empire, as Puerto Rico was dealt a heavy economic blow with the onset of the Depression period, hastened by Hurricane *San Felipe* in 1928, with levels of unemployment reaching over 60% in some areas. The dire economic situation was a catalyst for resistance among the poor working classes. Those who had previously understood work as necessary for subsistence were now required to look upon work in terms of capital (i.e., making more than what is needed in order to sell for profit). Many resisted the abusive and exploitative practices of the plantation overlords by creating secret labor associations.[54] Labor workers in the sugar industry who had made connections with the US labor movement (e.g., the AFL) began to strike; these actions gained momentum across the island in 1933 when sugar cane workers went on strike and brought "King Sugar" to a halt.[55]

It is not difficult to see how tensions must have run very high during this period; the economic pressure led to a boiling over of anger, resentment, and reactionary militancy. In 1935, the University of Puerto Rico was the site for the killings of nationalist militants by the US-controlled police force. In retaliation for these killings, in 1936 Nationalist militants assassinated the chief of police, Col. Francis Riggs. While not directly responsible for the assassination, the Nationalist leader, Albizu Campos, and others, were arrested, tried, and sentenced to federal prison in Georgia. The following year, a Palm Sunday demonstration of Puerto Rican pride and independence in the city of Ponce was the site of what has come to be known as "the Ponce massacre"; the police opened fire on a peaceful Nationalist organized parade, killing twenty and injuring over 200 Puerto Ricans. In 1938, the Nationalists attempted to avenge this massacre by making an assassination attempt on the life of Governor Winship. The decade of the 1930s was a bloody one, indeed.[56]

Those with the strongest fervor for independence tended to come from regions in Puerto Rico that were directly and adversely affected by the rise of the sugar cane industry, namely the central cordillera and western area of the island. These were the coffee producing regions that were forced to make way for the sugar industry's monopoly. As a result of having lost land and all means of subsistence, these were also the regions from which the greatest numbers of migrants to the continental United States originated, bringing with them the same disdain for the sugar monopoly that had displaced them as well as a passion for self-determination.[57]

From a political perspective, resistance took a number of different forms during this time, ranging from diplomatic negotiations to outright violence. A more organized opposition to US domination was beginning to take shape at this time. Rosendo Matienzo Cintrón founded the Puerto Rican Independence Party in 1912. In 1930, Pedro Albizu

Campos was elected President of the pro-independence Nationalist Party. At the same time, Luís Muñoz Marín, who would later become the proponent of a "middle ground" resolution, was studying and living in the USA where the political ideas of the liberal left were encountering Muñoz Marín's national pride and independent spirit. We now know that his shift toward a more "middle ground" resolution had less to do with learning the master's tools to construct a uniquely Puerto Rican democratic ideal, and more to do with fear and extortion asserted by the colonial overlord.[58] Albizu Campos, on the other hand, did not believe that the tools forged by a colonial master could ever serve any purpose other than domination and exploitation.[59]

From a religious perspective, this period saw the carving up of the island by various mainstream Protestant groups who were eager to bring Christianity to a people who were perceived as having "no religion whatsoever." While the Protestant missionaries provided the Puerto Ricans with services to which they previously had limited or no access, the people did not throw out their Catholic faith in exchange for Protestant education, hospitals, food pantries, etc. They may have become Presbyterian, Methodist, or Baptist on paper in order to obtain certain services, but they remained Catholic in belief and ritual practice. The preeminence of Marian devotion through the rosary is an example of a popular religious practice that survived the shift to Protestantism.[60]

Showing a resistance to Protestantism was a *de facto* affirmation of Puerto Rican identity over and against US Americanization through the Protestant churches, for the new colonizer believed that, to become a good American, the Puerto Rican had to strip away all vestiges of the Spanish legacy, including Catholicism. What the Protestant Americans failed to understand was that the Catholicism they encountered in Puerto Rico was more indigenously Puerto Rican than Spaniard, as it had been infused over four hundred years with Taíno and African belief systems, as well as influence from the Canary Islands.[61]

The resistance to religious imposition was deeply connected to the Puerto Rican's efforts to resist the ensuing social upheaval. As stated earlier, the shift from diversified subsistence farming to mono-crop plantation was a major upheaval in Puerto Rican life, which led to inter-island migration from rural to urban areas. As much as they possibly could, the Puerto Rican hill dwellers, or *"jíbaros,"* tried to maintain their way of life, characterized by a connection with the land, acquiring that which is needed for sustenance and no more, and a love of aesthetics and the beauty of "la naturaleza." They rejected the US American corporate work ethic of profit accumulation and, as a result, were seen as lazy and non-entrepreneurial in spirit. Such a perception has led to literature on the "docility" and "passivity" of Puerto Ricans, and their being labeled as indifferent and even apathetic to matters of political import.[62] Yet one can also understand such docility and passivity as a form of resistance to the American way of life, which was seen to value frenetic activity, aggression, and disrespect.[63] Here was a more subtle yet powerful rejection of the American mode of progress, a lack of which the Americans believed Puerto Rico had suffered under the rule of Spain, and which they were eager to increase in the next three decades.

ACT II: OPERATION BOOTSTRAP AND THE "EXODUS EFFECT"

Puerto Ricans transported much of this experience and history to the shores of the USA during the Great Puerto Rican Migration[64] of 1946–1964. During this eighteen-year period, over six hundred thousand (614,940) Puerto Ricans migrated to the USA, compared to less than one hundred thousand (97,129) in the years 1900–1945.[65] The migrants came mostly from the interior hill country where independent religious traditions (ones that were not dependent on ecclesial authority or rites) were vibrant. These periods of mass migration permanently transformed the Catholic, Protestant, and Pentecostal churches in the United States, particularly in the Northeast where many settled. For Catholic Puerto Ricans arriving in New York City, the basement church phenomenon developed to incorporate Puerto Ricans into already existing parishes without "disturbing" the established organization, liturgy, societies, etc.[66] These parishioners were relegated to the status of second-class citizens, a distinction that was merely carried over from the general society; Puerto Ricans were thus forced to make a way for themselves with little aid or welcome. Like the Catholic Church, so too the Protestant churches failed similarly to minister adequately to the influx of Puerto Ricans. Pentecostal churches fared somewhat better since they were established within smaller community pockets around a charismatic minister. They were less dependent on established institutions and were thus more autonomous and indigenous to Puerto Ricans.[67]

The imposition of the federally mandated "Operation Bootstrap" program was the primary catalyst for this exodus of Puerto Ricans from the island. This program aimed to industrialize the island and had significant political, economic, and social consequences. The political party that proved to be the support structure for the program was the PPD (*Partido Popular Democratico* or Popular Democratic Party), led by Luís Muñoz Marín. The general popularity of Muñoz Marín and his ideas for maintaining an autonomous yet dependent relationship with the USA, took even stronger hold. Many considered it to be the party of progress, for it pushed the industrial and manufacturing sectors to take advantage of the federally granted subsidies and tax relief to do business on the island.[68]

Economic power coalesced in the hands of the US capitalists who, once again, were able to partner with the island's governance to bring about rapid change and growth. Seen as positive progress by many, Muñoz Marín's PPD gained almost universal acceptance and support; all other dissenting or critical voices were seen as radical and anti-American, extended to mean anti-Puerto Rican, which could lead to imprisonment. The convergence of the PPD and Operation Bootstrap, at least from 1945 to 1968, solidified "autonomy," now known as free associated state status. Given the overwhelming popularity of the PPD, and Muñoz Marín as the party's main figure, the economic endeavors initiated by the USA were launched without much political opposition or impediment. The economic effect of Operation Bootstrap was extensive in scope. While the early decades of the twentieth century in Puerto Rico were marked by the shift from subsistence to commercial agriculture (with sugar as the monocrop), the Bootstrap period was marked by the shift from commercial agriculture to commercial industry, with light manufacturing as its mainstay.[69]

Thanks to tax incentives, subsidies, and low wage labor, manufacturers flocked to the island to set up shop. Puerto Rico proved a more desirable and lucrative environment than other "developing" countries since it was still under the jurisdiction of the USA and businesses did not have to contend with the laws and restrictions of foreign sovereign nations. The low-skilled, barely educated labor force was adequate for the types of manufacturing companies that relocated there. Yet, the supply did not meet the demand for jobs, and this contributed to the mass migration to the US at the onset of Operation Bootstrap. With such an exodus, the island became segmented into the low-skilled labor force and the highly educated governing elite, with little to no population in the middle, creating a tremendous gap between the upper and lower economic classes.[70]

While one-third of the population remained in the rural areas of the island, these people were the recipients of only one-sixth of the job market. As large agricultural companies bought out the land from the USA, the average rural peasant once again could not provide for his family and thus was forced to become an urban dweller, either on the island (San Juan, Ponce, Mayaquez) or in the continental US (predominantly New York, Chicago, Boston).[71] Unfortunately, only a small percentage of the capital profits made in those initial years of the Bootstrap program filtered their way back into the island's infrastructure. As an incentive to these companies, the federal government supported the efforts to build up the island's roadways, utilities, and other necessary infrastructure; this came at a price, which the Puerto Rican local governance structure had to manage in the form of debt repayment, which continues to choke the island to this day.

The island's reliance on US capital was not the only area of dependence. The manufacturing companies produced items for export and not consumption by the Puerto Rican people. In addition, the Puerto Rican people, influenced by marketing efforts of US companies, were beginning to consume items that were not being produced on the island. For example, canned foods from the States were now replacing homegrown staples from the island; it was more prestigious to have items from the States, since it indicated a person's ability to afford the more expensive goods.[72]

Operation Bootstrap altered the social life of the Puerto Rican people as well. In addition to the preference for imported foods, other US American products and customs were beginning to take root on the island. The role of women in the household and beyond began to shift as more women joined the manufacturing workforce. This also led to an increase in family planning and birth control, which is a distinct—albeit related—issue to that of forced sterilization of Puerto Rican women.[73] Puerto Rican women began to feel the impact of a clash in values once they entered the workplace: the place of employment required the women to work on an equal footing as men, and yet the home environment still demanded the same level of time, commitment, and energy (with children, household chores, cooking, etc.) as before.[74]

At the onset of Operation Bootstrap, Muñoz Marín was able to secure another "victory" which reflected the desire, under the banner of autonomy, to maintain and nurture Puerto Rican customs, traditions, and norms: Spanish was re-instituted as the official language of the island. In a parallel effort to the economic nature of Operation Bootstrap, "Operation Serenity" was Muñoz Marín's effort to push the importance of maintaining a distinct Puerto Rican culture and way of life in the midst of the growing US American influence.[75] This period of 1945–1968 can be characterized as one that both created and solidified the island's economic dependency, political ambiguity, and social uncertainty. While it marked the introduction of the first indigenous governor (as opposed to a US American politician planted on the island to govern), this period solidified the policy of US dominion over the island.[76] The island shifted from an agricultural to an industrial economy, which led to cultural loss and distortion through the mass migration of peasants within the island itself and away from the island to find sustainable employment. Operation Bootstrap created a situation in which two parallel Puerto Ricos began to develop: the rural Puerto Rico with little change in the day-to-day lifestyle, and the urban Puerto Rico with greater and greater dependence on and influence from the USA. Industrialization brought with it the rise of the cement industry from which the industrialist Luís Ferré, and subsequently his daughter Rosario, emerged. The notion of the Bootstrap begs the question, "Who's pulling up whom, whose foot is in the boot, and is the 'sole' of the boot coming loose at the seams in the process?"[77]

Resisting Operation Bootstrap: 1946–1968

Ongoing resistance to US occupation as well as the institution of "free associated state" status marked the years 1946–1968. Others saw this political status as a form of resistance to statehood, which would be the ultimate surrender of language, culture, and Puerto Rican identity. Through the institution of "free associated state" status, Spanish was restored as the official language of the island, and cultural activities that were distinctly Puerto Rican were encouraged by its supporters.[78] This new experimental status was not enough to keep Puerto Ricans from leaving their island home, however. The mass exodus was a means of protest and resistance, in my view, to the economic conditions created on the island.

Pedro Albizu Campos continued to raise concerns regarding the island's neo-colonial status, but began to see the futility of any amiable discussion with the USA to alter the course of Puerto Rico's sovereign future. Still, he maintained pressure on his people regarding independence and continued his activity in association with the Nationalist Party after his release from prison in 1947. Members of Muñoz Marín's PPD formed the Puerto Rican Independence Party (PIP) when they realized he had abandoned the vision of independence after supporting it for over two decades and instead "advocated" for the commonwealth.[79]

Many in political and non-political circles alike met the economic, political, and social erosion of Puerto Rican nationhood with anger and frustration. The desperate time called for desperate measures to maintain attention and focus on the plight of Puerto Ricans. One such demonstration of desperation was the Nationalists' futile attempt on the US government as a form of revolutionary defiance. In 1954, Lolita Lebrón led a group of Puerto Rican nationalists to the halls of the US Congress where she opened fire on the House of Representatives. Lebrón and the others were jailed; they were pardoned and released twenty-five years later by the Carter Administration.[80]

In the late 1960s and early 1970s, the Fuerza Armada de Liberación Nacional (FALN), described by US authorities as a terrorist organization, organized activities to keep the issue of Puerto Rico's independence alive and well in the streets.[81] However, since their tactics involved bombs and other forms of ammunition directed at strategic governmental sites, the FALN gained neither positive attention for the plight of Puerto Ricans in the USA nor support for the cause of anti-colonialism for the island of Puerto Rico.

In 1968, the political landscape changed with the election of millionaire industrialist Luís Ferré as the governor of the island. A man who had made his fortune in the cement industry creating the roads and infrastructure of the island to support the growing manufacturing and industrial sectors, Ferré was a proponent of statehood and his political party, the PNP (Partido Nuevo Progresista or New Progressive Party), overtook the decades of uncontested rule by the PPD.[82] In the midst of this seemingly two-party landscape, the hope of independence never waned; yet it did not gain widespread appeal from the majority of Puerto Ricans at this time.[83]

ACT III: BARRIO AS THE EPICENTER OF CURRENT STATUS

In general, the migration experience, which has continued to the present in a more "revolving door" fashion,[84] exacerbated feelings of "otherness," extreme isolation and social distance politically, ecclesiastically and socially. The US city environment itself was a culture shock since many migrants came from the rural *campos* of Puerto Rico. They were scattered all over the metropolitan areas of the Northeast to pocket neighborhoods. While from the outside these pockets may be regarded as communities, they lacked the ease of relationship typical of rural Puerto Rico, relationships more difficult to maintain in the stressful environment of crowded tenement houses or low income high rises of the barrios.[85] The barrio experience followed on the heels of the migration; it is an experience that has marked the existence of a majority of Puerto Ricans on the US mainland and on the island, and one which continues to plague our community with poverty, illiteracy, poor health and housing, substance abuse and violence.[86] This barrio existence has won Puerto Ricans the unique distinction of being named the "exception" to the growing socioeconomic success rate among Hispanics in the United States.[87]

Data obtained from the US Census Bureau bear out the facts of this "barrio" existence. In 1997, Puerto Ricans (who are US citizens by birth, since 1917) were 10% of the Hispanic population in the USA and 9.2% of the population in 2010,[88] yet represented 34.2% of Hispanics living below the poverty line (1997). While this figure dropped to 26.1% in 2002, and to 25.6% in 2011, it is still one of the highest percentages of poverty among Hispanics in the USA (second only to Dominicans at 26.3%) and at least twice the rate of poverty among non-Hispanic whites.[89] The majority of the Puerto Rican population in the States lives in the Northeast (72% as of 2010)[90]; while this part of USA is known as the financial capital of the world, the median household income was only 39,039 dollars in 2008[91]; this does not represent significant progress from the annual income of Puerto Ricans in the United States of 29,196 dollars in 2001.[92] Single mothers as heads of household represent over one-half of the Puerto Rican family structure (53.9% in 1997). This may account for the high rate of children living in poverty within the Puerto Rican community which was 49.5% in 1997, over four times the rate of non-Hispanic whites (11.4%). While this rate dropped to 33.3% in 2000, it is still the highest poverty rate of children among Hispanics in general.[93]

The point here is that if one lumps the numbers of all Hispanics together, one loses sight of the dire situation of the majority of Puerto Ricans in the USA. We must also remember that all Puerto Ricans are US citizens, and the majority are not recent "migrants" to the United States, which often accounts for the lower socio-economic status of communities transitioning to a new environment. The argument for the benefits of the current relationship between Puerto Rico and the USA seems to lose its relevance when one analyzes the economic data. This begs the question, "Who has truly benefited from this colonial relationship?"

Despite all of the economic advances of industrialization on the island of Puerto Rico, it seems as though many who live there as well as those of the Diaspora community continue to struggle desperately for survival. The promise of the American Dream has been overshadowed by the nightmare of violence, drug abuse, poverty, unemployment, gang warfare, welfare dependency, and disease (in particular AIDS, diabetes, asthma, high blood pressure, and obesity). All of the data point to the increase rather than a decrease of these factors in our community over time. Indeed as David Perez, member of the Young Lords Party, once said, "Puerto Ricans came to this country hoping to get a decent job and to provide for their families; but it didn't take long to find out that the American dream that was publicized so nicely on our island turned out to be the amerikkkan nightmare."[94]

From a political perspective, the barrio existence of the majority of our people has had significant implications. In many ways, the voices of our people are not heard in the halls of government, as is the case with any community living in poverty. The daily preoccupation with survival, with just getting by, does not allow the time, energy, and resources necessary to fight battles on the many fronts where battles are raging: for the quality and availability of education, housing, and other community services (e.g., medical, child care, employment, etc.). Those voices which, by incredible force and sacrifice, make it to the level of being heard to advocate for the needs of the people, are often repressed, silenced and/or demonized, as was the case with the Young Lords Party,[95] so that the people who would benefit most from such activism are led to distrust even their own (as with the case of Nydia Velázquez who ran for, and won, a seat in Congress in 1992 out of Brooklyn).[96] With limited access to appropriate political resources to enact significant changes, the barrio existence is perpetuated from one generation to the next. The community voices of protest, often emerging from poets, musicians, and writers, are no less than political forces rivaling those in the halls of government.[97] And while the barrio has made an incredible photo opportunity for many a political candidate, and even a Roman Catholic Pontiff,[98] it is still at the bottom of the priority list for our government, and Puerto Ricans continue to suffer because of such neglect.

The barrio existence for the majority of Puerto Ricans centers on the economic factors which led so many to leave Puerto Rico in the first place, as well as the cycles of dependence that make it so difficult to break free from poverty. The greatest number of Puerto Ricans left the island at a time of a major shift from agriculture to industry. Unlike other migrations, however, Puerto Ricans came to New York at a time when the city was experiencing a major shift of its own from being a manufacturing dominant economy to becoming a service/technology dominant economy.[99] The unique quality of the Puerto Rican migration experience was due, in large measure, to the economic conditions that greeted this community in a manner unlike that of any other immigrant group coming to New York.[100]

As a result, the low-skilled labor force, which expected to find menial labor in the city's sweatshops, was flooding a market that was in decline; this forced a large percentage of the community to live in the most poverty stricken areas for lack of any other options. This did not bode well for the subsequent generation of Puerto Ricans who were limited, by their location, to an inferior education, thus creating more of a cycle of dependency with higher drop-out rates and teenage pregnancies than their white contemporaries.

In addition to the economic difficulties encountered in New York City at the time, the federal government's policies did little to alleviate the situation. The decades of the 1970s (particularly the latter half) and 1980s witnessed cutbacks in the Food Stamp and other social assistance programs. This had a significant impact on the Puerto Rican community who, as a result of high unemployment, depend heavily on such support. The data indicate that Puerto Ricans are in a worse economic state now than we were twenty years ago.[101]

Life in the barrio was a far cry from the social fabric of the community in the rural mountains of Puerto Rico. If the culture shock of the urban environment were not enough, the Puerto Ricans who now called the barrio their home had to make a way of life in unfamiliar surroundings without the traditions and support systems from home. For the youth, the gang life and culture forged a new family bond. With both parents needing to work, children learned the ways of the street sooner than they learned the ways of math. The gap between the younger street-wise and the older homegrown generations became wider and wider until the family life and the street life were at odds with each other. The harshness of the environment has taken its toll on the Puerto Rican community; with no other outlet for the anger, frustration, and depression, people have lashed out within the community in the form of gang violence, drug trade activity, and abuse.

The religious traditions and support structures of the island were also difficult to maintain and perpetuate given the new environment, and seemingly useless as an effective response to a younger generation in crisis. The religious expression of the parent's generation was not easily transferred to the youth in this new environment with so many competing temptations and lures. The Cursillo Movement within the Catholic Church was an attempt to maintain the Puerto Rican population within the Catholic fold, while honoring the need for more vibrant religious expression, and with more lay leadership in the absence of Spanish-speaking clergy. In addition to the dearth of Spanish-speaking clergy, there were even fewer who overtly advocated for Puerto Ricans in the Archdiocese of New York at the time of their greatest influx. The mainstream churches, both Catholic and Protestant, did not welcome the Puerto Rican community. This led to a rise in Pentecostalism, which was able to fill the spiritual void of the community's pastoral care needs, and the physical void of not having a mainstream church within the barrio community. Life in the barrio also witnessed the rise in the influence of Santeria and Espiritismo.[102]

Resisting the Barrio: 1968–2004

Yet, there are signs of incredible resilience, hope, and life within our Puerto Rican community despite such conditions. From a political perspective, resistance in the barrio has taken the form of the various organizations that have pushed the concerns of the Puerto Rican community to the forefront. These include the Puerto Rican Socialist Party, El Comité–MINP (Puerto Rican National Left Movement), Puerto Rican Student Union, Movement for National Liberation (MLN), Armed Forces for National Liberation (FALN), the Nationalist Party, and the Puerto Rican Independence Party (PIP). The Young Lords Party, while purported to be a gang in the most negative sense by governmental authorities, served to consolidate power and resistance in the hands of youth who wished to make a difference in the lives of their people.[103]

By the late 1960s, almost all of these groups employed some form of Marxist analysis in their strategy and ideology. From an economic perspective, the resistance at this time took the form of involvement in the labor movement and strikes; many of these organizations were actively involved in efforts to improve the economic and social conditions facing Puerto Ricans in the barrio, such as the Garbage Offensive and the Lincoln Hospital Offensive, both initiated by The Young Lords Party.[104] It was also marked by the increased involvement of women in both the workforce and the movement for labor justice and anti-poverty efforts. One of the greatest and most significant accomplishments of these groups was that, through the combination of community activism and an anti-colonial bent, they were able to avoid the annexation of Puerto Rico to the USA (i.e., statehood), which, in their view, would have been the ultimate defeat.[105]

In addition, the cultural institutions that developed during this time, such as the Nuyorican Poets' Café and the Museo del Barrio, continued to preserve and nurture the cultural expressions of Puerto Ricans in the New York area and which can be understood as a form of resistance to an environment that was hostile to them.[106] Even in the midst of the English dominant USA, the Spanish language continues to be spoken and taught to our children. The poets and writers of the barrio era speak to the horrific conditions in which Puerto Ricans live, and yet point to a vision of greater quality of life for the community. The newspapers/ media that developed gave a voice to the people to confront the daily onslaught of negative forces, and were effective in pushing certain issues to the forefront.[107]

These aspects of our lives which continue in the midst of the devastating social ills can be understood as an effort of resistance: of resisting despair and depression, of resisting a loss of faith, of resisting the impulse for destruction and responding with creation and hope and life. It was a clear indication that, for the Puerto Rican community in the USA, the issues of racism and discrimination could not be severed from the issue of freedom; to face one meant having to battle the other.

Although the image of the tough "Nuyorican" has emerged from this period as a caricature of the abrasive urban Puerto Rican with a fierce attitude, this persona can also be seen as a form of resistance to the stereotype of Puerto Rican docility and passivity, embodied as the person allowing others to control him/her with little, if any, reaction. The Nuyorican persona instilled fear and intimidation (e.g., the biker type, bad boys) as a defense against the sense of powerlessness in the face of the looming power of the USA.[108]

"Nuevo Despertar"[109]: 2005 to the Present

Puerto Ricans are confronting the barrio existence that has remained at the center of our experience in the new millennium with a renewed fervor. "Nuevo Despertar" or new awakening was a phrase used to refer to the late 1960s when the US Puerto Rican community, spurned by a number of national and international events/movements, began to assert its voice and radicalism on the state-side front in solidarity with the island community. I use it here to make the point that, with the new millennium, Puerto Ricans are, once again, being shaken up from their slumber in order to confront the new conditions with which we are now faced.

While the barrio existence of our community continues to be a pressing concern, we have witnessed a number of victories that provide opportunities for hope and change. The 1980s and 1990s witnessed the emergence and growth of Puerto Rican studies programs at a number of colleges and universities in the New York area, such as those at Brooklyn College, Hunter College, and Fordham University. These programs have sparked the consciousness of a new generation who are, indeed for the first time for many, learning the history and struggle that I have presented here.[110]

Raised consciousness has also led to movement building in the 2000s. In media, publications like *La Respuesta* have arisen as a site of meaning-making for Puerto Ricans in the United States Diaspora.[111] On and off the island, individuals came together to organize and fight for the freedom of Puerto Rican political prisoner Oscar López Rivera who spent over three decades in jail under "seditious conspiracy" charges for his organizing around Puerto Rican independence.[112] Artists like Calle 13 have used music and art to raise consciousness around the issues plaguing Puerto Ricans and their connection to the rest of Latin America and the world. And surely with the rise of a new diaspora in places like Florida we are sure to see a new movement once more—particularly with the impetus of Puerto Rico's present debt crisis.[113] This "nuevo despertar" of Puerto Rican consciousness has gained traction within the international human rights community as well. According to its report, "The Negative Impact of US Foreign Policy on Human Rights in Colombia, Haiti and Puerto Rico," the Human Rights Council recommended that the USA cease its colonial relationship with Puerto Rico and remove all vestiges of its colonial legacy.[114]

The story of oppression, resistance and new awakening calls all Puerto Ricans to remember the shared history of who we are, how we suffer, and the direction of our hope. In doing so, others can participate in solidarity toward the transformation of a community in crisis. Such is the purpose of the stories that I present in following chapters. The stories of Esmeralda Santiago, Pedro Juan Soto, and Rosario Ferré emerge out of this history of Puerto Rican oppression and resistance, and yet are not bound by it. Their stories suggest something beyond the history where dreams of the imagination create a prophetic vision of freedom from colonization for our people.

NOTES

1. According to the 1997 Population Survey of the Census Bureau, 58% of Puerto Ricans living in the continental United States reside in the Northeast region of the country. As of 2010, however, "about two-fifths (41%) of the Puerto Rican population lived in two states, New York (1.1 million) and Florida (848,000)" (Ennis, Sharon R., Merarys Ríos-Vargas, and Nora G. Albert, *The Hispanic Population: 2010* [United States: US Census Bureau, 2011], 8). While this population shift, particularly to Florida, has continued up to the present, the northeast focus of this piece remains pertinent to telling the Puerto Rican story on the island and in the Diaspora.

2. Eldin Villafañe, *The Liberating Spirit: Toward an Hispanic American Pentecostal Social Ethic* (Grand Rapids, MI: Eerdmans, 1993), 23.

3. Both Ferré and Santiago structure their respective narratives around the various dualisms which characterize Puerto Rican experience: industrial vs. agricultural (Ferré), island vs mainland (Santiago), fact vs. fiction (Ferré), child vs. adult (Santiago). These dualisms parallel the relationship between Puerto Rico and the US in varying degrees, thus making the categories essential to both the history and the stories.

4. My telling of my family story is based on the stories I heard as a child from my mother and father, my aunts and uncles, my grandmothers and grandfathers. I do not purport that they are "fact" in the sense that the stories have been corroborated by others. Rather, they serve as "truth" by the fact that they held meaning and power within the family, and were passed on to me, some willingly and others reluctantly, some intentionally and others unintentionally.

5. Not all of the siblings sold their land; to this day, there are members of my extended family who own significant acreage in Barranquitas. The percentage of this remaining land to what was originally owned is unknown.

6. After developing diabetes, she had to leave work. It is unclear to the family exactly when her diabetes affected her health to the point that she stopped working.

7. At a basic level, the religiosity of the Taínos and the slaves imported from the African continent shared a common sense of the connection among the many "worlds" we inhabit: natural, spirit, material. This was then syncretized with Roman Catholic Christianity of Spain, shaped by the Reformation and Counter-Reformation of the sixteenth century.

8. The island's name has also been spelled Borikén and Borinquen; see Darrel Wanzer-Serrano, *The New York Young Lords and the Struggle for Liberation* (Philadelphia, PA: Temple University Press, 2015), 31–32.

9. See Antonio M. Stevens-Arroyo, *Cave of the Jagua: The Mythological World of the Taínos* (Albuquerque, NM: University of New Mexico Press, 1988); and Sadi Orsini Luiggi, *Canto al cemi: leyendas y mitos taínos* (San Juan, PR: Instituto de Cultura Puertorriqueña, 1974).

10. Luís N. Rivera-Pagán, *A Violent Evangelism: The Political and Religious Conquest of the Americas* (Louisville, KY: Westminster/John Knox Press, 1992), 220–221.

11. Ibid., 201.

12. Ibid., 244. De las Casas still believed in a vision of a Christian world but one which would be achieved by free will rather than force (234). De las Casas ironically sought indigenous liberation in order to oppose "civilizing" African slaves (see Jackson, John P. and Nadine M. Weidman, *Race, Racism and Science: Social Impact and Interaction* [New Brunswick, NJ: Rutgers University Press, 2006], 20–21).

13. Kal Wagenheim, "Puerto Rico: A Profile," in *The Puerto Rican Experience*. Francesco Cordasco and Eugene Bucchioni, eds. (Totowa, NJ: Littlefield, Adams and Co., 1973), 98.

14. Gordon K. Lewis, *Puerto Rico: Freedom and Power in the Caribbean* (New York, NY: Monthly Review Press, 1963), 59.

15. Ibid., 56–58.

16. Adalberto López, "The Evolution of a Colony: Puerto Rico in the 16th, 17th and 18th Centuries," in *The Puerto Ricans: their history, culture and society*, Adalberto López, ed. (Rochester, VT: Schenkman Books, 1980), 27. This entire chapter provides an excellent background of the economic, political, military, and religious influences on Puerto Rico during this period.

17. Arturo Morales Carrión, *Puerto Rico: A Political and Cultural History* (New York, NY: W. W. Norton and Company, 1983), 80.

18. Ibid, 28.

19. Lewis, *Puerto Rico*, 47.

20. Ibid., 49.

21. López, "Birth of a Nation: Puerto Rico in the Nineteenth Century," in *The Puerto Ricans: their history, culture and society*, Adalberto López, ed. (Rochester, VT: Schenkman Books, 1980), 51–53.
22. Ibid., 64.
23. Eric Williams, *From Columbus to Castro: The History of the Caribbean 1492–1969* (New York, NY: Random House, 1970), 291. Williams makes the argument that Puerto Rico was unique in the Caribbean at the time based on the fact that the percentage of slaves to the total population was around 5% in 1872; given its economy as a food producing agricultural system, slavery was not necessary as a "productive element" and should therefore by abolished. In contrast, the Cuban slave population in 1867 numbered approximately 24% of the total population, 290.
24. López, "Birth of a Nation," 75.
25. Both Matienzo Cintrón and de Diego broke with the policy of "autonomy as a first step" and advocated complete independence after the U.S. became the occupying colonial power in 1898. See López ("Birth of a Nation," 73–90) for a more detailed discussion of the debate, including the influence of other independence movements within the Spanish colonial empire taking place at the same time. For the purposes of this study, I have highlighted only the main points of the three political positions. I find it interesting, and not in the least coincidental, that the three positions argued in the nineteenth century (autonomy, stepping-stone autonomy and independence) are carried into the twentieth and beyond (status quo, statehood, independence) in relation to a different, nevertheless colonial, empire.
26. Betances was exiled for the majority of his adult life for his separatist views, but continued to work for Puerto Rican independence from exile until his death in Paris in 1899. In his last written piece, he voices his disillusionment with his Puerto Rican compatriots who, in his opinion, have let the perfect opportunity to assert their freedom slip away: "What are the Puerto Ricans doing? Why don't they take advantage of the blockade to rise up in a mass? It is essential that when the vanguards of the American army land they be received by Puerto Rican forces waving the flag of independence, and that it be the latter that give them their welcome," in López, "Birth of a Nation," 91. See also Iris Zavala's "Introduction" in *The Intellectual Roots of Independence: An Anthology of Puerto Rican Political Essays*, Iris M. Zavala and Rafael Rodríguez, eds. (New York, NY and London, UK: Monthly Review Press, 1980).
27. Morales Carrión, *Puerto Rico*, 111.
28. Lewis, *Puerto Rico*, 62–63.

29. Roberto Santiago, "Introduction," *Boricuas: Influential Puerto Rican Writings—an Anthology* (New York, NY: Random House Publishing Group, 1995), xviii.
30. Lewis, *Puerto Rico*, 58–59. The emancipation of slaves in the United States did not occur until 1863 with the Emancipation Proclamation, leading to the ratification of the Thirteenth Amendment in 1865. Its provisions substituted the concept of "property" to that of "criminal" as a precondition of acceptable slavery.
31. For a complete description of the components and branches of the fledgling system, see Morales Carrión, *Puerto Rico*, 120–125.
32. Jerry Floyd Fenton, *Understanding the Religious Background of the Puerto Rican*, B.D. Thesis (Union Theological Seminary, 1964), 11–12.
33. Father Sherman, chaplain to the US American occupying army in Puerto Rico wrote, "Puerto Rico is a Catholic country without religion whatsoever....Religion is dead on the island." In this case, he seems to be equating institutional clerical presence with the viability of religion. In any case, such a sentiment fueled the Protestant missionary effort which considered the Catholic legacy superstitious, anti-social, undemocratic, crude and illiterate. See Arthur James, *Thirty Years in Porto Rico: A Record of the Progress since American Occupation* (San Juan: Porto Rico Progress, 1927) Chaps. 4 and 7; Clement Manly Morton, *Kingdom Building in Puerto Rico: A Story of Fifty Years of Christian Service* (Indianapolis, IN: United Christian Missionary Society, 1949).
34. As cited in Eldin Villafañe, *The Liberating Spirit*, 90–95.
35. See Fenton, *Understanding the Religious Background of the Puerto Rican*, 29–37 and 53–58.
36. The Monroe Doctrine, while understood, in origin, as "a prohibition of European imperialist adventure in the hemisphere became transformed...into a mandate for American imperialism," in Lewis, *Puerto Rico*, 82.
37. In *War Against All Puerto Ricans: Revolution and Terror in America's Colony*, Nelson A. Denis notes that the devaluation of the Spanish *peso* imposed by the American Colonial Bank in 1899 occurred virtually at the same time that Hurricane Ciriaco hit the island. This hurricane was one of the worst in the island's history creating a "perfect storm" for the economic degradation of Puerto Rico: with a devalued *peso* and devastated homes and lands, the Puerto Rican people fell into the hands of their new [economic] colonizer; (New York, NY: Nation Books, 2015), 25–31, especially 29.
38. Angel G. Quintero Rivera, "Background to the Emergence of Imperialist Capitalism in Puerto Rico," in *The Puerto Ricans: their history, culture and society*, Adalberto López ed. (Rochester, VT: Schenkman Books, 1980), 113–118.

39. Lewis, *Puerto Rico*, 88–93.
40. Zavala and Rodríguez, eds. "Historical Chronology" in *Intellectual Roots of Independence* (New York, NY and London, UK: Monthly Review Press, 1980), 6.
41. Morris Morley, "Dependence and Development in Puerto Rico," in López, *The Puerto Ricans: their history, culture and society* (Rochester, VT: Schenkman Books, 1980), 171–177.
42. It should be noted that this autonomy was only a political reality for eight days. On July 17, 1898 Puerto Rico's autonomous government came into power, but was quickly relinquished on July 25, 1898 when the United States invaded Puerto Rico's shores.
43. Morales Carrión, *Puerto Rico*, 121–125. The manner in which the United States engaged Spanish land grants in Puerto Rico is reminiscent of their engagement with similar land grants across the now U.S.-Mexico border during the ratification of the Treaty of Guadalupe-Hidalgo (see Daisy L. Machado., "The Historical Imagination and Latina/o Rights," *Union Seminary Quarterly Review*, Vol. 56. Nos. 1–2 (2002): 162–165, especially 164).
44. Lewis, *Puerto Rico*, 107–108, 111; Morales Carrión, *Puerto Rico*, 155–161.
45. Morales Carrión, *Puerto Rico*, 200–201; Lewis, *Puerto Rico*, 111; López, "The Evolution of a Colony," 51, quoting Kal Wagenheim states, "[Puerto Ricans] automatically became United States citizens unless they signed a document refusing it. But this refusal deprived them of numerous civil rights, including the right to hold public office, and made them aliens in their own birthplace."
46. EPICA Task Force, *Puerto Rico: A People Challenging Colonialism* (Washington, DC: Epica Task Force, 1976), 68–69; Morley, "Dependence and Development in Puerto Rico," 173–174.
47. Max Weber's classic *The Protestant Ethic and the Spirit of Capitalism*. [Translated by Peter Baehr and Gordon C. Wells from the original German text, 1905 (New York, NY: Penguin Books, 2002)] links the rise of industrial capitalism in the West to a particular Protestant theological understanding of human value related work. While many have critiqued his sociological theory, I believe his thesis continues to lend credibility to the existence of false and racially biased stereotypes regarding Puerto Ricans as lazy, docile and lacking of initiative.
48. Luís Nieves Falcón, "The Social Pathology of Dependence," in *Puerto Rico: The Search for a National Policy*, Richard J. Bloomfield, ed. (Boulder, CO and London, UK: Westview Press, 1985), 51–56; Angel G. Quintero Rivera, "The Development of Social Classes and Political Conflicts in Puerto Rico," in López, *The Puerto Ricans: their history, culture and society* (Rochester, VT: Schenkman Books, 1980), 214–215.

49. See his speech given before the Associated Press (1936), in Santiago, ed. *Boricuas*, p. 27–29; also Morales Carrión, *Puerto Rico*, 221–224, 234–236; Nelson A. Denis, *War Against All Puerto Ricans*, 109–131; and Laura Briggs *Reproducing Empire: Race, Sex, Science, and US Imperialism in Puerto Rico* [Berkley and Los Angeles, CA: University of California Press, 2002], 74–81; all provide more background information on Albizu Campos.

50. See Alfredo Lopez, *The Puerto Rican Papers: Notes on the Re-emergence of a Nation* (Indianapolis, IN: The Bobbs-Merrill Company, Inc.), 57–58.

51. See his poetry translated by Santiago in *Boricuas*, particularly "Hallelujahs" and "The Final Act."

52. Alfredo Lopez outlines the drastic and devastating effects of the shift from a natural-agricultural to an urban-industrial lifestyle that "fractured the Puerto Rican consciousness." This was the after effect of the mechanization of the sugar industry which led to the loss of sugar cane cutter jobs in the thousands; *The Puerto Rican Papers*, 72–73.

53. Cordasco and Bucchioni, *The Puerto Rican Experience*, 102–103.

54. Adalberto López, *The Puerto Ricans*, 214–215.

55. Morales Carrión, *Puerto Rico*, 183–184, reminiscent of the sugar cane workers strike of 1915; López, *The Puerto Ricans*, 142.

56. Ibid., 234–235, 238–239.

57. Dale Nelson's article, "The Political Behavior of New York Puerto Ricans: Assimilation or Survival," asserts that Puerto Ricans who migrated to New York City do not fit the assimilation model of theorists as other ethnic groups from Europe, suggesting other cultural factors which preclude the desire to behave politically as part of the "melting pot"; in *The Puerto Rican Struggle: Essays on Survival in the US*, Clara E. Rodríguez, Virginia Sánchez Korrol and Jose Oscar Alers, eds. (New York, NY: Puerto Rican Migration Research Consortium, Inc., 1980), 90–110.

58. Denis (*War Against All Puerto Ricans*, 81–107) observes that while in the United States Muñoz Marín developed an addiction to opium. By 1940, Muñoz Marin was well established in the Puerto Rican political scene, but this addiction would plague him. As the son of a man who fought for Puerto Rican independence, and himself having been an advocate for independence heretofore, in the 1940s Muñoz Marin "repeatedly opposed the Tydings independence bill" that would have granted Puerto Rico full self-determination (98). "He even travelled to Washington in 1943 and 1945 to lobby against it, saying that Puerto Rico 'was not ready for self-government'" (98). Many were concerned at the soon-to-be governor's change of heart and rightfully so. As Denis

notes, his political shift was due to the fact that the FBI had a file on Muñoz Marin proving his opium addiction. Were this to be released, his political career would have ended. As a result, Muñoz Marin was at the bid and mercy of the FBI and any other government official for the remainder of his political career. As a compromised political figure in Puerto Rico, Muñoz Marín opposed Puerto Rican independence, passed a Public "Gag" Law 53 (which made it a felony "to own or display a Puerto Rican flag [even in one's home]; to speak in favor of Puerto Rican independence; to print, publish, sell, or exhibit any material that might undermine the insular government; and to organize any society, group, or assembly of people with a similar intent") and was placed in office as the first "elected" governor of Puerto Rico (102–107).

59. See Zavala and Rodríguez (*The Intellectual Roots of Independence*) for Albizu Campos; see Morales Carrión (*Puerto Rico*) for an excellent discussion on the influences which shaped the different approaches toward Puerto Rican political and economic viability of both Albizu Campos and Muñoz Marín, 221–241.

60. According to Ana María Díaz-Stevens (*Oxcart Catholicism on Fifth Avenue*), a good percentage of the people did shift from Catholicism to Protestantism, while others actually "converted"; today approximately 35% are Protestant, some never having been Catholic at all.

61. See Ana María Díaz-Stevens, "Aspects of Puerto Rican Religious Experience: A Socio-Historical Overview," in *Latinos in New York: Communities in Transition*, Gabriel Haslip-Viera and Sherrie L. Baver, eds. (Notre Dame, IN: University of Notre Dame Press, 1996).

62. René Marques' book, *The Docile Puerto Rican* (Philadelphia, PA: Temple University Press, 1976), is representative of this; Gordon Lewis, in his acclaimed work, *Puerto Rico: Freedom and Power in the Caribbean*, makes suggestive comments which convey, in my opinion, a belief that the Puerto Rican, particularly in political terms, would rather play up to the powers that be rather than confront them head on. See Lewis, *Puerto Rico*, 62–65.

63. The stories of Juan Bobo, as part of Puerto Rican folklore, seem to convey this subtle subversion and resistance. Often in the disguise of children's tales, Juan Bobo (John the Fool) takes on the persona of the trickster to convey a more profound message of self-determination associated with jíbaro consciousness: "Manrique Cabrera says this name is preferred by locals because it signifies the mentality of a true jíbaro: The character of Juan Bobo, under all its forms and costumes, seems to show, prima facie, an evolution in the stories where he is the main character. The simple fool transforms himself into a person that pretends to be a numskull using his foolishness as a disguise. This evolutionary

slanting seems to reflect the assimilation of a trait attributed to the jíbaro's psychic. It refers to what has been called "jaibería," an attitude which feigns dullness to throw off those who come near. It is a defensive weapon whose ultimate efficacy is worth investigating." Translated from Manrique Cabrera, F. (1982). *Historia de la literatura puertorriqueña.* Rio Piedras, PR: Editorial Cultural, p. 62.

64. See Ana María Díaz-Stevens, *Oxcart Catholicism on Fifth Avenue*, 12–15.
65. Operation Bootstrap, an economic development plan instituted by the United States to hasten the pace of "industrialization" on the island, was a major catalyst for the massive migration; in fact, the migration which ensued was an essential part of the Bootstrap plan. Ibid., 12–15.
66. Ibid., Chap. 4.
67. Fenton, *Understanding the Religious Background of the Puerto Rican*, 59–66; Joseph Fitzpatrick, *Puerto Rican Americans: The Meaning of Migration to the Mainland* (Englewood Cliffs, NJ: Prentice Hall, 1987), Chap. 8 "Religion," 117–138.
68. María E. Pérez y González, *Puerto Ricans in the United States* (Westport, CT: Greenwood Press, 2000), 31–37.
69. Morales Carrión, *Puerto Rico*, 267–273.
70. EPICA Task Force, 23; Lewis, *Puerto Rico*, 143–164.
71. Adalberto López, *The Puerto Ricans*, 190.
72. Lewis' (*Puerto Rico*) chapter on "The Problem of Economic Dependency" gives a fair and balanced assessment of the complex issues facing Puerto Rico as a result of the policies enacted with the Operation Bootstrap program and beyond; 189–213; also, López, *The Puerto Ricans*, 180–188.
73. In many respects the rise of "family planning" is directly connected to an "overpopulation" (and eugenic) rhetoric that began permeating Puerto Rico from the 1920's. Briefly, the United States infiltrated Puerto Rico during a rise in Neo-Malthusian thinking, which suggested that economic poverty was directly connected to overpopulation. Applied in Puerto Rico, this thinking conveniently ignored the issue of Puerto Rico's colonial relationship with the United States and diagnosed the cause of Puerto Rico's rising poverty as overpopulation. At first, some in power began to address the issue through encouraging emigration. Charles Allen and Arthur Yager, the first governors of the island (placed in power by the US government), encouraged Puerto Ricans to leave the island and find work elsewhere to alleviate the overpopulation of the island. This encouragement was further facilitated through the Jones Act of 1917 that gave Puerto Ricans United States citizenship and thus freedom to travel across the US. Over time, however, Neo-Malthusian logic manifest in more sinister ways as emigration was

pushed alongside sterilization. As Iris Lopez (*Matters of Choice: Puerto Rican Women's Struggle for Reproductive Freedom* [New Brunswick, NJ: Rutgers University Press, 2008], 7) writes, "The reshaping of the Puerto Rican population and economy was not accomplished by emigration alone. A complementary government policy of sterilization arose simultaneously and the Puerto Rican and US governments developed Puerto Rico's economy through both emigration and sterilization, especially during the industrialization phase known as Operation Bootstrap [which began in 1948]. In essence, migration was used as the temporary response to Puerto Rico's overpopulation problem, while sterilization became the permanent solution." While it would take until Operation Bootstrap for sterilization to rise significantly, the structural foundations for its rise began in the early twentieth century through a rising birth control movement facilitated in the creation of various birth control and health clinics across the island. Muñoz Marin in the 1920s, for example, advocated strongly for birth control options offered by Margaret Sanger and what would become Planned Parenthood. She, alongside Clarence J. Gamble (an independently wealthy individual who founded the Asociación pro Salud Maternal e Infantil in 1936), worked to repeal Comstock Laws, establish eugenics boards, and later would push for testing the Birth Control Pill on Puerto Rican women—many of whom became sterilized in the process. This push for family planning directly arose from the clinics and propaganda of Sanger, Gamble, and others which inherently stemmed from a Neo-Malthusian ideology implemented into practice. Thus, one needs to ask how much choice Puerto Ricans, generally, and Puerto Rican women, particularly, were given in thinking about family planning. For more, see Briggs, *Reproducing Empire*, 93; Angela Franks, *Margaret Sanger's Eugenic Legacy: The Control of Female Fertility* (Jefferson, NC: McFarland & Company, Inc. Publishers, 2005), 132–137; Iris Morales, "Sterilized Puerto Ricans," in *The Young Lords: A Reader*, ed. Darrel Enck-Wanzer (New York, NY: New York University Press, 2010), 165–166; Jennifer A. Nelson, "Abortions under Community Control," in *Journal of Women's History* 13.1 (2001): 157–180.

74. Edna Acosta-Belén, "Women in Twentieth-Century Puerto Rico," in López, *The Puerto Ricans: their history, culture and society* (Rochester, VT: Schenkman Books, 1980), 273–282.

75. Lewis, *Puerto Rico*, 187; Morales Carrión, *Puerto Rico*, 273, 315.

76. As a result of the change to Free Associated State status in 1952, the United States put forth the argument that it was no longer required to report to the United Nations regarding the condition of its "non-autonomous territory"; thus the US could operate unchecked and

unregulated in Puerto Rico without any recourse by the Puerto Rican people or the international community. See Juan Mari Bras, *The Case of Puerto Rico at the United Nations*, as cited in EPICA Task Force, 101–103.

77. An artist's illustration depicting the same, the sole of the boot coming loose to expose the bare foot, can be found in the EPICA Task Force text, 28.
78. Morales Carrión, *Puerto Rico*, 273–282.
79. Adalberto López, *The Puerto Ricans*, 159–160; Morales Carrión, *Puerto Rico*, 276; Denis, *War Against All Puerto Ricans*, 103–107.
80. Morales Carrión, *Puerto Rico*, 293–294.
81. Fitzpatrick, *Puerto Rican Americans*, 32.
82. EPICA Task Force, 29; Morales Carrión, *Puerto Rico*, 308–309; Bloomfield, *Puerto Rico*, 19–21; Adalberto López, *The Puerto Ricans*, 164–165.
83. Ibid., 331–332; Bloomfield, *Puerto Rico*, 141–156, 173–177; Morales Carrión, *Puerto Rico*, 288–289.
84. Díaz-Stevens, *Oxcart Catholicism on Fifth Avenue*, 19.
85. Ibid., Chap. 2; Fenton, *Understanding the Religious Background of the Puerto Rican*, 59.
86. See socioeconomic data compiled by David Traverzo, "Towards a Theology of Mission in the US Puerto Rican Migrant Community: from Captivity to Liberation," *Apuntes* 9.3: 51–54.
87. See Linda Chavez' chapter, "The Puerto Rican Exception," in *Out of the Barrio: Toward a New Politics of Hispanic Assimilation* (New York, NY: HarperCollins Publishers, 1991), 139–159. While Chavez' thesis is staunchly conservative, advocating a relinquishing of culture and community in order to assimilate more easily into a changing environment, she outlines the unique aspects of Puerto Rican life in the northern cities that suggest the negative impact of the weight of colonization, unequaled in the experience of other Hispanic groups.
88. The Hispanic population in the United States includes the following groups identified as such via the US Census Bureau Current Population Survey by type of origin: Mexican, Central and South American, Puerto Rican, Cuban and Other Hispanic. This population universe does not include residents of the island of Puerto Rico; those statistics are captured on the International Database set of the Census Bureau. Sharon R. Ennis, Merarys Rios-Vargas, and Nora G. Albert, "The Hispanic Population: 2010," 3.
89. The poverty rate of non-Hispanic whites in 1997, 2002 and 2011 was 8.6%, 7.8%, and less than 14% respectively; see also Suzanne Macartney, Alemayehu Bishaw, and Kayla Fontenot, "Poverty Rates for Selected

Detailed Race and Hispanic Groups by State and Place: 2007–2011," in *American Community Survey Briefs* (Washington, DC: United States Census Bureau, 2013), 5.

90. As of 2010, the top five states where Puerto Ricans lived are: NY: 1,070,558; FL: 847,550; NJ: 434,092: PA: 366,082; MA: 266,125. Sharon R. Ennis, Merarys Rios-Vargas, and Nora G. Albert, "The Hispanic Population: 2010," 8.

91. Sonia G. Collazo, Camille L Ryan, Kurt J. Bauman, "Profile of the Puerto Rican Population in United States and Puerto Rico: 2008" (presentation, Annual Meeting of the Population Association of America, Dallas, TX, April 15–17, 2010).

92. Meizhu Lui, et al., "The Economic Reality of Being Latino/a in the United States," in *Race, Class and Gender in the United States*, Paula Rothenberg and Kelly Mayhew ed., 9th edition (New York, NY: Worth Publishers, 2013) 373.

93. The percentage of children living below the poverty level among other Hispanic groups is as follows: Mexican 36%, Other Hispanic 38.1%, Central and South American 33.2%, and Cuban 20.7%. In addition, over one-half of children under the age of 18 in Puerto Rico live in poverty; in 2000, the percentage was a staggering 58.2% (Source: "Children and the Households They Live In: 2000" Census 2000 Special Reports [Censr-14]). More recent data demonstrates that not very much has changed; see Lui, "The Economic Reality of Being Latino/a in the United States," in *Race, Class and Gender in the United States*, 371–374.

94. The Young Lords Party, *Palante* (Chicago, IL: Haymarket Books, 2011), 10. Originally published in 1971.

95. Pérez y González, *Puerto Ricans in the United States*, 50–51; Andrés Torres and José E. Velázquez, *The Puerto Rican Movement: Voices from the Diaspora* (Philadelphia, PA: Temple University Press, 1998), 223–224, on this point specifically, although a number of essays in this anthology speak about the activities of the Young Lords Organization and the Young Lords Party in Chicago, Philadelphia and New York City.

96. During her campaign, Congresswoman Velázquez' medical records were released unlawfully, on the eve of the 1992 primary, demonstrating that she had undergone therapy for depression and an attempted suicide. In spite of the disclosure and perhaps due to her unflinching defense and perseverance, Velázquez won the primary and subsequent election; she continues to serve as the first Puerto Rican woman elected to the U.S. Congress. See A. Rubin, "Records No Longer for Doctors' Eye Only," *Los Angeles Times*, September 1, 1998, A1.

97. See María Teresa Babín, "A Special Voice: The Cultural Expression," in Morales Carrión ed. *Puerto Rico: A Political and Cultural History* (New York, NY: W. W. Norton and Company, Inc., 1983), 319–352.

98. Pope Francis visited Our Lady Queen of Angels R.C. School in East Harlem during his visit to New York City on September 25, 2015, where parishioners—mostly black and brown working class and immigrant—had fought to keep the church from closing to no avail in 2007.

99. Clara E. Rodríguez, *Puerto Ricans: Born in the USA* (Boston, MA: Unwin Hyman, Inc., 1989), 85–91.

100. Joseph Fitzpatrick, *Puerto Rican Americans*, 26, 101.

101. See Mercer Sullivan's essay on the Puerto Rican community of Sunset Park in Brooklyn, "Puerto Ricans in Sunset Park, Brooklyn: Poverty Amidst Ethnic and Economic Diversity," in *In the Barrios: Latinos and the Underclass Debate*, Joan Moore and Raquel Pinderhughes, eds. (New York, NY: Russell Sage Foundation, 1993), 1–25; Pérez y González, *Puerto Ricans in the United States*, 63–84.

102. Díaz-Stevens, "Aspects of Puerto Rican Religious Experience," 168–169; Fitzpatrick, *Puerto Rican Americans*, 128–138, although the author details the few programs which specifically benefited New York Puerto Ricans such as the San Juan Fiesta.

103. For more on The Young Lords Party see: Jennifer A. Nelson, "'Abortions Under Community Control'," 157–180; Wanzer-Serrano, *The New York Young Lords and the Struggle for Liberation* (Philadelphia, PA: Temple University Press, 2015); Johanna L. del C. Fernández, "Radicals in the Late 1960s: A History of the Young Lords Party in New York City, 1969–1974," (Dissertation, Columbia University, 2004); Elias Ortega-Aponte, "Young Lords Party," in *Hispanic American Religious Culture, Encyclopedia*. Ed. by Miguel De La Torre. Pages 583–585. United States: ABC-CLIO, 2009; Darrel Enck-Wanzer, *The Young Lords: A Reader* (New York, NY: New York University Press, 2010); The Young Lord Party, *Palante*.

104. See "Dirty Love: Collective Agency and Decolonial Tropicalization in the Garbage Offensive," in Wanzer-Serrano, *The New York Young Lords and the Struggle for Liberation*, pp. 122–143; and pp. 59 and 169 for information on the Lincoln Hospital Offensive.

105. Torres and Velázquez, *The Puerto Rican Movement*, 5–22, although the entire volume is a chronicle of the vibrant and active movements of the Puerto Rican diaspora community.

106. Ibid., 45–46, 155; Jorge Duany, *Puerto Rican Nation on the Move: Identities on the Island and in the United States* (Chapel Hill, NC: University of North Carolina Press, 2002), 185–207.

107. Torres and Velázquez, *The Puerto Rican Movement*, 212–213, 155–172; Pérez y González, *Puerto Ricans in the United States*, 50–51.
108. Alfredo Lopez names this persona "Slick," a new urban hero replacing the stereotype of the folk hero of the jíbaro, which resonates more accurately with the urban experience. However, Lopez acknowledges that this persona is an unhealthy one, as it glorifies the life of a hustler, "Slick was an illusory prototype, a folk hero who did not create new values but mimicked the very values of American society in a perverted way." In *The Puerto Rican Papers*, 181–187.
109. See Andrés Torres' "Introduction" to *The Puerto Rican Movement: Voices from the Diaspora*.
110. See Anthony M. Stevens-Arroyo and María E. Sánchez, eds. *Toward a renaissance of Puerto Rican studies: ethnic and area studies in university education*. (Boulder, CO: Social Science Monographs; Highland Lakes, NJ: Atlantic Research and Publications; New York, NY: Distributed by Columbia University Press, 1987).
111. http://www.larespuestamedia.com/
112. As one of the last executive actions of the Obama administration, Oscar López Rivera's 55-year prison sentence was commuted in January 2017 after serving almost 36 years in federal prison. See Oscar López Rivera, *Between Torture and Resistance*, ed. Luis Nieves Falcón (Oakland, CA: PM Press, 2013).
113. James Gibney, "As Cuba rises, Puerto Rico keeps on slipping: Caribbean U.S. Policies Raise Questions," *Bloomberg View*, March 27, 2016.
114. Submission to the United Nations Universal Periodic Review, Ninth Session of the Working Group on the UPR Human Rights Council (November 2010), "THE NEGATIVE IMPACT OF U.S. FOREIGN POLICY ON HUMAN RIGHTS IN COLOMBIA, HAITI AND PUERTO RICO," "Recommendations: 1. The United States should expedite the process to allow Puerto Ricans to exercise fully their inalienable right to self-determination and independence, in conformity with General Assembly Resolution 1514 (XV) and the applicability of the fundamental principles of that resolution. 2. As part of that process, the United States should withdraw its military, courts, the FBI and other repressive forces from Puerto Rico; disclose all documents documenting the repression of the independence movement, including those documenting the assassination of its members and leaders; and release Puerto Rican political prisoners serving prison sentences for cases relating to the struggle for the independence of Puerto Rico."

CHAPTER 3

Bridging the Puerto Rican Story and Christian Doctrine

Shroud me, moments after my death,
with the shield of my nation.
Shroud me, head to foot,
with the three colors of my flag.

Above my tomb,
as patient as the sea,
will sit a lonely Hope,
testing the patience of eternity.

But there will arrive a great day when
my tomb will be unsealed.
And Hope's joyous cry will ring.

My bony remains will lift that shield.
And I will rise, holding a flag once a shroud.

Hoisted high, before the world, before Infinity.
           José de Diego, "The Final Act"[1]

This poem, written by nineteenth-century Puerto Rican revolutionary José de Diego, makes an explicit interdisciplinary connection between Puerto Rican literature/story and Christian theology. The poem, part of Puerto Rico's literary legacy, is contextual because it reflects the long struggle and patience of people waiting for a new day. Its reference to

© The Author(s) 2017
T. Delgado, *A Puerto Rican Decolonial Theology*, New Approaches to
Religion and Power, DOI 10.1007/978-3-319-66068-4_3

the Easter promise of the tombstone pushed away to reveal the one who is risen gives it a central theological motif. The poem embodies Puerto Rican identity, suffering, and hope, themes which the following chapters will explore through the literature of Esmeralda Santiago, Pedro Juan Soto, and Rosario Ferré, and with which the Christian doctrines of anthropology, soteriology, and eschatology can dialogue.

Our identity, suffering, and hope cannot be separated from each other if our complete story as Puerto Ricans is to be told. Likewise, our literary tradition, socio-history, and theological sensibilities must remain in conversation in order to maintain the integrity of who we are and what we value as a people. The poem reflects the conversation between our present reality and our future vision, the "now" and the "not yet." This dialogue and dialectic are central because the willingness to engage the conversation reflects a belief that something else happens beyond death, something perhaps more important than the fact of death itself. The poem reflects the hope that outlasts all despair; it speaks of an eschatological hope in the resurrection, in the life to come that does not bypass suffering and death but does not see it as the final act either.

Puerto Rican literature has always maintained this tension between the discontent of the "now" and the promise of the "not yet." It has been preoccupied with the transcendence of freedom in a state of captivity, as de Diego's poem illustrates. Central to the work of Santiago, Soto, and Ferré, the three Puerto Rican authors I highlight in the next chapters, is this theme of transcending captivity and finding freedom.

In his controversial and still relevant book of essays entitled *The Docile Puerto Rican*, author, playwright, and literary/cultural critic René Marqués also focuses on transcending captivity; in fact, he identifies the mission of the writer as one who aspires "to defend humanistic values, to search for the truth, the truth of his own circumstances, to be a rebel, to be free and therefore never to abandon the cause of freedom."[2]

The mission of the creative writer and that of the theologian share this common search for elusive truth. Although the devices and methodologies may differ, the purpose is the same. Good writing and good theology[3] do not claim to be the final word; rather they open our souls to possibilities and questions of ultimacy that our human existence and experiences reflect. David Jasper, in his concluding remarks to his edited volume *The Study of Literature and Religion*, makes this point: "In literature we glimpse, at times, the fulfillment of our nature, cast in the imaginative genius of great art, and continuing to persuade us of the value and ultimate truth of the theological enterprise as a seeking for utterance of the divine mystery as it is known and felt in our experience."[4]

The relationship between creative literary production and freedom is a close one. The literature of Puerto Rico and, more recently, of Puerto Ricans of the Diaspora has been one of the very few areas where freedom of content and form has continued to be exercised within Puerto Rican scholarship. This connection between the creative act of writing and independence of thought without fear of reprisal (although reprisal has come in many forms to many of the writers) is central for the Puerto Rican writer.

Thus, the very act of writing is an act of rebellion, evidence of a revolutionary spirit and impulse in a repressive environment where the silence of those numbed by the weight of colonialism is preferred. Puerto Rican journalist Roberto Santiago said of the works he compiled in the anthology *Boricuas*, "[I]t isn't possible to separate Puerto Rican art from its politics. Strip one aspect away and you're left with an incomplete portrait."[5] Rosario Ferré, in her essay "The Writer's Kitchen," states similarly, "imagination is irreverence to the establishment... [it is] always subversive."[6]

The creative writer, or any writer who understands his/her creation in this way, does not attempt to reach the absolute truth or solutions to the contradictions witnessed and experienced in the community and in life. From a Puerto Rican perspective, these creative writers have positioned themselves outside of the realm of solutions and finality. For them, good writing is not ultimately prescriptive, but it is more than simply descriptive. The Puerto Rican writers I have chosen, through the process and content of storytelling, speak a prophetic word to the reader with the hope, I believe, that the reader will act upon that word. "Take heed," they seem to tell us, "we are living in a time of crisis and some action is required if we are to be faithful to ourselves, to our children, and to our God." Through their gift of imagination, they are calling us into action by their critique. They are speaking truth to power: the abusive power of those who oppress, and the transformative power of those who hope.[7]

Both literature and theology have transformative power, both within their respective disciplines and as I bridge the conversation between them. First, literature by Puerto Ricans has continued a tradition of subversive rebellion and freedom. It has served the purpose of waking the sleeping conscience of Puerto Rican people. It has maintained a tradition of Puerto Rican anti-colonialism, sovereignty, and self-determination.

This is not to say that every Puerto Rican author, or even the ones I have utilized, is an *independentista*, an advocate of political sovereignty from the United States. Regardless of whether they have expressed their political beliefs outwardly or not, all three writers—Santiago, Soto and Ferré—show a preoccupation with the issue of freedom and what that means for Puerto Rican people.

Second, creative writing (inclusive of prose, poetry, *cuento* and novel) shows us the contradictions evident in the context of the writer, specifically, and in the context of the human community in general. The most memorable literary creations are the parabolic ones, as John D. Crossan describes in *The Dark Interval*: they push us to the edge of our reality and leave us there with the responsibility of finding a conclusion.[8] They expose the contradictions at work in the lives of the characters we read and quite possibly in our own lives in ways that may have gone unrecognized. Contemporary Puerto Rican writers, as they expose these contradictions, raise existential questions about our human condition: Can one exist when one's existence is denied? Is salvation possible in the midst of suffering? Is there hope in the midst of utter despair?

Third, I believe that our response to the contradictions, to the disjuncture between the "is" of our reality and our conviction of how things "ought to be," constitutes our developing theology. The way in which we live out a hope/doubt/search-filled faith in the midst of those contradictions is a fundamental aspect of a theology that is active as well as reflective, that both perceives and responds to our earthly condition. Jon Sobrino, Salvadoran Jesuit priest, activist, and theologian, proposes three prerequisites for a genuine and concrete spirituality, which I believe can be upheld as prerequisites for a genuine and concrete Puerto Rican decolonial theology as well: (1) honesty about the real: a willingness to look the contradictions squarely in the eye and confront the ugliness of our situation with hope; (2) fidelity to the real: a recognition that faithfulness to eradicating the contradictions will lead to carrying a burden of love that those who choose to "escape" from reality do not shoulder; and (3) participating in the "more" of reality: a willingness to be an active player in the building of a more just society, which is our ethical mandate to strive towards the "ought."[9] For Sobrino, a more just society is one that understands and tries to live out a profound notion of freedom.

Fourth, a decolonial theology that emerges from a Puerto Rican context as illustrated through our stories must also embody liberating action while maintaining the prerequisites Sobrino describes. In this sense, our Puerto Rican literature is testimony of our theology of decolonization; to write, as Rene Marqués claims, is to choose to see oneself as a free being: free to create and to determine one's creative destiny. Our creative writers have not, in general, separated the spirituality of the people from their political expressions or desires, as have the institutional churches.[10] They have been faithful to our interconnected Christian and cultural roots, and thus do not turn away from the political/economic "king-dom" which has served to numb our senses, crush our spirit, dull our vision, and separate us from our very being. Their "honesty about the real" compels them to write and struggle with the ambiguities and contradictions of being Puerto Rican in the United States. Theirs is an attempt to come to some sort of understanding about our situation as a people in crisis, with some hope that an answer, implicit in raising the question itself, will be revealed in the process.

Finally, a decolonial theology that emerges from a Puerto Rican context will be experienced through the connection of cultural identity and faith, which can only be fully encountered within community and relationship. The dynamic between our culture and faith provides the opportunity to scrutinize and embrace both, depending on how each serves the goal of justice and freedom for our people. This dynamic helps us maintain a hermeneutic of suspicion[11] toward all that may diminish our vision of hope for the future.

I believe it is important to note that the literature/stories of Santiago, Soto, and Ferré all pay close attention to the lives, experiences, and voices of women through their narrative. This attention to the experience of women is critical for a number of reasons. First, Puerto Rican women in Puerto Rico and in the Diaspora have been the bearers and godmothers of spiritual traditions and rituals, often those not associated with the institutional churches, passing these on to future generations. Theirs is a story outside of the established history; it is subaltern and critical to the telling of the entire story. Second, Puerto Rican women's lives parallel that of a colonial existence. As Ferré states in *Eccentric Neighborhoods*, they understand the dynamics of colonialism better than men do because they live it daily. The literature of Puerto Rican writers, then, serves a dual function of describing the underside of Puerto Rican history by using the lives of women as a metaphor for Puerto Rico itself; and of challenging that same Puerto Rican history by allowing us to examine in a critical way the reality in which we live. As such, these writers truly stand on the margins of the margins and, from that vantage point, continue to give voice to what would otherwise remain unspoken. Through their creativity and vision, Santiago, Soto, and Ferré engage in a process of "prophetic imagination"[12] through their literary production. Their *cuentos* (short stories and novels) are prophetic; they proclaim the coming of a new era for Puerto Rican people, and reveal messages that are both disturbing and necessary for Puerto Ricans to hear. These same *cuentos* are imaginative because, while emerging from the lived experience of Puerto Rican people, they create a vision of what does not exist in the lives of Puerto Rican people as a collective: humanity, salvation, and hope. Through the use of literary devices, such as metaphor, they communicate their vision indirectly, almost catching us off guard. Perhaps they know, as good writers, that readers often hear and understand a message when it is presented parabolically, so that we are forced to think about its meaning in relation to our lives. The stories will haunt us otherwise. My task is to move forward the process of breaking both an historical and theological silence by articulating a decolonial perspective that makes meaning from the identity, suffering, and hope of Puerto Rican people. The story creates a new space where, as Emma Pérez affirms, "the decolonizing subject negotiat[es] new histories."[13]

"To try to understand ourselves and, by the way, to find God...You have to be independent in your own soul." These words were spoken in *Eccentric Neighborhoods* by Clarissa Rivas de Santillana de Vernet from her deathbed to her defiant and troubled daughter Elvira who believed divorcing her husband would finally bring her freedom. In this novel, Rosario Ferré suggests that her character found such freedom but that it was short-lived because it was only superficial, and that the deeper internal transformation of freedom had yet to take shape. Her inner freedom came later and was not dependent upon external circumstances. Her story suggests that, like peace in the midst of turmoil, freedom can exist in the midst of bondage. Once the inner freedom is attained, the outer freedom can be realized because it is drawn to the one who believes she is free. Her inner soul exudes the light of freedom, thereby ushering in the same from the outer world.

I understand this deeply because I have lived it personally. Much of my own journey was a quest for social justice—regarding women's issues, the status of Puerto Rico, racism and ethnic bias in the USA, and children's advocacy. I believed that once the outward conditions were made right, once others changed their attitudes and belief systems, then freedom from oppression could be achieved. What I had yet to learn was that, given improved conditions, true freedom of mind, body, and soul was not automatically achieved if a person were still enslaved by their own internalized state of colonization.

When I think back on my own life story, I am overwhelmed by the silence of my people. I think of my immediate family and in particular my parents who rarely spoke of their life stories or that of their parents. This silence felt uncomfortable and unnatural because my parents, particularly my mother, did enjoy recalling memories of the past when in the presence of her own siblings. Whether this silence was conscious or unconscious, the result was that my sisters and I were left with a gap in ourselves; we had little to stand on, little into which to grow our own roots.[14] Unable to see ourselves in relation to what had gone before us, we have gone about the business of gathering anything we could find— memories, achievements, *detalles*, things we could carry with us forever, things we could leave behind— so that we would not be so empty inside. We needed a history—a story.

A turning point occurred when my paternal grandmother died in November of 1988. Because she was no longer around for me to ask directly, I then began to ask my parents questions about her life. I witnessed something then that has helped me to understand why the silence about our past had been so prominent in our home: it was extremely painful for both my parents to speak of their past because their stories had to do with hardship, shame, welfare, uprootedness, non-identity, alienation, racism, shattered dreams, and death. By telling their stories, the past would be brought to life and transported into the present. By hearing them, the stories would be transformed into something I could take with me, something either pleasant or discomforting. For no other reason than to keep the past where it was and instead to make something new of the future, especially for their children, my parents had remained silent. Even the language of their stories, Spanish, was kept in the past; the language of our future was English.

It is no coincidence to me that I first began to see myself as a whole person—one connected with the spirits of the past, present, and future— when I began to uncover and claim the stories of my people as my own. It began with reading books about the history, culture, and politics of Puerto Rico and the Puerto Rican migration to New York; this enabled me to make connections in my own family (as far back as I could) with the conditions of the time. I then had a context from which I could approach my parents and ask them pointed questions about our people. From here, I was able to see myself as part of the same continuum as they were, not separate from their story but at a turning point in their story where the setting, language, and emphases changed. And while it took me a long time and a painful journey on my own part to see this, I am still very much a part of the story.

I now think back to my younger self and see a little girl straining to hear the stories my mother told only when she was with her sisters around the kitchen table playing Scrabble (in English, no less) on holidays when the extended family got together. I loved being around them at this time because I loved hearing the stories, even though I had heard them many times before. The stories made me feel that I was important, that I was a part of something special that had come before me but still remained with me. Those stories were mine to claim, even though I could only understand bits and pieces of the Spanish–English mixture that is common to Diaspora Puerto Ricans. Because I felt complete when I heard the stories, even when the parents encouraged me to go and play with my cousins, I invariably stayed with the adults. Perhaps I sensed then what I know now without a doubt: that my life depended on the telling and hearing of the stories of my people.

My parents had good intentions in not telling me their life stories. They meant to spare me the pain, anger, frustration, and alienation that seemed to envelop their lives and those of their parents. What they did not anticipate was that their silence would perpetuate those very feelings of pain and alienation that they wished to keep at a distance and from which they sought to protect us. Thus, we were wrapped in a silence that choked us, whereas the stories of our people, as difficult as they may have been to tell/hear, could have nurtured a sense of freedom. The captivity of silence in the absence of story kept me in an exile of sorts, a wandering state with no place to call home, a place with no ground, no stories into which to root myself. Yet, from this experience of being in exile, of trying to root myself in something, I have found my history and have made a people for myself.

Rosario Morales, Puerto Rican writer/poet/activist, has written a poem entitled, "I Never Told My Children Stories."[15] She says it was because she liked to stick to the truth of things, that she was not good at making things up. But that was before she realized that the truth is only someone's belief in his or her own story. When I began to claim the stories of direct and indirect ancestors as my own, my confidence in my ability to tell a story—namely their stories and by extension our stories—blossomed. Specifically, I began to tell stories about my paternal grandmother, whose life had been silenced by her stormy relationship with my mother. And since a story is not complete without pictures, I went on a search for hers. In all the hundreds of pictures taken of the family over the years, the only one of her was from my parents' wedding. From that point on, she became invisible.

Even without pictures of her, I have made it my labor of love to bring her and my other Puerto Rican ancestors back into the story. Doing this tells me something about how they strove to survive in the face of incredible obstacles. Doing this also bridges my life's story with the wider story of Puerto Rican people and our struggles. In the process, I have found strength and resolve in their stories, not to glorify the struggle to claim their identity, or to idolize their suffering, or to get stuck in a pit of hopelessness. Rather, I have found tremendous hope in the ways my Puerto Rican ancestors have affirmed their identity in the face of its erasure; have claimed joy in the midst of suffering; have dared to hope when presented with despairing circumstances. Despite the anguish, invisibility and silence, their stories always seem to find a way into the lives of those who continue the legacy; they find their way into the contemporary stories which are really new and creative interpretations of age-old tales. Some may credit this occurrence to inspiration or obligation. Considering the immense weight of colonial assimilation, I call it miraculous.

I don't think it is coincidental that I went in search of my paternal grandfather—"Gollo" Delgado—when I was pregnant with my daughter Francesca, my first child, in 1993. Never mentioned by my paternal grandmother who we called Mamá, and rarely mentioned by his namesake, my own father, Gregorio's presence in my life was a looming absence, as was that of my four uncles and one aunt, my father's siblings. Sometimes, when I would question my own physical characteristics, with brown eyes, black hair and olive skin that was darker than my green-eyed sisters, my father would tell me that I looked just like his sister Judy. But that was about as much as he would share with me about her, about any of them.

Without telling my father of my plan, I reached out to my Madrina who had kept in touch with my father's family; she knew where they lived in New Jersey and New York, and how to contact them. And one day in the July heat of New York City in 1993 from my apartment on

123rd Street and Broadway, I made a call to my grandfather. While I can't recall the exact words I spoke (although I can still hear the nervousness in my voice), I said something like this: *Abuelo, yo soy Teresa, la hija de su hijo Gregorio, su nieta. I know we have never met, but I am tired of not knowing you and my family. And you are about to have a great granddaughter. I want her to know who you are. I want her to know where she comes from. Yo quiero que ella conoce su familia.*

The next thing I knew, I was speaking with my Tía Judy, to whom my grandfather handed the phone in shock and surprise. We spoke for a very long time that, in retrospect, felt like the blink of an eye. Our conversation led to an August 1993 gathering where, at age 27, I met my Abuelo and my Tía Judy (along with her husband, my Uncle Peter) for the first time. My father and mother, as well as my sisters, joined my husband and me that day in our apartment; I cooked pernil and arroz con gandules to mark the occasion that was simultaneously sorrowful and joyful. That meeting led to many years of shared memory, including births, weddings, baptisms, my grandfather's death in 2003 and my Tía Judy's death in 2016.

José de Diego's poem, my own personal struggle, and the stories of writers Santiago, Soto, and Ferré that I explore in the next chapters, all converge on this one point: without the intervention of God's miraculous power, ours would be a story of arrested development, of eternal waiting, of choking silence, of "la isla nena," of stunted growth, of being only "almost a woman." Our history tells us that this is all there is, that this is all we are, a "lost cause," but our faith tells us otherwise. It is our negotiated history as decolonized subject.

Literature as a descriptive source for theology demonstrates the "is" of Puerto Ricans' identity, our suffering, and our sense of hopelessness amidst the oppressive conditions and environment under United States rule. Our Christian faith affirms that what appears to be our reality is not all there is. As a prescriptive source for theology, our literature also projects a vision of the "ought" of our reality. It is as if the stories are saying: "This is what our identity as Puerto Ricans can be," "this is how our suffering as Puerto Ricans can be alleviated," and "this is where our hope as Puerto Ricans is renewed." In relation to identity, suffering, and hope, Christian theology offers the same hope that there is more.

Who the world says we are and what God calls us to constitute the bridge between our story and God's story, between literature and theology. I believe this in-between liminal space, according to Crossan, is where God meets us if we choose to turn toward God's infinite grace.[16] The Puerto Rican literature of Santiago, Soto, and Ferré reflect the ongoing struggle of the "is" and the "ought" of Puerto Rican life: the described identity, suffering, and hopelessness and the prescribed humanity, salvation, and hope toward which we are called by God as Puerto Ricans and as God's children.

NOTES

1. Translated by Roberto Santiago in *Boricuas: Influential Puerto Rican Writings—an Anthology* (New York: Ballantine Books, 1995), 347.
2. René Marqués, *The Docile Puerto Rican*, Essays translated with an Introduction by Barbara Bockus Aponte (Philadelphia: Temple University Press, 1976), xvi.
3. Co-editor (with Robert Detweiler) Gregory Salyer, in his "Introduction" to *Literature and Theology at Century's End* (Atlanta: Scholars Press, 1995), speaks of the literature and theology dialogue/enterprise as "a viable hermeneutical avenue because it values the inherently self critical dimensions of life on the borders," which will continue into the coming century because of "its refusal to proclaim itself in its various incarnations as the final word," 3–4.
4. David Jasper, ed. *The Study of Literature and Religion* (Minneapolis: Fortress Press, 1989), 138.
5. Roberto Santiago, ed. Introduction to *Boricuas*, xxi.
6. Rosario Ferré, "The Writing Kitchen," in *Feminist Studies* 2 (Summer 1986): 243–249.
7. Robert MacAfee Brown, *Persuade Us to Rejoice: The Liberating Power of Fiction* (Louisville: Westminster/John Knox Press, 1992), 20–29.
8. John Dominic Crossan, *The Dark Interval: Towards a Theology of Story* (Sonoma, CA: Polebridge Press, 1988), 1–30. Related to the effectiveness of "story limit," René Marqués, in his essay "Literary Pessimism and Political Optimism," describes a study where an educational pamphlet geared toward country-dwellers in Puerto Rico presented two stories, one ending in reconciliation and the other in open-ended tragedy. The people were more affected, and responded more acutely, to the latter where no solution/conclusion was provided. In *The Docile Puerto Rican*, 22–23.
9. Jon Sobrino, *Spirituality of Liberation* (Maryknoll, NY: Orbis Books, 1988 [English trans.]), 14–20.
10. See Samuel Silva-Gotay, "The Ideological Dimensions of Popular Religiosity and Cultural Identity in Puerto Rico," in *An Enduring Flame:*

Studies on Latino Popular Religiosity, Anthony M. Stevens-Arroyo and Ana María Díaz-Stevens, eds. Program for the Analysis of Religion Among Latinos [PARAL], Study Series Volume 1 (New York: Bildner Center for Western Hemisphere Studies, 1994), 133–170.

11. The philosophy of Paul Ricoeur has been fundamental for the discipline of literature and theology, particularly his theory of interpretation where he identifies distinct hermeneutic styles such as the hermeneutic of suspicion and the hermeneutic of restoration. See *The Philosophy of Paul Ricoeur*, ed. Charles E. Reagan and David Stewart (Boston: Beacon, 1978). While I have yet to delve fully into his volumes of post-modernist philosophy, my initial and cursory investigation of Ricoeur's *The Symbolism of Evil*, tr. Emerson Buchanan (Boston: Beacon, 1967) identified many useful tools for future theological analysis of Puerto Rican and Hispanic literature.

12. Although Walter Brueggemann's *The Prophetic Imagination* (Philadelphia: Fortress Press, 1978) shares this phrase in its title, it focuses primarily on the ministry of the church, which must respond with justice and compassion in order to remain faithful to the Mosaic/prophetic covenant with God. While this theme resonates with my work in this essay, I have not depended on Brueggemann's analysis for my own.

13. Emma Pérez, *The Decolonial Imaginary: Writing Chicanas into History* (Bloomington and Indianapolis, IN: Indiana University Press, 1999), p. 5.

14. This concept comes from a piece entitled "Gardens" by Aurora Levins Morales in which she writes, "I am barefoot, and I feel the earth under my feet. From the soles of my feet, roots grow down into the earth, deeper and deeper. Very deep. A voice behind me says, 'The most sacred thing you can do with the earth is to sink roots into it.'" Rosario Morales and Aurora Levins Morales, *Getting Home Alive* (Ithaca, NY: Firebrand Books, 1986), 133.

15. Rosario Morales, "I Never Told My Children Stories," in Ibid., 167–176.

16. Crossan, 1–30.

CHAPTER 4

The Works of Esmeralda Santiago: Puerto Rican Identity and Christian Anthropology

Esmeralda Santiago arrived in New York City at the age of thirteen along with her mother and eight siblings; her father remained in Puerto Rico where the family had lived all of her life. By the time she was twenty-one, the family had grown to eleven children of which Esmeralda was the eldest. Her upbringing can be characterized as volatile since Esmeralda's mother supported her children without any support from their multiple fathers. Yet, she was a very strict mother who closely monitored Esmeralda's every move.

Esmeralda attended New York City's Performing Arts High School where She focused on dance (particularly Indian dance) and theatre/drama. She traveled and worked directly after high school and, after eight years of part-time study at community colleges, she was accepted to Harvard University. She graduated magna cum laude in 1976 with a degree in film production. Now married with two children and living in Katonah, New York, Ms. Santiago and her husband produce documentary and educational films through their film and media production company. In fact, Ms. Santiago began her career writing and producing

This chapter is a more extensive development of my earlier work published as "Freedom is Our Own: Toward a Puerto Rican Emancipation Theology," in *Creating Ourselves: African Americans and Hispanic Americans on Popular Culture and Religious Expression,* Anthony B. Pinn and Benjamín Valentín, eds. (Durham and London: Duke University Press, 2009), 139–172.

© The Author(s) 2017
T. Delgado, *A Puerto Rican Decolonial Theology*, New Approaches to Religion and Power, DOI 10.1007/978-3-319-66068-4_4

documentary films with her husband through their production company, Cantomedia. She has since received a Masters of Fine Arts degree from Sarah Lawrence College and numerous honorary doctorates.[1]

Santiago's works read like a good screenplay, in which one can easily visualize the characters and the events taking place in all their detail. In fact, her second memoir, *Almost a Woman*, was adapted in 2002 into a PBS film as part of their Masterpiece Theatre American Collection and her novel *América's Dream* was adapted into a feature Spanish language film, *América*, in 2011.[2]

LITERARY ANALYSIS: "WHO AM I?"

The writings of Esmeralda Santiago, particularly her novel *América's Dream*[3] and her second memoir *Almost a Woman*, communicate a prophetic call for freedom on many levels, including the personal, relational, and national. All encourage the reader to question and challenge the assumptions behind the prescribed identities of the characters she presents. In other words, Santiago's work asks the reader to consider, "What does it mean to be a woman, in general, and a Puerto Rican woman, in particular?"

Her first publication, an autobiographical account titled *When I Was Puerto Rican*,[4] details Santiago's youth in rural Puerto Rico, the culture shock of moving to New York, her coming of age straddling two cultures, and her graduation from Harvard University with high honors. Her autobiography sustains the myth of the American Dream: poor country girl overcomes all the odds and climbs the ladder of societal success to the highest rung that is Harvard. Her story sets itself up to support of the myth of meritocracy: if you work hard and sacrifice enough in American society, you will certainly succeed. Myth, according to John Dominic Crossan, leaves us feeling at ease, our conscience assuaged because, "what myth does is not just to attempt the mediation in story of what is sensed as irreconcilable, but in, by and through this attempt it establishes the possibility of reconciliation."[5] For Santiago, the myth of the American Dream is made reality for her through the telling of her life story...or so it seems.

The title of her second publication, *América's Dream*, plays into this American mythology; but now it is America with a Spanish accent who pursues this dream. The protagonist is América[6] González, a single mother working as a maid at the only hotel on Vieques. It begins with the words, "It's her life, and she's in the middle of it." Indeed, América's life is centered on her suffering. The novel begins with the occasion of

América's fourteen-year-old daughter, Rosalinda (Beautiful Rose-flower), running away with a young man. Her daughter's impulsive action stands in the tradition of similar conduct by América and América's mother Ester (Star); Rosalinda is but the latest in a long line of fatherless illegitimate daughters of a mother maid.

América is abused, physically and otherwise, by Rosalinda's father Correa (Belt/Strap) who, at ten years her senior, impregnated but refused to marry her when she, too, was fourteen. While married to another woman and with three children of his own, Correa continues to possess/oppress América; he does not permit her to be with, or even speak to, other men since he must know her whereabouts at all times. Even the slightest provocation, interpreted as such through his chauvinistic paranoia, could lead Correa to beat América. But he always does his penance; Ester's house (where América and Rosalinda live) is full of his penitential offerings: "Electronics typically mean he knows he's really hurt her, but chocolates always mean she deserved it.... A coffee brewer for a split lip. A toaster oven for a black eye. A rocking chair for a broken rib that kept her out of work for a week."[7] Correa, with all his charm and good looks, is the quintessential abuser; América is the archetype[8] of the battered woman.

Without giving away the entire story, I will jump to its ending which is all too familiar. Now with Rosalinda working as a maid in an exclusive midtown hotel in New York, América takes a moment to stand in front of a mirror to examine her reflection. Noting the changes on her face after her many dances with death, the narrator has this to say:

> It's a reminder of who she is now, and who she was then. Correa's woman was unscarred, but América González wears the scars he left behind the way a navy lieutenant wears his stripes. They're there to remind her that she fought for her life, and that, no matter how others may interpret it, she has the right to live that life as she chooses. It is, after all, her life, and she's the one in the middle of it.[9]

The story seems to end as it begins; despite all that has happened to her—"freedom"[10] from Correa, re-locating to New York City, claiming her daughter back—América remains in the same psychological state. There is no transformation or reconciliation in the story itself. *América's Dream* is no myth; rather, it is a parable. "Parable is always a somewhat unnerving experience," Crossan says, "You can usually recognize a parable because your immediate reaction will be self-contradictory: 'I don't know what you mean by that story but I'm certain I don't like it.'"[11] I had this precise reaction after reading this novel; it made me feel as if I had been strung along on a cruel and painful ride to nowhere.

While myth mediates reconciliation, or at least its possibility, parable undercuts reconciliation showing that it, too, is a myth of our own making. Again, Crossan's definition is useful:

> The surface function of parable is to create contradiction within a given situation of complacent security but, even more unnervingly, to challenge the fundamental principle of reconciliation by making us aware of the fact that we made up the reconciliation…You have built a lovely home, myth assures us; but, whispers parable, you are right above an earthquake fault.[12]

I believe this story is a parable about/for the Puerto Rican people. In other words, "Puerto Rico/Puerto Ricans is/are like a battered woman." We are, the story suggests, victim, survivor, and accomplice of our current condition. From the names alone, we can understand the parallel Santiago makes with the history of Puerto Rico—the "shining star of the Caribbean" (Ester),[13] the island paradise in full bloom (Rosalinda), America with a Spanish accent (América)—and América's story, shared with her mother (past) and daughter (future). Correa is the (Operation Boot) strap that binds, cutting off circulation, squeezing out the breath of life; when pulled up by the bootstrap, so to speak, América finds herself in target range of being struck down again.

How América and Puerto Rico/Puerto Ricans have been victimized is obvious from reading the story and knowing the history. The fact that Puerto Ricans have continued to live to tell the story has been a formidable task given the continuous oppression and annihilation; it is evidence of our determination to survive. But how can I say that América, and Puerto Ricans, act as accomplices to our own victimization and struggle to survive? This is not what Puerto Ricans are prepared, nor wish, to hear. But Puerto Ricans must hear precisely this message if we are to have an authentic response to the prophetic imagination of the author. This prophetic message for freedom jolts our complacent consciousness and makes us think about our condition in a new way while the messenger/author refuses to prescribe an easy solution. When we say we are accomplices in our continued captivity, it is, at the very least, an acknowledgment of the theft of our spirit and, more importantly, a recognition of our inner, collective power, our moral agency, to reclaim it.[14]

In a 1993 essay entitled "Island of Lost Causes" published in the *New York Times* Op/Ed section the day of the plebiscite to *recommend*[15] independence, statehood, or commonwealth status for Puerto Rico, Santiago wrote:

> We are taken for granted by the U.S., and that sharpens in us a stubborn nationalist streak - yet we don't demonstrate it at the ballot box. In our hearts, we want to believe independence is the right choice, but our history forces us to see it as a lost cause. Still, we are not willing to give up so completely as to vote for statehood. It would be the ultimate statement of our surrender.
>
> This is why so many Puerto Ricans will vote for the status quo. It fosters the illusion of choosing a destiny, neither capitulating nor fighting. But it continues to evade the question of who we are as a people.
>
> An elusive cultural identity lies at the heart of our unwillingness to declare ourselves either a nation or a state. A vote for the commonwealth insures that we don't have to commit one way or the other.
>
> Ironically, neither violent insurrection nor the democratic process seems able to solve that question.... We need to look at ourselves hard and stop hiding behind the status quo. It is not a choice. It is a refusal to choose.[16]

The refusal to make a choice is, as América's story reveals, as deadly as choosing the path of life and freedom. Her story illustrates how the silence that envelops such a refusal slowly but certainly leads to greater isolation and alienation. América hardly communicates her inner thoughts and feelings to her mother or her daughter; she is resentful and suspicious even of them, thus severing all possibility of mutual wisdom gained from relationship. Her involvement in any meaningful community is non-existent; she listens to the sermons of the Pentecostal preacher from the rocking chair on her own porch as they are broadcast to the neighborhood on a Saturday night. When América comes to New York to work as an *au pair* for a wealthy white family in Bedford, she is cautious of the other *empleadas* (nannies) she meets at the playground. While they share the same childcare and housekeeping tasks, they are different, she reasons, since they are Latin American and she is American. Like Puerto Rico in relation to Latin America, América González fears relationship because it will somehow break the silence of her true condition of oppression and domination, a condition that she has escaped only temporarily and superficially.

América's silence and self-perpetuated isolation, fueled by justifiable fear, puts not only herself at risk but those for whom she is responsible: the children she cares for and her own daughter. Without a support system, a community of solidarity, she becomes an island unto herself ("It's my life and I'm in the middle of it") without recognizing that her life includes the lives of those with whom she is in relation and who will come after; she is still responsible for their well-being. While it may be true that "it is all uphill from *Esperanza* (Hope) to *Destino* (Destiny),"[17] the two need not be exclusive of each other when the path is paved with the wisdom of community. By walking away from hope and identifying herself as a victim whose life is caught in a cycle of dependency, América puts her daughter into a situation that will be difficult to change, to break a cycle of a destiny without hope.

Santiago conveys the incredible hardship of breaking such a cycle given the history of oppression. Can we expect anything more from América, or Puerto Rico, given the circumstances? Can we call her an accomplice after acknowledging her victimization and survival? Her story is tragic[18] indeed. Yet, the author allows us to catch glimpses of revelatory moments in América's life: for five days a month, when she takes her blue placebo birth control pills, she is in tune with her natural hormonal cycle and true emotions. She sees her situation clearly, in all of its desperation she cries tears of "hurt and anger, fear and frustration."[19] But on the sixth day, she goes back to her usual self: humming and singing, sedated from her reality, numbed. In these bursts of revelation, América talks to herself more and seems assured to make some change; she even fights for her daughter to stay when Correa has made plans to take her away. These moments, however short-lived, carry the seed of transformation; they are nonetheless ineffective because no one else witnesses them. No one else participates with her in the transformative process that will lead her toward freedom. These revelatory moments are like seeds that fall onto rocky ground; without the nourishment of a community of solidarity, they do not take root and flourish.

Santiago's second memoir, entitled *Almost a Woman*, chronicles her life after coming to live in New York City at the age of thirteen. It is a tale of adolescence and, more importantly, it is a tale about choices. While her first memoir can be seen as a myth of the American dream, and her novel as a parable of the same, this memoir can be likened to a quest, a coming of age tale, the hero's journey. We are not privy to the actual arrival at her destination—womanhood—but we know that she has in fact arrived by the telling of the story itself. We can see that the choices she makes along the way have as much to do with her desire to attain "womanhood" as with not wanting to be the same kind of woman she considers her mother to be. In this sense, Santiago tells us more about the negative choices— what she chooses against, or rejects—than the positive choices—what she affirms and claims as her own. In either case, Santiago tells the story of her adolescent quest for freedom through her maturity into womanhood; she ends up telling us more about her desire to achieve freedom *from* the most influential and controlling force in her life: her mother. "To become a woman... I must rebel against my own mother."[20]

The quest upon which Negi embarks entails many relationships with different men, each with a varying degree of intimacy. She is offered many tantalizing gifts from men in exchange for her portraying the persona of the hot Latin vixen, the Anita of West Side Story. The frequency of men's advances increased upon her graduation from high school, a time of indecision and flux for Negi when she passed her time and earned some cash doing office work. These relationships helped shape Negi's own personal expectations of the man she wanted to be with, but more importantly they shaped her notions of the person she wanted to become.

Neftali was the first of her suitors; he was drafted into the army and, upon his return, died not of his heroin addiction, surprisingly, but at the hands of the police. Then there was Sidney, the Jewish salesman she met on the job. Otto was next, the brawny German man in whose arms she felt more like a woman than with anyone else, but who returned to Switzerland and soon forgot about her. After that, there was Andy, the pageboy at NBC whom she met with her friend Shoshanna and shared a platonic friendship. There was also Sammy, the pre-med student, with whom Negi was not impressed despite his book smarts. Shanti followed in line, the photographer who was mysterious and kind, yet distant and detached. Then there was Avery Lee, the Texan who lavished Negi with all the attention, material and otherwise, that she could imagine. Next was Jürgen, who refused to explain what he did for a living yet asked for Negi's hand in marriage anyway. Finally, was Ulvi, the film director twice her age with whom Negi became lovers, eventually leaving her family and friends in New York to follow him to Florida as he fulfilled his filmmaking dreams.

How does this coming-of-age story, a recollection of memory in the service of the quest for womanhood/identity, function in the broader picture of Santiago's work? Further, how does that purpose inform us of her perspective regarding the plight of Puerto Rico and Puerto Ricans? By asking these questions, I presume that Santiago is, in fact, making a statement regarding Puerto Rico, using her life and memory as a parallel to the life and memory of the island and her people. Her life and memory demonstrate, above all else, that often we know what we *do not* want in our lives before we discover what we do. The *via negativa* is clearer than the path our life's journey is bound to take.

In this sense, Negi was very clear about the reasons she chose not to be in relationship with the various suitors in her life; and less clear about the reasons for choosing to be with Ulvi, the man whose destiny she chose to accompany. Negi did not choose Neftali because his eyes made her uneasy. She did not choose Sidney because she refused to be defined as a "shikse." Negi did not choose Otto because he wanted her, body and soul, more than she could give. She did not choose Andy because he didn't really want her enough. She did not choose Sammy because he loved himself way too much. Negi did not choose Shanti because he could see in her things she refused to see in herself. She did not choose Avery Lee because she did not want to become a mistress, a kept woman. She came closest to choosing Jürgen, accepting his marriage proposal and all, but finally rejecting him as well because she could not bear to spend her life with someone she was not sure she loved. But she wanted to be with Ulvi for reasons she could not explain except that his life was the antidote to her own: ordered, planned, without expectations, quiet, suspended in time and space. When asked by her best friend, Shoshana, why she chose him, Negi could not answer the question.

> No, he wasn't as handsome as Neftali, Otto, Avery Lee or Jürgen. In the week we'd been together he hadn't taken me to any restaurants, the theater, not even the movies. He'd spent no money on me. He hadn't asked me to be his girlfriend, his mistress, his wife. He'd made no promises whatsoever. He seemed to have no expectations except that I show up at his apartment at the agreed time...In his arms, I didn't have to think, didn't have to plan, didn't have to do anything but respond to his caresses. When he held me, I didn't question or challenge him, because I knew nothing.[21]

Negi does not seem to recognize in the same way as Santiago, the writer, does (by the inclusion of this affair in the story) that the two lives—with her mother and with Ulvi—are strikingly similar in their opposition. Both try to mold her into the woman they believe she should become: how to dress, walk, listen, speak, eat, etc. The fact that Negi allows herself to be molded, assimilated, appropriated in such ways demonstrates that she is not yet a fully matured woman on the inside, despite her chronological age at the end of the memoir (21). Her movement toward Ulvi comes at a time when her mother begins to let go, easing up on the restraints that have been placed on Negi for so long. Once freed from that grasp, Negi is drawn immediately into the grasp of another who aims to control her as much as, if not more than, her mother did.

> He needed a disciple; I needed to be led. I felt myself submerge into his need like a pebble into a pond, with no resistance, no trace I'd ever been anywhere, or anyone without him. With Ulvi I wasn't Negi, daughter of an absent father, oldest of eleven children, role model for ten siblings, translator for my mother. I wasn't Esmeralda, failed actress/dancer/sec-retary. My head against Ulvi's chest, my arms around his neck, I was what I stopped being the day I climbed into a propeller plane in Isla Verde, to emerge into the rainy night of Brooklyn. After seven years in the United States, I had become what I stopped being the day I left Puerto Rico. I had become Chiquita—small, little one. Little girl.[22]

Just as Santiago uses the story of a battered woman to tell the story of Puerto Rico, she is similarly using her memory of her coming of age to tell the story of Puerto Rico's coming of age in the twentieth century, a process which has yet to reach maturity even after more than one hun-dred years. For example, even before meeting Ulvi, Negi is fearful of the telltale signs of aging in her physical appearance. In the context of applying makeup for a class on theatre, Santiago reveals her fear of "get-ting old," of becoming the old woman she sees reflected back to her in the mirror, a face that bears a striking resemblance to her grandmothers Tata and Abuela.[23] Negi's identity is Puerto Rican identity: the fear of maturing as a community, a Puerto Rican nation, of being almost, but not quite, a full-fledged adult, politically and otherwise. Santiago seems to suggest that, like herself, Puerto Rico has made a choice to align itself with a more modern way of life (Ulvi) with the promise that Puerto Rico will be molded into the shape and form that American modernity deems best for Puerto Rico. What is unrecognized to Santiago as she reflects on this moment in her life is the realization that American modernity is linked to its sinister underbelly—colonialism—and the benefits of one cannot be assumed with the detriments of the other.[24]

Negi values the relationship she has with Ulvi because it allows her to maintain her youthfulness, her childlike persona in a seemingly adult relationship. All this is done under the guise of stewardship, but the relationship is far from being equal or reciprocal. On the contrary, the relationship of Negi/Puerto Rico and Ulvi/USA is based on the imbalance of power, where the terms of the relationship are not mutually agreed upon but based rather on the best interest of the powerful. The striking reality which Santiago, through her memoir, is trying to convey, is that for all the calm, quiet, ordered façade of "liberty in law," there is a sinister erasure of all that has come before and that has shaped the identity of the Puerto Rican to this day. It is as if we are now an empty slate with no history, upon which a future that is amenable to US American interest can be designed. And yet, the relationship has its many benefits, like those bestowed by the parent upon the perennial child: to be taken care of, directed, molded into the form that makes the parent proud, but never to be in the position of the parent itself: arrested development at its finest.

Santiago also uses this coming of age memoir as an opportunity to identify the challenges that accompany the quest for identity and for womanhood, and suggests that these challenges are rarely overcome once and for all. As she is on the cusp of making the transition from high school to the world beyond, Negi becomes painfully aware that she is in the midst of at least two worlds at any given time; her challenge is to straddle all of them without losing her own balance. The world of her family in Brooklyn, that of her father in Puerto Rico, as well as the world she gladly inhabits at Performing Arts, all beckon to her simultaneously. She comes to this realization in moments of epiphany.

The first epiphany comes when, at the onset of her mother's ninth pregnancy, a social worker pays a visit to their home: "I seethed but I had no outlet for my rage, for the feeling that so long as I lived protected by Mami, my destiny lay in the hands of others whose power was absolute. If not hers, then the welfare departments…It was not funny anymore to laugh at ourselves or at people who held our fate in their hands. It was pathetic."[25]

The second epiphany comes at the point of her final high school performance as the Virgin Mary where her role is danced in Martha Graham style in a costume which, unbeknownst to Negi, is transparent. Despite the rave reviews for her performance, her mother and grandmother are aghast. And yet, Negi is proud of herself while feeling "pulled by Mami, Don Carlos, and my siblings in one direction, while my peers and teachers towed me in another. Immobile, I stood between them both, unable to choose, hoping the party wouldn't move one inch away from me and that my family would stay solidly where they were. In the end, I stood alone between both…".[26]

The third epiphany comes at the point of her graduation from Performing Arts, as she celebrates her accomplishment without knowing about, or planning for, her immediate future. Negi realizes that she embodies three distinct realities within her, and that she would have to find some way to negotiate these allegiances, often conflicting, in order to be a success on her terms. "I'd have to learn to straddle all of them, a rider on three horses, each one headed in a different direction."[27]

In the year after graduation, Negi accepted a number of different jobs to put money in her pocket, but had no luck in finding acting work. Her burgeoning independence and self-determination were not left unmitigated by her mother who refused to allow her daughter, even at the age of eighteen, to go out with a man without a chaperone, much less have an official boyfriend. Her coming of age can be understood as parallel to that of Puerto Rico itself: trying to assert its own identity and power only to be pulled back by a power more absolute and encompassing that is the USA.

> The home that had been a refuge from the city's danger was now a prison I longed to escape...I was tired of the constant tug between the life I wanted and the life I had...I wanted to become La Sorda, deaf to my family's voices, their contradictory messages, their expectations. I longed to cup my hand to my mouth, the way singers did, and listen to myself. To hear one voice, my own, even if it was filled with fear and uncertainty. Even if it were to lead me where I ought not to go.[28]

We are left at the end of the memoir without knowing for sure whether Negi chooses to follow Ulvi to Florida or to stay with her mother and siblings in New York. It is only upon a second reading of the memoir that we recognize in a line near its beginning that Negi made the choice to leave her mother and the life she shared with her family for twenty-one years, "to begin my own journey from one city to another."[29] We are left wondering how she finally lives into her own womanhood, and we hope for a glimpse of how that transformation can be translated to the process for Puerto Rican political maturity and, in fact, Puerto Rican identity. Indeed, we are left the same way we began each of Santiago's works: without clear answers but with more questions than ever regarding the nature of identity and personhood, of community and nationhood. As a good writer, Santiago leaves that constructive work to the reader and beyond.

PUERTO RICAN IDENTITY IN DIALOGUE WITH THE DOCTRINE OF ANTHROPOLOGY

Esmeralda Santiago's literary works, while unique and diverse creations, all seem to converge around the question, "Who am I?" Her writing reflects a preoccupation with the issue of Puerto Rican identity, as suggested in the titles of her two-part memoir *When I Was Puerto Rican* and *Almost a Woman*. Even her novel, *América's Dream*, can be read metaphorically as the identity of a woman, América, mirroring that of Puerto Rico itself.[30]

The picture Santiago paints of Puerto Rican identity is not the most becoming. Through the character of América, we see the identity of Puerto Rico aligned with that of a battered woman who tries to escape her situation by a change in scenery, only to discover that she cannot run away from her past. América goes on the "hero's journey" but is not affected by her journey; she remains in the same psychological state from beginning to end. Santiago begins with one character and ends with the same, offering no change of consciousness in between.

In the form of a parable, *América's Dream* allows us to see the condition of Puerto Rican women in particular, and Puerto Rico in general as unjust to the core. Santiago does not suggest otherwise. While we Puerto Rican women have been treated unjustly, we have also participated in the unjust treatment of ourselves by failing to recognize the grace-filled moments of revelation that startle our consciousness out of stupor.

Similarly, the character of Negi in *Almost a Woman* is a study in thwarted identity formation and arrested development. Through the recollection of her own life in New York, from when the fatherless family left Puerto Rico until Esmeralda/Negi left her mother's home at age twenty-one, Santiago suggests that her chronological age and life experience had little effect on her maturation process. While considered a woman by legal and societal standards, Negi was "almost a woman" when measured by her own level of self-esteem and independence. She moved out of one sheltered dysfunctional environment—her mother's—only to move into another—her lover's. Again, Santiago suggests that the external change of scenery, from Puerto Rico to New York, or from mother's to lover's house, has little to do with the internal state of dependence that is perpetuated over and over. She suggests that through these relationships—even with all the opportunities afforded, economically and otherwise—something vital is missing: knowledge of one's self, one's place and purpose in the world. This is the missing link in Negi's ability to approach full womanhood.

In both scenarios, Santiago tells us that our journey in life through many experiences both shapes and discloses our true identity. Yet, when that journey is mired in abusive experiences and relationships, we become identified with abuse; when the journey is filled with dependent experiences and relationships, we become identified with dependence. The characters of both works parallel the history of Puerto Rico; the identities of those characters parallel the identity of Puerto Rico and Puerto Ricans, similarly.

Santiago's literature illustrates another characteristic of Puerto Rican identity that is just as important to consider and affirm among our people: the value of relationships as a significant factor in shaping a healthy identity. Relationships within the Puerto Rican community are critical for the development of self-understanding as Puerto Rican. Santiago illustrates both the negative and positive aspects of such relationships, but the relationships and the community are important nonetheless. When América González says, "It's my life and I'm in the middle of it," at the beginning and the end of her story, we hear a woman trying to cut herself off from the negative repercussions of the unhealthy relationships she has experienced. Yet, our identity as Puerto Ricans, Santiago proposes through her characters, need not be "either/or." We do not have to choose between being either self-sufficient women or good wives, dutiful daughters or ambitious career women, committed mothers or sensual lovers, Puerto Ricans or US Americans. We must, however, find a way to strike a balance among all of these aspects of our identity, even as such harmony requires embracing the seemingly contradictory elements of our own being. When we refuse to embrace those ambiguities we embody, we forfeit the opportunity to reconcile ourselves, as Puerto Ricans, with our past history, our present reality, and our future potential.

Santiago leaves the story and the reader with all but a hint of reconciliation. Reality has been presented, imaginatively and in sharp relief, with neither conclusion nor the possibility of conclusion in ways that will ease our conscience. We are forced to confess our complicity on many levels and make a choice: either live like América and Negi allowing circumstances and others to govern our identity, or choose another way that is not made explicit but left to the reader to discern. Santiago, by giving us the big panoramic picture of our existence, is asking us the question, "Given what we now know of ourselves, do we have the courage to change?" We are poised to respond. Through her authorship, Santiago has broken América's silence and Negi's secrecy; she has testified and we are her witnesses, the community neither América nor Negi ever had. As a community of witnesses, our lack of response would be a betrayal of our very spirit, serving to negate the legacy of freedom of our people and sacrifice ourselves to the status quo. América and Negi's world is devoid of hope for the future because they cannot respond from their current state of arrested development. The patron demands compliance and submission; the abuser winds himself up for the ultimate blow.

Finally, Santiago shows us the future of our identity as a community if we refuse to choose the path of freedom: our children will suffer an even worse fate because they will know our betrayal of them and their destinies. But if we share our struggles with them, allow them to see the contradictions we embody in ourselves as América and Negi concurrently, and communicate our most profound visions and deepest fears, we will have given them tools to break the cycles of despair, even as we may despair ourselves. Our Puerto Rican children will know who they are in all their ambiguity and confusion. They will struggle valiantly for their right to redefine their identity because they will have seen the destructive elements of themselves. Our theological tradition attests that life can be made new by facing fear and death with hope and promise.

Myth vindicates the world we know; parable subverts that world. Taken together, Santiago's literary works act in tension with one another; as an author, she justifies her own identity, while undermining it at the same time. Puerto Ricans, and Puerto Rican women in particular, face and embody this very same contradiction. The story/history may be despairing, a lost cause, but our response to it need not be. And, our response to that contradiction will bear the fruit of our labor: love and freedom.

WHO WE ARE: TOWARDS A PUERTO RICAN DECOLONIAL ANTHROPOLOGY

The question of identity is one that resonates with Christian theology articulated as the doctrine of anthropology and grounded in the biblical tradition. Jesus himself asked his disciples, "Who do you say that I am?"[31] What it means to be human is significantly influenced by our belief in God's intention for our humanity. Within the Christian tradition, we are provided the ultimate point of reference in the life span of Jesus Christ through whom our human identity gains meaning and purpose. Illustrating how identity emerges from Puerto Rican literature as an important theme, I will now explore how this theme corresponds with the Christian theological definition of human identity.

"Coming to terms with who we are is thus seen in Christian faith to be inseparable from coming to terms with who God is in Christ through the Holy Spirit."[32] As Christians, we believe that our identity as human beings is revealed to us through the life, death, and resurrection of Jesus. Through our connection and relationship with his life, both scripture and tradition confirm, we are fully and completely human. Christopher Morse states,

> To be sure, we are identified within many frames of reference, from genea-logical charts and census reports to our career records and medical files, but none of these tell us what is the primary news about ourselves in the gospel message, that we are ultimately loved, that our life belongs irre-placeably with God's own.[33]

As Puerto Rican Christians, then, how do we do both? Believing that our identity is a gift from God that makes us unique and special, how do we come to know who God says we are through both our Puerto Ricanness and our Christianity? In a world where we struggle to know and feel the love of ourselves as Puerto Rican, where we are continuously mandated to negate our identity, how do we come to know that God loves us as Puerto Rican?

Puerto Rican stories resonate with Christian theology and tradition. By using these same stories as a source for developing a decolonial theol-ogy, I claim that the stories reflect a tendency toward freedom aligned with the Christian understanding of freedom. While each author tends toward a particular theme, taken together, these themes of identity (Santiago), suffering (Soto), and hope (Ferré) tell the story of what it means to be Puerto Rican.

To this end, Christopher Morse's comprehensive work on doctrine, *Not Every Spirit: A Dogmatics of Christian Disbelief,* is an essential tool for "testing the spirits" or discerning what Christian faith calls us to believe and, as importantly, to reject. Morse's methodology—draw-ing out the rejected belief behind the accepted belief—parallels my own methodology of drawing out the silence behind the dominant speech, as well as the decolonial methodology of affirming "the epistemically disa-vowed colonial subjects" of Western modernity.[34] Morse's methodology applies to this effort because it maintains an element of suspicion toward tendencies to interpret the Christian tradition with "naïve dogmatism," and a critical eye toward expectations to comply unquestioningly with such dogmatism, much like the colonial power in relation to its subjects. Both Morse's and Mignolo's hermeneutic urge us to take a second look at those elements of our belief systems that we've taken as universally true for all—or "zero point epistemology" in Mignolo's words—in order to discover another side of that belief which has suppressed any and all challenges to its hegemony.

Morse points us to the First Letter of John as a reference for the scriptural tradition of "faithful disbelief." There the apostle warns the early Christian community, "do not believe every spirit, but test the spirits to see whether they are from God; for many false prophets have gone out into the world."[35] Morse reminds us that the ever-present struggle of faith and doubt is not the main question when we are called to test the spirits. Instead, he is calling us to examine our experiences, even "our struggles to be faithful, with all their doubts,"[36] as an opportunity to discern what originates in the love of God and what does not.

There are two concerns at stake here in relation to a Puerto Rican decolonial theology. First, what do the stories of Santiago, Soto, and Ferré tell us about ourselves as Puerto Ricans that conflicts with our understanding of ourselves as Christian? Second, what does the Christian tradition tell us that contradicts the way we understand ourselves as Puerto Rican? The history of Christianity tells us that not everything done in the name of Christ, or the Christian Church, has been "of God." Third and finally, which story do we, as Puerto Ricans, believe and which are we called, by faithfulness, to disbelieve?

These are not rhetorical questions for me. They are essential to a theology that is both true to the Puerto Rican experience and consistent with the Christian theological tradition. I contend that the answers to these questions can be found in the *relationship* and *dialogue* between the Puerto Rican story and the Christian story because each is a constitutive element of the other. In other words, I believe that as Puerto Ricans, our story is essential to the overall Christian story; similarly, the Christian story is essential to the Puerto Rican story, when both are centered on love and freedom. Neither story can be told fully without the other; God's work in history continues to unfold in particular times and places, and among particular people. I am suggesting that God's unfolding historical project can be witnessed within the Puerto Rican community.

Therefore, the way in which we are able to discern what to believe and disbelieve evolves out of the dialogue/relationship between the story of a particular people—Puerto Ricans—and the Christian story. The call to faithful disbelief is a call to test what the Puerto Rican story has told us, as well as to test what the Christian story has told us, both grounded "by the Spirit that [God] has given us."[37] Our inherited Christian tradition has been a rich spiritual foundation, in all its denominational manifestations. But it has also served us poorly in some respects when its message has been distorted to create guilt, depression, alienation, and rejection within our Puerto Rican spirit. These distortions demand a critical voice that reclaims the best of the tradition in the service of love and freedom for our people.

Thus, I initiate this dialogue between Puerto Rican identity and Christian identity with the categories of Christian anthropology as outlined by Morse, that our identity as human beings is (1) foreknown and predestined, (2) called, (3) justified, and (4) glorified, noting the principles of the doctrine that can be used for, and have been used against, the Puerto Rican community.

Foreknown and predestined: Through the methodology of identifying the "refusals" of Christian doctrine, Morse helps us understand what "foreknown and predestined" means by articulating first what it does not mean. The affirmation of God's foreknowledge and predestination of humanity is not a "foreclosure of our freedom"[38]; it does not mean that we relinquish our free will by making this claim. On the contrary, it means that God is first and foremost, as our creator, the one who has inscribed a purpose in our life even when that purpose is unclear to us. It means that God knows who we were, who we are now and who we will become; God will lead us into our becoming when we open ourselves to God in Christ through the Holy Spirit. Our human identity is made manifest through God's design, not our own. "In believing that human life is constituted by God's decision, Christian faith disbelieves that who we are consists ultimately in our own decisions. God is for us even when we are not."[39]

This is an incredible affirmation to make from a Puerto Rican perspective. Believing that God is for us and on our side even when the world rejects us and when we reject ourselves, is a radical affirmation of our current identity of brokenness and arrested development. It's as if God is saying to us, "I love you just the way you are at this moment in time, but I know that does not reflect the entire you." It's as if God is telling us, through the witness of Jesus' humanity and divinity, that there is much more in store for us.

The affirmation of God for us as Puerto Ricans tells us something else about our identity. It issues a warning to us to not be so quick to ascribe to either this or that, to make the "either/or" decision, but to discover what God has in store for us in the middle ground, the borderland, where we find ourselves between two worlds that "grate against each other and bleed, *una herida abierta*," as Gloria Anzaldúa reminds us.[40] If we believe that God loves us as Puerto Rican in the here and now, then we believe that God loves us in the midst of the ambiguity and contradiction; these are now a gift from which we may learn and grow. Our exercise of freedom entails a discovery of that which is freeing of our identity in the present moment in the midst of the identity crisis. When we acknowledge that our development has been arrested and thwarted, stifled and repressed, we are free to uncover that which has created such conditions in order to change them. Either way, we know that God has a plan for us and loves us through it all.

Called: Our Christian tradition claims that all creation is good because God, in the act of bringing all things into being, affirmed its goodness. Through the creative act initiated by God, we are, as human beings in relation to all creation, called forth; both goodness and relationship are intrinsic elements of our humanity. Morse states that the creation account in Genesis

> portrays human life not only as foreknown and predestined but also as called for and called forth. This portrayal of being called provides the most comprehensive element in Christian self-understanding. Who we are called to be is pronounced as good, as made in the very image of God to live in covenant fidelity. This calling to image God in faithfulness to God's covenant is what is said to give human life its purpose, its real vocation.[41]

Morse offers a wonderful analysis of the difference between the meaning of "vocation" and "occupation" in relation to an understanding of how all human beings are called by God. In refuting the widely held assumption that "clergy are called by God, but everyone else has to find a job,"[42] Morse demonstrates that, regardless of one's occupation, "the call to be whole is the one vocation to which all are summoned by the gospel."[43] This affirmation illumines a crucial disbelief that has been overlooked all too often within the history of Christianity: "Christian faith refuses to believe that God calls anyone to reject the particular gifts that God gives uniquely to each human life to make it whole."[44]

On the one hand, our Christian tradition, at its best, says that who we are, our identity, is good; our identity is intrinsically relational, in terms of God and neighbor; our identity makes us whole, which is as God intends us to be. On the other hand, our stories demonstrate that who we are, our Puerto Rican identity, is far from good, relational, and whole. Our stories tell us that our identity is shaped by uneasiness and discomfort, ambiguity and contradiction, by abuse and dependence, isolation and alienation. Herein resides the gift of the dialogue between the two visions of identity: By viewing the doctrine through the Puerto Rican lens, we can say that our identity may be all that the stories reflect, and God affirms its goodness, relationality, and wholeness regardless.

This does not mean that everything we have come to identify with ourselves as Puerto Rican affirms our goodness, relationality, and wholeness. It does mean that when we begin with the premise that God calls us into being as Puerto Rican, bestowing upon us the particular gifts of that identity, we are allowed to affirm the goodness, relationality, and wholeness of who we are in God's eyes, even when the eyes of the world hold us in contempt. With this foundation of God's love, we are allowed to be self-critical about those aspects of our own identity that undermine the goodness, relationality, and wholeness of our humanity. Applied to both the external environment and the internal community, this critique and examination can take the form of guiding questions which, in light of the gospel message, summon us all to the one who called us forth: What is good in us as Puerto Rican, and what in us undermines our goodness? What in us affirms our relationship with each other and God as Puerto Ricans, and what in us undermines those relationships? What in us promotes our wholeness as Puerto Ricans, and what in us undermines our wholeness?

These become the guiding questions that enable us to shape a new and transformed identity that lives out our vocation—our God-given birthright—in a particular Puerto Rican fashion. These questions can function like a compass, providing the sense of direction and purpose in a continuous changing landscape that our Puerto Rican identity has traveled over the centuries.

Justified: Christian theology has a great deal to say about justification as an inherent aspect of our humanity. Derived primarily from the letters of Paul, particularly to the Romans, Christian theology affirms that we are justified by faith in Jesus Christ, and not by anything we do, control, design, or earn. Our justification, that is our right to exist/be, comes from God; God alone "who is righteous makes human life righteous."[45] We are not justified by our own actions, by the institutions, political and otherwise, in which we live, or by our own self-perceptions, for good or ill. Morse states clearly that the affirmation of Christian faith in justification,

> is faith in the way God looks upon us, that is, as those whose own life cannot be separated from the life promised in Jesus Christ. This confidence is therefore not so much a faith in our knowledge of God, but rather,..., a faith in how we are known by God (Gal. 4:9). God sees us as no one else does, as being within the relationships of ultimate love and freedom... God acts to claim us for love and freedom precisely where we have suffered from the rejection of love and freedom, and does so in such a way that we are brought home to the uniqueness of who we are as God's own.[46]

Our right to be as Puerto Ricans comes from God alone, not from politicians nor from the garment factory boss, nor from military power. It means that our existence is justified in the eyes of our creator, even when that existence is precarious and unsettled. As Puerto Ricans in the United States, we do not have to justify our existence to Puerto Ricans on the island in order to make ourselves more legitimate in their view by purporting to be something we are not. As hotel workers, nannies, cab drivers, or day laborers, we do not have to second guess ourselves or make excuses for the things we need to live in dignity. All we have to know, our Christian tradition attests, is that God claims us for love and freedom when the world denies us the same.

Our stories demonstrate that, in terms of our Puerto Rican identity, we walk on shaky ground; we are in a state of flux and are trying to come to concrete conclusions about who we are as a people. In the midst of such confusion, we can rest assured in the belief that God sees our value and the value of our struggle to be who we want to be, united with the promise of life in Jesus Christ.

Glorified: While the Christian tradition is consistent in its claim that all of humanity has fallen short of the glory of God, it is equally consistent with its assertion that humanity is created in the image of God, in all of God's glory. Humanity, via our relationship with Christ, is thus understood as glorified, "through him, with him, in him, in the unity of the Holy Spirit." Morse clarifies this assertion further by stating that,

The glory of being human is that God's love for us in Christ proves stronger than whatever is against us in our life and death...Adherence to this testimony enjoins an equal refusal to believe that human life is ever glorified by rendering suffering invisible, or that there is any glory in suffering other than in its overcoming...The one true glory of every life is that God's love for it does not fail.[47]

Our stories tell us that the Puerto Rican quest for self-understanding and wholeness is a journey mired in snags and obstacles, and one in which we cannot simply run from one situation to another in search of truth and meaning for our lives. Using the metaphor of her female characters, Santiago suggests that the core of our identity must be sought from a place deep within our being. To illumine that search, the Christian notion of glorified humanity holds up a spotlight for Puerto Ricans by affirming that God sees the glory in our existence, even when that existence seems anything but glorified. Our current condition as a community demonstrates that the society in which we live does not see us "in the image and likeness of God"; unfortunately, neither do we perceive ourselves. And it is not enough to say that the glory of our humanity overrides the suffering we experience. On the contrary, by affirming this glory as Puerto Rican, we are mandated to speak a prophetic word against the very suffering that prevents us from witnessing the glory of our humanity.

RACHEL'S IDENTITY IN GENESIS AND PUERTO RICAN IDENTITY

The biblical story of Rachel is a powerful trope and serves as a bridge between the Puerto Rican story and a decolonial interpretation of Christian doctrine focused on love and freedom. Of course, I'm not the first to do this. In *Not Every Spirit*, Christopher Morse uses Rachel's story as a springboard for his discussion of "faithful disbelief," asserting that our Christian witness has as much to do with what we refuse to believe as with that which is affirmed. "In each of these instances, [Genesis, Jeremiah and Matthew], the figure of Rachel personifies the human encounter with whatever in nature and history seeks to destroy the hope of the world." If we affirm Rachel's life as a crucial person in the lineage of Israel and indeed of Jesus as a descendant, then not only do we refuse to accept that which undermined her life, but more important, we refuse to accept any false hope that attempts to console her without taking seriously the forces that undermined her life. In other words, we take her story seriously as evidence of God working God's way—the way of love and freedom—within human history.

The reference to Rachel in three distinct books and moments within the biblical text also hold a striking similarity to the predominant themes that emerge from the stories of Puerto Rican authors Santiago, Soto, and Ferré. We meet Rachel first in the book of Genesis, where the identity of a people, God's chosen people, is being shaped into a community. The second reference to Rachel occurs in the prophetic works, specifically the Prophet Jeremiah, during a period of tremendous suffering of a people in exile. The third reference to Rachel is found in the Gospel of Matthew, specifically the infancy narrative of Jesus, at a moment of hope and promise amidst a violent slaughter of innocents. These biblical references to Rachel draw us to consider her and her people's identity, suffering, and hope as a bridge to and from our own similar stories. In doing so, both our Puerto Rican stories and the story of Rachel can serve as a source for developing a fresh interpretation of the Christian doctrines of anthropology (identity), soteriology (suffering), and eschatology (hope).

Rachel's story is an empowering one in itself and in the way her life is referenced in other parts of the biblical text. She "has inspired the largest creative response in the history of art and literature, a response confirmed a thousand-fold by the people of Israel, for Rachel is among the most beloved figures in all of Jewish history and in the history of the Jewish psyche." In Genesis (29–35), we hear the story of her life, her marriage to Jacob, the birth of sons and her death on the road to Bethlehem, the land of her kin by marriage. She dies not in her own homeland or that of her children, but in transition, en route, somewhere in the middle ground. Her identity, in both life and death, is liminal. The accounting of Rachel's life highlights the complex relationships within her world and indeed in the Hebrew Scriptures. Her identity is comprised of a variety of distinct yet interwoven relationships. Rachel's identity is understood traditionally as centered on her role as Jacob's wife and Joseph's mother. However, her identity as a woman and as a matriarch of Israel offers some interesting clues as to how the text demonstrates God's allegiance and affinity to those who are relegated to the margins. "The God of Genesis...is partial to marginal people of both genders. On some level, that god is the god of the tricksters who use deception to deal with the power establishment, whether the power establishment is the elders of one's family or non-Israelites."[48] In the story, we learn that Jacob favors Rachel, the younger of Laban's daughters. But Jacob is tricked into taking Rachel's older sister Leah as his wife, and must work for seven years on Laban's land as the bride price. Jacob still desires Rachel and will have no substitute; he works for seven more years to satisfy the bride price. After working twenty years on Laban's land, Jacob takes his family to his own homeland. Upon departure, Rachel, in an audacious act of spite, takes important statues from her father's house, knowing that these have spiritual significance for him. When Laban tracks down Jacob's family in search of his teraphim (household gods), Rachel hides them from her father, using her own menstrual cycle as a deterrent to his search. On the way to the land of Jacob, Rachel dies after bearing her second son, Benjamin, and is buried along the way. Her grave rests neither in the land of her birth, her father's land, nor the land of her sons, which is Bethlehem.

Rachel can also be viewed as a colonized woman, a woman whose ownership is not her own but rather that of her father's and then of her husbands. She is valued insofar as she brings worth to each relationship: first, as a daughter whose betrothal to Jacob brings her father seven years of indentured servitude; then, as a wife whose fertility (after some time) brings Jacob two sons, Joseph and Benjamin. The men of her past (father), present (husband) and future (sons) have claimed her life as their own; yet, no one can claim her death as she is buried in a "no man's land." While she belongs to all—father, husband, and sons—she belongs to no one. Her death and her life take place in an in-between ambiguous place where she has no sovereignty over her own destiny. She is like Negi in Santiago's *Almost a Woman*, and América in *América's Dream*; her identity is not her own and thus her destiny is overshadowed by the men who determine it.

Yet, these fictional women differ from Rachel because the story tells us that God looked upon Rachel and made a destiny for her. God saw that her life on the margins was valuable in itself, evidenced by the way she is remembered and revered as a matriarch of a chosen people. There is something about Rachel that also suggests a certain bravado and freedom unlike other women in the Scriptures. As her father's shepherdess, Rachel had to roam the fields with her flock alone; this is how she meets Jacob at the well. She demonstrates a good deal of cunning as she "repudiates her father by leaving him and taking his idols."[49]

Rachel contrasts with the typical image of woman as an "interior" (home or withdrawn) figure. The quality of self-reliance, even audacity, which Rachel as shepherdess represents, continues in her lifetime and in legend after her death...Rachel, the outdoor, roaming shepherdess, was destined to serve her people and is laid to rest along the roadside, that she might rise up to console the exiles when they would pass on the way to Babylon.[50]

Rachel's identity defies strict definition or interpretation. She is on the margins of definitive categories; her ambiguous and multifaceted identity becomes an intrinsic aspect of her election by God.

THEOLOGICAL PERSPECTIVES ON ANTHROPOLOGY

The marginalized identity, and God's option for the marginalized, are not original theological perspectives. Virgilio Elizondo's work, from *Galilean Journey* (1983) to *A God of Incredible Surprises* (2003), has focused on the issue of Mexican-American identity in relation to Jesus of Galilee as a relationship of promise and salvation, because both identities are centered on suffering, rejection, and lowliness. He claims that "the identity and mission of the Mexican American people will not only continue but will be purified, ennobled, and strengthened by the discovery of its fundamental identity and mission in its acceptance and following of Jesus of Nazareth as the Lord of history and life."[51] He is not saying that all Mexican-Americans must convert to Christianity in order to understand their true identity and mission. Rather, he believes that those who confess Jesus as Lord need to see his identity—one who emerged from Galilee and chosen by God—as particularly significant because it parallels what Elizondo calls the Mexican-American identity of *mestizaje*.[52] Notwithstanding the critiques that have been voiced since his introduction of this theological perspective, Elizondo speaks of *mestizaje* as a gift of identity that is offered to Mexican-Americans and, in fact, to the world. Speaking of his own journey toward self-acceptance of his personal and communal *mestizaje*, Elizondo relates this to the larger human family:

I am always both kin and foreigner at the same time. This "in-between" is the pain and the potential, the suffering and the joy, the confusion and the mystery, the darkness and the light of Mestizo life. As I claim this ambiguity and recognize it for what it truly is, I become the bearer of a new civilization that is inclusive of all the previous ones. No longer do I carry the burden of shameful news but rather become the bearer of the good news of the future that has already begun in us.[53]

More than a personal quest for identity and self-understanding, the promise of *mestizaje* lies with its connection to Jesus Christ himself who, as a Galilean, is affirmed as the savior through his own *mestizo* identity. The *mestizaje* of Jesus gives both evidence and hope of God's promise fulfilled in choosing those whom the world considers absurd (1 Corinthians 1:28). "This marginal identity certainly fits into the pattern of who God chooses.[54]

James Cone suggests something similar in *A Black Theology of Liberation*.[55] Here, he outlines a black theological anthropology, stating that the critical element of a black perspective on the question of human identity is the rejection of the dominant theology's claim of a universal God and a universal Jesus. Instead, Cone invites us to look at the particularity of Jesus as the Oppressed One, the fundamental element of his human and divine nature. "The basic mistake of our white opponents is their failure to see that God did not become a universal human being but an oppressed Jew, thereby disclosing to us that both human nature and divine nature are inseparable from oppression and liberation. To know who the human person *is* is to focus on the Oppressed One and what he does for an oppressed community as it liberates itself from slavery."[56] For Cone, the constitutive elements of a black theological anthropology are oppression, resistance to oppression and liberation from oppression, all circumscribed by the life, death, and resurrection of Jesus, the Oppressed One who is made free. Therefore,

> To say that Christ is black means that God, in his infinite wisdom and mercy, not only takes color seriously, he takes it upon himself and discloses his will to make us whole—new creatures born in the spirit of divine blackness and redeemed through the blood of the Black Christ. Christ is black because...Christ really enters into our world where the poor, the despised and the black are, disclosing that he is with them...[57]

The authentic identity of black people is defined by God whose own oppression and liberation through Jesus Christ demonstrates the true nature of human existence.[58]

A Puerto Rican Decolonial Anthropology

"In God's eyes, no life story is ever without promise."[59] This is the true nature of humanity viewed from the divine perspective. We are justified not because of how we know God or what we know of God. We are justified in our very human existence because God knows us and, with all of our flaws, sins and failings, loves us. "What is proclaimed to justify our right to be as God has created us is that God acts to claim us for love and freedom precisely where we have suffered from the rejection of love and freedom, and does so in such a way that we are brought home to the uniqueness of who we are as God's own."[60] This understanding of ourselves as humans takes on a profound significance when considered from a Puerto Rican perspective. In other words, God claims the Puerto Rican community for love and freedom because we have suffered from the rejection of love and freedom, and God does so in such a way that we, as Puerto Ricans, are restored to the uniqueness of who we are, our identity, as God's own children.

How can such a claim have any bearing upon us when we have been defined for so long through the lens of such socio-economic factors which distill our identity into lawlessness, violence, out-of-wedlock births, illiteracy, substance abuse, domestic violence, child abuse, ...and the list goes on? How can we say that God chooses us precisely because of these conditions in order to restore us to our own true selves? And what is our own true identity when the vision of such has only been glimpsed, overarched by our depressing reality? Accordingly, what clues does the literature offer in our self-understanding, our identity, which has been circumscribed by the overwhelming reality of colonization that can speak to our relationship as a particular people with our God?

First, I believe that the reality of colonization lays bare the dream of decolonization; the colonized do not wish to remain so, deep in their souls. They dream of freedom, if only as a dream, and maintain that dream at all costs; the title of Santiago's novel implies as much, although her protagonist's dream falls short of reality. The colonized know that it is better to be free from colonization than to be governed by it—on every level—just as those who are enslaved know that the absence of slavery is better than its perpetuation. Even while maintaining the dream of the demise of colonialism, the colonized learn much from that same system: subversive tactics, trickery, and even silence, which mask pain and vulnerability. It also teaches survival tactics of creativity, adaptability, compromise, resilience, acceptance of the "other" within our own identity.[61]

4 THE WORKS OF ESMERALDA SANTIAGO ...   99

Puerto Rican identity is a precarious term, one that has been and continues to be debated by many scholars. Yet, these scholars agree that Puerto Rican identity is both fixed and fluid, static and dynamic, the same as it has been yet ever changing. Even the title of the book, *The Puerto Rican Nation on the Move: Identities on the Island and in the United States*,[62] suggests a notion of nationhood that is not geographically bound nor comprised of one definition of identity. In an "uneasy" coexistence of colonialism, nationalism, and transnationalism,[63] the author suggests that Puerto Rican national identity is both fluid and tenacious "across many kinds of borders, both territorial and symbolic."[64]

Thus, the reality of colonization, as a starting point for a Puerto Rican theological anthropology, suggests the discomfort of living in a liminal space, an in-between state on the boundaries of existence that are not concrete. This is certainly an uneasy existence, when an entire people have no sense of where they belong in relation to themselves or others. We would be much happier as a people if we knew exactly what our identity consists of, what are its fundamental markers and attributes, whether it is language, culture, geography, etc. But the comfort of a certain identity can lead to complacency, an acceptance of things as they are—the status quo—and a lack of questioning or critical perspective that brings about change. I propose, then, that the discomfort or uneasiness of what it means to be Puerto Rican is a desirable place because it is a catalyst for creativity, not complacency; it highlights the contradictions of one's reality, rather than status quo acceptance; it challenges the existing reality by asserting a critical perspective. In fact, what emerges out of a place of dis-ease is the voice of the prophet, which can motivate a people to change that which is seemingly unchangeable. The prophetic call is a voice from God giving the words the prophet must speak "to uproot and to pull down, to destroy and to overthrow, to build and to plant." (Jeremiah 1:10)

If we understand the identity of Jesus as the oppressed one (Cone), as the mestizo (Elizondo), and as the divine/human "other" (Segovia), we can also see him, from a Puerto Rican perspective as the colonized Jew in a land ruled by the Romans. As a colonized Jew from Galilee, Jesus' own identity is ambiguous and highlights the ambiguity of our own Puerto Rican identity, the main attribute of which is our collective colonization. Yet that same ambiguity, the belonging to all and nothing, is also a place of fruitfulness; in fact, it is the place that was chosen by God as the location of his incarnation, precisely for its ambiguity, as if to say that no one in their exclusive particularity can claim Jesus' life as salvific exclusively for themselves. On the contrary, everyone in their exclusive particularity can claim his life as salvific. That is the promise of Jesus' identity which we come to know through his life, death, and resurrection.

The story of Rachel, and her identity as a woman God chose, may shed some light on the mystery of this promise. When we consider Rachel by the factors that identify her in her society, we see a woman who should not have been chosen, really. She was the younger daughter when the eldest place is reserved and revered. She is barren in the story until close to the end of her life, when fertility is honored. She steals her father's things and then lies about what she has done. She pits herself against her sister in competition for their husband. She dies suffering through a difficult childbirth experience and is not buried in her own land. She is a transition figure, an exile, a daughter who suffers the rejection of her father's love by being sold to another man for greater wealth and benefit. And she knows this; she knows that her only value to her father is as a commodity. Yet, God sees what the society in which Rachel is born and lives does not see. God sees in her something special and unique; her life story holds a promise: that she will always be remembered not only for the fruit of her womb. Her story will be remembered because it is part of God's option for those on the margins, the lowly and the weak, those who are in-between reality with no secure place to stand. Her story is, in fact, the message of the gospel through Jesus since "the Messiah will not come from Galilee," (John 7:41) or so it was believed. The gospel story is precisely the Puerto Rican story as we share the same rejection of our ambiguous and conflicted identity; still, we are God's chosen within the rejection and suffering of our identity. While Ramón Grosfoguel speaks of Puerto Rican transnational identity formation as "constructions that emerge out of political strategies within specific power relationships,"[65] I would add that the story of Rachel and our Puerto Rican story confirm to us that the worldly structure of our identity must never be our exclusive focus if we believe that God knows us, calls us, justifies us and glorifies us into being.

NOTES

1. From the author's official web site www.esmeraldasantiago.com@ Cantomedia 2012.
2. http://www.ncteamericancollection.org; Sonia Fritz, *América* (Puerto Rico: Isla Films, 2011), film. *América*, directed by Sonia Fritz (Isla Films, 2011).

3. Esmeralda Santiago, *América's Dream* (New York, NY: HarperCollins, 1996).
4. Esmeralda Santiago, *When I Was Puerto Rican* (New York, NY: Vintage/ Random House, 1993). Santiago received some criticism for the title of this work because it suggests that she does not consider herself to be Puerto Rican any longer, based on the use of the past tense. However, I believe her use of such a title highlights the dichotomy and tension that exists between the island Puerto Ricans and the mainland Puerto Ricans, each claiming an identity to be more authentically Puerto Rican. I believe Santiago is intentional in her choice of such an ambiguous title as it emphasizes the ambiguity of Puerto Rican identity itself.
5. John Dominic Crossan, *The Dark Interval: Towards a Theology of Story* (Sonoma, CA: Polebridge Press, 1988), 32–37; he makes the distinction of myth, as a perpetuation and support structure of the status quo, and parable as a subversion or undermining of the status quo.
6. The name America is quite common among Spanish speaking peoples. In Santiago's novel, the name has a number of layers of meaning and reference: for the protagonist herself, as well as a metaphor for Puerto Rico (America with a Spanish accent), and for the United States of America. I believe the author is deliberate about the ambiguity of the reference as a literary tool for illustrating the ambiguous nature of Puerto Rico's relationship with the United States and vice versa.
7. Santiago, *América's Dream*, 91.
8. Archetypes: content of the collective unconscious; meaning original model after which other similar things are patterned; synonym: prototype; birth rebirth death hero child demon trees wind fire rings weapons trickster…; not to be regarded as fully developed picture in the mind but as a negative that must be developed by experience; persona, anima, animus, shadow, self: important archetypes for Jungian psychology; archetypes can form combinations and interact with each other; archetypes are universal; everyone inherits the same basic archetypal images (i.e., infant with mother archetype); archetype functions as a magnet attracting relevant experiences to form a complex; in this way the archetype gains consciousness on the surface. From Calvin S. Hall and Vernon J. Nordby, *A Primer of Jungian Psychology* (New York, NY: Penguin Books USA, Inc., 1973).
9. Santiago, *América's Dream*, 325.
10. Freedom, in this instance, refers to América's physical freedom from her abuser who will never hurt her or her daughter directly again.
11. Crossan, *The Dark Interval*, 39.
12. Ibid., 40.

13. For many years, Puerto Rico was portrayed in tourism advertisements as the shining star of the Caribbean. The name Ester is a derivative of the word "estrella," meaning star.

14. Throughout the writing of this book, I have been nurtured, sustained, and brought back by Clarissa Pinkola Estés' work *Women Who Run With the Wolves* (New York, NY: Ballantine Books, 1992). The notions of capture, theft, and returning to the self resonate throughout her work but are brought into sharper focus in her chapter "Homing: Returning to Oneself," 255–296.

15. I emphasize the word "recommend" here because, in truth, the plebiscite had no real power of persuasion for those in whose hands the power to change Puerto Rican status lies, namely the United States Congress and the Executive Office of the President. The plebiscite is also questionable because it was conducted by the colonial power, not by an independent party, as would be required by United Nations standards for a legitimate vote.

16. Santiago, *Boricuas*, 24.

17. Santiago, *America's Dream*, 19. *Esperanza* and *Destino* are two actual towns on the island of Vieques; in the novel, América physically walks away from the former (hope) to the latter (destiny).

18. Nathan Scott states of tragedy: "In the tragic universe, life is experienced as having broken down: that the congruence between the highest aspirations of the human spirit and its world environment, apart from which existence seems utterly futile, is no longer discernable," *The Broken Center* (New Haven, CT: Yale University, 1966), 122. He claims it is the communion of the Eucharist, of the celebration of the defeat of tragedy, which mediates/reconciles the tragic vision. In this sense, the community of those who maintain the memory, like those who read/know América's story, can respond in spite of tragedy.

19. Santiago, *America's Dream*, 78–79. The motif of the birth control pill is significant for the Puerto Rican woman since reproductive rights have been exploited through forced sterilization and unethical "experiments" with birth control pills on Puerto Rican women by US pharmaceuticals. See Edna Acosta-Belen, ed. *The Puerto Rican Woman: Perspectives on Culture, History and Society* (New York, NY: Praeger, 1986); and Cynthia T. García Coll and María de Lourdes Mattei, eds. *The Psychosocial Development of Puerto Rican Women* (New York, NY: Praeger, 1989), 147–148, 217.

20. Santiago, *Almost a Woman*, 283.

21. Ibid., 275–277.

22. Ibid., 306. Santiago's final installment of the memoir trilogy, *The Turkish Lover* (Cambridge, MA: De Capo Press/Perseus Book Group, 2005) details this seven-year relationship exclusively.

23. Ibid., 82–83.
24. Walter Mignolo, *The Darker Side of Western Modernity: Global Futures, Decolonial Options* (Durham, NC: Duke University Press, 2011).
25. Santiago, *Almost a Woman*, 136–137.
26. Ibid., 145.
27. Ibid., 153.
28. Ibid., 210.
29. Ibid., 2.
30. Santiago's most recent novel, *Conquistadora*, delves into these same ambiguities and complexities of identity as well, as the protagonist is a nineteenth-century aristocratic slave-holding woman in Puerto Rico (New York, NY: Knopf-Doubleday/Vintage Books, 2011).
31. Matthew 16:15; Mark 8:29; Luke 9:20.
32. Morse, 257. Whereas Morse's chapter on the doctrine of humanity follows his discussion of the doctrine of salvation, I have intentionally reversed the order in this work. The Puerto Rican story, as I have chosen to tell it, compels me to address the question of identity first and foremost because our identity as Puerto Rican, in a racist and ethnically hostile US environment, has determined the conditions for our economic/social/political suffering. In turn, our ability to transcend this suffering will depend, in part, on our ability to come to terms with our current identity, which is in the process of transformation.
33. Christopher Morse, *Not Every Spirit: A Dogmatics of Christian Disbelief* (Valley Forge, PA: Trinity Press International, 1994), 263.
34. Mignolo, *The Darker Side of Western Modernity*, 80–81.
35. 1 John 4:1, in Morse, *Not Every Spirit*, 3.
36. Ibid., 6.
37. 1 John 3:24. The words preceding these (3:18ff) tell the community of how they are to know they are on the path of truth: "Our love should not be just words and talk; it must be true love, which shows itself in action. This, then, is how we will know that we belong to the truth; this is how we will be confident in God's presence."
38. Morse, *Not Every Spirit*, 263–264.
39. Ibid., 264.
40. Gloria Anzaldúa, *Borderlands/La Frontera: The New Mestiza*, Fourth Edition (San Francisco, CA: Aunt Lute Books, 2012), p. 25: "The US –Mexican border es una herida abierta where the Third World grates against the first and bleeds. And before a scab forms it hemorrhages again, the lifeblood of two worlds merging to form a third country—a border culture...A borderland is a vague and undetermined place created by the emotional residue of an unnatural boundary. It is in a constant state of transition."

41. Morse, *Not Every Spirit*, 265.
42. Ibid., 267.
43. Ibid.
44. Ibid.
45. Ibid., 270.
46. Ibid., 270–271.
47. Ibid., 272–273.
48. Carol A. Newsom and Sharon H. Ringe, eds. *The Women's Bible Commentary* (Louisville, KY: Westminster/John Knox Press, 1992), 18.
49. Samuel H. Dresner, *Rachel* (Minneapolis, MN: Augsburg Fortress, 1994), 35.
50. Ibid., 35–36.
51. Virgilio Elizondo, *Galilean Journey: The Mexican American Promise* (Maryknoll, NY: Orbis, 1983), 1.
52. First articulated in *Galilean Journey* and carried through subsequent publications, Elizondo maintains that the Mexican-American experience of mestizo identity parallels that of Jesus: the societal rejection of each is overarched by the divine election of each.
53. Elizondo, *The Future is Mestizo: Life Where Cultures Meet, Revised Edition* (Boulder, CO: University Press of Colorado, 2000), 129. Arturo Bañuelas' edited volume *Mestizo Christianity: Theology from the Latino Perspective* (Maryknoll, NY: Orbis Books, 1995) was so titled based on the premise that all Latino theology is *mestizo*, a mixture, in content and method.
54. This belief in the gift of marginalized people to salvation history is addressed more fully in Elizondo's more recent book, *A God of Incredible Surprises: Jesus of Galilee* (Lanham, MD: Rowman and Littlefield Publishing Group, Inc., 2003), 53; Chapter Five, "Where are you from?" delves into the question "Why Galilee?" Presuming that Galilee was a borderland in its own time, Elizondo offers this answer: "Precisely because of its ethnic mixture, it was a good place to begin the new universal fellowship that Jesus came to initiate…It was a great place for the reign of God as lived and proclaimed by Jesus to begin. From among the peoples who were considered the least by the greats of this world, the greatest of this world would emerge," 55.
55. James H. Cone, *A Black Theology of Liberation, Second Edition* (Maryknoll, NY: Orbis, 1986).
56. Ibid., 85.
57. James H. Cone, *God of the Oppressed* (San Francisco, CA: Harper and Row Publishers, 1975), 136.

58. Cone's theological anthropology continues to identify the main elements of human nature, when oppression is the starting point, as 1. the human being as endowed with freedom; and 2. the human being as a fallen creature; see *A Black Theology of Liberation*, 87–109.
59. Morse, *Not Every Spirit*, 271.
60. Ibid., 270–271.
61. This is what Elizondo calls the "gift" of mestizo identity, that we can do and be both. Fernando Segovia confirms this perspective from a biblical vantage point (see *Mestizo Christianity*).
62. Jorge Duany, *The Puerto Rican Nation on the Move: Identities on the Island and in the United States* (Chapel Hill, NC: University of North Carolina Press, 2002).
63. Ibid., 284.
64. Ibid., 285.
65. Ramón Grosfoguel, *Colonial Subjects: Puerto Ricans in Global Perspective* (Berkeley, CA: University of California Press, 2003), 143.

CHAPTER 5

The Works of Pedro Juan Soto: Puerto Rican Suffering and Christian Soteriology

Pedro Juan Soto was born in Cataño, Puerto Rico in 1928 and moved to New York City at the age of eighteen to attend Long Island University where he received his bachelor's degree (1950). During this time, he supported himself financially by taking jobs as a mail carrier, movie usher, bus boy, and reporter for a Spanish language newspaper. He was drafted into the US army upon graduation and served in the Korean War from 1950–1951. He received a Master of Arts degree from Columbia University (1953) and his doctorate from the University of Toulouse (France) in the late 1970s. He taught Puerto Rican Studies as a professor at SUNY Buffalo, then returned to Puerto Rico to teach at the University of Puerto Rico as Professor of Spanish and Literature.

This background allowed Soto to develop within a literary genre of Puerto Rican writing known as the Generation of 1940 that exhibited a style and manner different from that of prior generations. Other notable Puerto Rican authors of this group are René Marqués, Jose Luís González, Luís Rafael Sánchez, and Emilio Díaz Valcarcel. These authors were the first generation of artists to experience fully the imperialism and

---

This chapter is a more extensive development of my earlier work published as "Freedom is Our Own: Toward a Puerto Rican Emancipation Theology," in *Creating Ourselves: African Americans and Hispanic Americans on Popular Culture and Religious Expression*, Anthony B. Pinn and Benjamín Valentín, eds. (Durham and London: Duke University Press, 2009), 139–172.

© The Author(s) 2017   107
T. Delgado, *A Puerto Rican Decolonial Theology*, New Approaches to Religion and Power, DOI 10.1007/978-3-319-66068-4_5

domination of the USA: In 1917, United States citizenship was imposed upon all Puerto Ricans, not incidentally making all adult Puerto Rican men eligible for the draft to fight in World War I.

A recurrent theme in Soto's work, as in the other authors of this Generation of 1940, is the confrontation with and struggle against some sort of oppressive force, be it industrialization, economic exploitation, or political militancy. In the introduction to her translation of Soto's short story collection *Spiks*, Veronica Ortiz writes

> In their handling of these various themes, the Generation of 1940 reflects a confident step toward redefinition of a national spirit, the reinstitution of familiar and appropriate worldviews and the rejection of imposed and poorly digested alien structures. As such their work most often emerges as a cry of despair...Their characters are tortured by real or imagined demons, twisted by agonies of mysterious origins; the worlds revealed are fraught with violence and tragedy, populated by grotesque and pathetic monsters; and the human interaction they depict is characterized by mis-understanding and cruelty, by victimization and brutalization.[1]

Violence and tragedy, misunderstanding and cruelty, victimization and brutalization can be said of Soto's own personal life as much as with the characters his literature animates. His own son, Carlos Soto Arrivi (age 18), along with Armalvo Dario Rosado (age 24) were killed by Puerto Rican police in what has been termed the Cerro Marrovilla Massacre in 1978. Initially accused of being terrorists planning an anti-government action, the young men were exonerated posthumously of any criminal activity (other than being pro-independence activists like Soto) and a number of government officials (including police, detectives, district attorneys) were either jailed or fined.[2]

In the following section, I focus on Soto's stories of Puerto Rican suffering and desperation, particularly the novels *Hot Land, Cold Season* and *Usmaíl*, as well as the collection of short stories, *Spiks*.[3] In foregrounding the experience of Puerto Rican people through our literary tradition, I am privileging the voices of a people in anguish, to which the Christian doctrine of salvation, or soteriology, is called to respond.

LITERARY ANALYSIS: "WHY IS THIS HAPPENING TO ME?"

Soto's novel *Hot Land, Cold Season* begins in flight, neither on the island of Manhattan in New York nor on the island of Puerto Rico. It begins ambiguously in the middle of nowhere: not belonging to either place but not disassociated from the two. The novel's protagonist, Eduardo Marín (the same name as Puerto Rico's embattled proponent of the "middle ground" Luis Muñoz Marín), is taking an airline flight back to Puerto Rico, only his second time on a plane, the first being the trip his entire family made when they moved from the Puerto Rican coastal town of Caramillo to the barrio of East Harlem. He was eight years old then, and now, ten years later, he and his fellow Puerto Ricans in flight are like "prodigal sons returning home."[4]

Eduardo is reminded of his own alcoholic father when he helps an old man to his feet, a man who, as he emerges from the plane, stoops to kiss the ground, his beloved *tierra*. Eduardo imagines that it is not a "stranger's hand he is holding but his own father's: a man returning to his homeland with his son after countless defeats and endless years in captivity."[5] To Eduardo, hope for the future is associated with *la naturaleza* (nature/wilderness), the openness of the land, the vastness of the sky, the colors and spaces as the language of the earth.[6] Through the character of Eduardo, the author suggests that when one is in touch with the natural world, one feels most free. Eduardo begins to associate his own coming of age into adulthood with the openness and freedom he feels in Puerto Rico.

Upon his arrival, Eduardo therefore immediately begins to associate Puerto Rico with all things positive and New York City with all things negative, including the notion of captivity. He does not want to meet the same fate as his best friend Lefty Fernández who, like Eduardo, wanted to become an engineer, but died at too young an age. Lefty was a "free spirit" who hitchhiked his way around the country every summer in search of "wide open spaces, peace, natural beauty,"[7] rather than work a "normal" job like Eduardo in the local supermarket or pizza joint. But when a neighborhood bad boy sexually abused Lefty's sister, Lefty took justice into his own hands and stabbed the perpetrator to death. He was finally cornered on a rooftop after outrunning the police and made the fateful choice to jump to his death rather than be arrested and live the rest of his life in prison.

Yet for all his desire to associate Puerto Rico with the good and the positive, on his return to Caramillo, the town of his birth, Eduardo is shocked by the reality of poverty. The creek in which he swam as a child is now polluted; there is no place for the children to swim other than the ocean, which is too strong for their young and frail bodies. The homes he remembered from his childhood as being quaint and lovely he now sees are ramshackle huts with corrugated tin walls and roofs. Eduardo decides to make peace with his past after staring poverty's cruelty in the face for the first time and witnessing its torment without the patina of nostalgia. He decides to swim in the ocean as a loving ritual of reconciliation.[8]

Haunted by the poverty he now recognizes yet also moved to make a difference, Eduardo resolves that he will not go back to New York but stay in Puerto Rico to attend the university. He has visions of becoming an engineer in order to help his hometown of Caramillo develop a new infrastructure. He sees himself volunteering his time and efforts to improve the town, living as a hermit or missionary barefoot and with ragged clothes. The true goal of his philanthropy he envisages is proving to the people of his town that he has not forgotten them, that he is not a "sell-out," and that he has not become a US American.[9] Yet his efforts are unsuccessful; those in the town continue to refer to him as a *gringo Americano.*

"The loneliness of feeling unwanted in his own country"[10] is the worst kind of loneliness he has ever experienced. Eduardo dreams of combating the loneliness by putting himself in a stupor of liquor, sex, drugs, and repressed anger[11]; he will never again be at peace. When he meets an old friend, Foron, the epileptic with whom he used to play as a child, Eduardo realizes that the world is full of mean people who say and do mean things without any regard for others' feelings. He realizes that he came back to Caramillo looking for something and found nothing, and that the nothingness includes him.

The sense of nothingness is personified by acquaintances who Eduardo and Jacinto (Eduardo's older brother) call "the others," a group of colorful characters. At the center of the group is Fran, born in Brooklyn to Puerto Rican parents who, after separating from her husband Luís and two kids, decided to move to Puerto Rico to live carefree and uninhibited, without any commitments. There is Monsita who tries to follow Fran's footsteps very closely. There is Julie, another friend and roommate of Fran's, who is in love with Jacinto and with whom she is having an affair. There is Nick Baez, the founder of the exclusive club for New York Puerto Ricans, or displaced Nuyoricans unwelcomed in Puerto Rico; Baez is both an opportunist and a bit of an exhibitionist. There is Millie, who tries to seduce Eduardo the night of the big club party. Rather than being exclusive, the club is a lonely-hearts club, people who try to drown out their sadness and loneliness—their sense of being nothing—with unbridled sex, excessive drugs and alcohol, and other self-destructive activities. The club meets in an old building in the heart of Old San Juan, where old Spanish and modern American styles meet, a broken and incongruous city with drug dealers and prostitutes on every corner.

Eduardo, feverish and ill from his evening with "the others," begins to lose the naïve nostalgia that had brought him back to Caramillo in the first place. Eduardo remembers the science notes he took as a child in school in Puerto Rico in which he wrote about the characteristics of elephants:

> The elephant has a prodigious memory. His ivory tusks are very valuable. The elephant also has the longest life span of any mammal on earth. He knows at an early age where the elephant graveyard is. He is a peace-loving animal who attacks only in self-defense. His diet consists of fruit and plants. The jungle is his home. When he feels death approaching, he heads for the elephant graveyard, lies down and dies.[12]

These characteristics come to mind when he sees his hometown Caramillo, the place of his birth, as a graveyard. He realizes that the place of his birth at this point in his life holds nothing more for him than disappointment and disillusionment. He likens himself to the elephant as one who remembers too much; he also reveres the elephant for its ability to live in the jungle freely, free from the curse that memory has become for him.

Eduardo also remembers the story of the lilies in Don Eulogio's fields, a story that few others seem to recall. The lilies were originally planted as a memorial to the twenty soldiers from Caramillo who died in service to the United States military in a war "on foreign soil." Now the lily fields are shared by squatters who were fighting eviction by a landowner, a man who had once welcomed them for their cheap labor. The lilies, planted as a loving marker for the sacrifice of Caramillo, are now only as valuable as their market price. Don Eulogio's name proved quite fitting for him:

in fighting the squatters for the rights to the land, he was eulogizing the memory of the past, dead men who could not be brought back to life. The lilies, usually associated with rebirth, beginnings, purity, and spring (the classic flower of Easter), are representative of both death and life, just like the elephant.

Eduardo's brother Jacinto represents another image of the life/death struggle characterized by Eduardo's recollections. Although Jacinto wants to be supportive of his younger brother, he is annoyed and frustrated at what seems to be Eduardo's nostalgic romanticizing of the island. Jacinto, in contrast, has lived on the island long enough to know that it holds in tension many contradictions; one cannot romanticize life in Puerto Rico if one is to survive there. At the same time, he is held captive by his pessimism and by the bitterness he maintains toward his own father.

Yet, for all his conviction and commitment, Jacinto seems unable to communicate with his wife Adela about his dreams and aspirations for their future because he has become increasingly cynical with every passing day on the island. The future holds no hope, Jacinto reasons, only the constant struggle of the moment. He does not want to have children because he sees as a lost cause the world they would inherit. Instead he escapes the tension in the household by having affairs with other women, Julie in particular. And Adela, seeing the change her husband has undergone, wants desperately to have children and return to the "good old days" in New York City. Jacinto, for all his activism and commitment, has become fearful of hope for he does not wish to be disappointed by it. He is, in the end, saved by his brother who, despite his naïve optimism and nostalgic outlook, helps him to see that living without hope is like living in a cage, tentative of each step and fearful of approaching the limits of one's circumscribed existence. Eduardo gives his brother permission to forgive his father, his wife, and even himself so that he can regain a bit of promise for tomorrow and hope for today.

Twice in the story Eduardo returns to his birthplace, the town of Caramillo. In the genre of migration literature, the town/city plays an important role as a protagonist like any other character. The city has a life and personality of its own, and this life has a number of functions for the writer of the migration story. First, the city is a wilderness, a barren land. It is a place of alienation and loneliness. Second, the city is a seducer/seductress, drawing the person to its boundaries, appealing to the aspects of our personalities that need the city and what it has represented in the past. Third, the city is the trickster, yielding unexpected surprises at a moment's notice.[13] Both New York City and Caramillo serve this function in the story. The first time he visits, Eduardo searches for memorable aspects of his childhood: certain people, special places, and familiar smells. But now one of those places—the creek in which he used to swim—is polluted and seems so much smaller than what he remembers. Where there were abundant food and shelter, there is now poverty in abundance: children with no undergarments or shoes, begging on the street. Though he returned to Puerto Rico optimistic and excited about seeing the place of his birth, Eduardo leaves feeling that something has died: his nostalgic and romantic notion of Puerto Rico.

The second time Eduardo returns to Caramillo, he does so after a wild evening with the "others" (from the Nuyorican club). With clothes tattered and soaked from rain, his body burning from fever, Eduardo feels as if he is going to die. His birthplace, he realizes, will become his graveyard as well. There can be no healing in this place, Eduardo concludes. While something did die—his illusions of Puerto Rico and the people of Caramillo—something else was born the day he realized this. Eduardo leaves with a new realization that is necessary but not easy to bear: there is no dichotomy of good Puerto Rico and bad New York; there is a "both/and" quality to being Puerto Rican that is both ambiguous and freeing. While he had come to Puerto Rico initially to look for flowers and wide-open spaces like his deceased friend Lefty, Eduardo returns to New York City knowing things there are the same, that flowers and wide-open spaces are a rarity there as well. We are left with the image of Eduardo going back to the same geographical place but having found a different spiritual interior place as a result of his experiences. His story informs us that we cannot run away from our pain but that, like Eduardo, we do best to live through it wherever we are and to seek healing even in the place of our greatest pain and vulnerability.

In his collection of vignettes, *Spiks*, Soto addresses similar themes as in the novel, but now the setting is the barrio of New York. As a literary technique, Soto utilizes the "pre-story" vignette as a prelude to the larger story. In each, there is at least one character who will also appear in the larger story; this character's setting or environment is glimpsed in the miniature and gives the reader a clearer sense of what life must be like for that character. It is a microcosm/macrocosm relationship of each vignette to the larger story; the relevant issues of pain, struggle and desperation are evident in both.

In the vignette "Captive," seventeen-year-old Fernanda is in love with her sister's husband. In order that all parties maintain the proper distance, her mother decides to send Fernanda to Puerto Rico to live with a brother who will keep a watchful eye on her. The only named person in the story is Fernanda; her brother-in-law/lover and mother are not named even though they wield a great deal of power. In a sense, both the story itself and Fernanda's preoccupation with her brother-in-law are all about her and no one else. Like Santiago's character, América González, "it's [Fernanda's] life and she's in the middle of it."

The vignette "Miniature One" and its subsequent and related short story, "Scribbles," tell the tale of Rosendo, an unemployed artist with two children and a wife expecting their third child. Though his art essentially makes him no money, he maintains it as the passion of his life. On Christmas Eve, he decides to draw a mural in the bathroom of their small tenement apartment; his vision for the mural is that it will be a beautiful depiction of his love for his wife, Graciela. By the next day, Graciela has erased all of it, down to the very last detail. Upon hearing what his wife had done, Rosendo falls apart: "When he rose from the chair, he felt all of him emptying out through his feet. All of him had been wiped out by a wet rag and her hands had squeezed him out of the world...The wall was no more than the wide and clear gravestone of his dreams."[14]

"The Innocents" depicts the limited resources available to the Puerto Rican family living in the barrio that has a host of emotional, physical, and psychological issues to deal with. Hortensia is Pipe's sister, who is trying to convince their mother to have Pipe placed in a home for the mentally disturbed. Despite the numerous scars Pipe has left on her from his violent tirades, Mami cannot face the possibility of turning her back on her son when he is in such need, even if it means sacrificing her very life for it. For Mami, the most intense natural disaster could not be worse than the tragedy of her daily life. "Facing the immense clarity of a June midday, she longed for hurricanes, eclipses and snowstorms."[15]

In "Miniature 3," Chano the taxi drivers' insults and temper lead to his death at the hands of the barber. Chano's death is alluded to in the next story, "Absence" in which a young woman insists that her husband, who abandoned her three and a half years earlier, has begun to haunt her in her apartment. She is drawn to the idea of the man she loves, even though that man is merely a figment of her dreams and nothing more.

In "Miniature 4," two men are leaving a hospital, one a new father who believes he has bad luck (*mala suerte*) and drops pennies from his pocket to eliminate it. The discussion between the two suggests that tensions are high, a mood which leads right into the following story, "Bayaminiña." This mood suggests that the new father of the prelude is the same character as the short-tempered police officer in the second. The fate of the struggling vendor, whose cart is in disrepair, will ultimately end up in the hands of the officer who can think of little else but the mounting bills caused by the addition to the family. In the end, one life is brought into the world and one is taken away, both by the same person.

In "Miniature 5," we glimpse a classroom of young Puerto Ricans in which a white US American teacher is trying to communicate the meaning of the "sound of English" but is not quite accurate in her own pronunciation of Spanish surnames. The students take pleasure in mocking her. This transitions into the next story, "Champs," in which a game of pool between the sixteen-year-old Puruco and the ex-con Gavilán risks becoming violent. Puruco's arrogant bravado displayed in the prelude is nowhere to be seen in the story; the young man is no match for the experienced and savvy professional. Both pieces illustrate how easy it can be to take advantage of and exploit perceived weakness: in the first case the males, regardless of age, exploiting the woman, and in the second, a professional exploiting the novice. They are both stories of how people abuse power.

In "Miniature 6," an unnamed woman goes to a fortune-teller, a seer, to find out whether the son she is carrying in her womb will love her in the future. She is pregnant and unmarried; we meet her by name, Nena, in the next story "God in Harlem." Nena, meaning little girl, is a prostitute who has tried to get out of the business, only to find herself at the service of one man only, Microbio (microbe/germ), the father of her unborn child. As his name suggests, Microbio is a minor figure in the world at large, but he has an incredible impact and influence on those he "infects" with his deceit, manipulation, and violence, in this case Nena. She is lured into thinking that he is changing his ways as a result of the pregnancy, but she continues to mistrust him in the midst of her longing for him and for a better life for all three of them. She lives with the hope that "God is watching over all three of them."[16]

She is lured as well by the suggestive flyers that rain down from the sky from an anonymous source which state, "Await ye the Lord," and "The Lord is Nigh." Nena is drawn to the revival where, in the end, she hears the words that allow her to begin to heal after having lost the baby at the hands of a drunken Microbio. "I am the door. He who passes through me will be saved…" She comes to the understanding that, in God, all will be protected and there is no room for fear: "She knew neither pain, nor hate, nor bitterness. She was being born."[17]

How can Nena feel saved? How does she experience God in the midst of her life wrought with pain, deceit, degradation, and loneliness? A similar question is posed by Usmaíl, the main character of Soto's novel of the same name, at the end of this tragic tale; facing the likelihood of lifetime imprisonment, at best, or capital punishment at worst, Usmaíl asks,

> "God, God what have you got to say?" And he listened to the silence, to the darkness of the corners. "God, aren't you everywhere? How about it old man? How about it?"

> Then he thought about Nana Luisa, about the scent of the herbs, about Vieques, about Cisa…Guimbo was dead, his father and mother dead, the marine dead: all dead in that bar by his own hand. But what had he gained? Ah, a little bit of peace. A little bit of peace that would have been a bigger bit if they hadn't hung that name on him in the police station. A little bit of peace on the man. On *The Man* as Nana Luisa said. Creature of God, abandoned to his own resources. Because God's back was turned and *The Man* with his chest to the wind was isolated. Waiting for some Christmas, some distant solace. With his hands on this face.[18]

Usmaíl believes he is cursed because of the strange name his mother bestowed upon him at his birth—also the moment of her death—and so had left the familiar place of his upbringing, Vieques, to travel to San Juan to make an official change of his name and his life. The character does not realize, as with América in Santiago's novel, that no superficial change of a name or place can alter one's existential prison and captivity. It follows like a curse for which there is no antidote.

Set in the 1930s and 1940s on the island of Vieques, *Usmaíl* chronicles the life of a young Viequense mulatto boy, told in three distinct movements, each bearing the name of the women who have the most significant influence in the shaping and sustaining of Usmaíl's life: his mother, grandmother and lover. Josefa "Chefa" Laugié, his mother, described as a beautiful young black woman with high cheekbones and glistening skin, takes care of her father, Quico el Morrocoyo,[19] who seems to be suffering from a number of mental ailments that engender both sympathy and scorn from neighbors. Chefa becomes enamored with Mr. Adams, the US American government official sent to Vieques (where he doesn't want to be) to manage the Puerto Rican Emergency Relief Administration (PRERA), followed by the Puerto Rican Reconstruction Administration, instituted by President Roosevelt in 1933 and 1935 respectively.[20] Unable to resist the lure of Mr. Adams' flaming red hair, "an intense red, provocative...; perhaps like the apple that seduced Adam and Eve,"[21] Chefa responds to Mr. Adams' advances and embarks on a "secret" affair that leads to her pregnancy and, as a result, her abandonment by Mr. Adams. Agonized by his sudden departure without a word or sign of return, Chefa seeks consolation for her melancholy by visiting the pier where the postal ferry arrives each day, hoping for a letter from Mr. Adams (she never learns his first name) that will satisfy her dreams of a future together with their child:

> Hadn't the *americano* come to pull Vieques out of its moratorium, to resolve its hunger? Well, she too was an island. An island where everything languished, where everything faded, where everything had fallen into moratorium; all that could save her was the miracle of a man who would take care of her.[22]

Her dreams languish at the "dark and tranquil bottom of a sea without water," upon giving birth to the son she names Usmaíl, after weeks of hoping for salvation that would be delivered by way of the US Mail.

The second movement is named for Usmaíl's grandmother of sorts, Nana Luisa. Usmaíl grows up believing Nana Luisa is his biological grandmother, but she is really the local midwife, healer and wise woman "cure-it-all" who Chefa, by default, entrusts with Usmaíl's care and upbringing. Nana Luisa is cautious about Usmaíl, protecting him physically as well as from the disdain the townspeople held for his parents, but "imbuing him with a certain monitored independence sufficient to permit him to be some steps away from her skirts."[23] She tries to instill in Usmaíl a belief in his own capacity to chart his own destiny, regardless of the circumstances into which he was born. And he witnesses her frustration with her own people who seem to accept the forced appropriation of their lands by the US military in silence. But Nana Luisa's fervor, and wrath, is revived when plans for a naval base that would occupy at least a third of the island are made public:

> She now saw something more than the black flags and the furious clamor of so many for the cause of unemployment and consequent hunger. Little had been gained by such manifestations (hunger still persisted and the protests of many had been diminished or silenced by the lack of hope, sickness or death) but something valuable came out of it. There remained a long and wide trace of anguish and resentment that now signaled the true route to follow: rebellion.[24]

The third movement is named for Narcisa "Cisa" Lomeña, who becomes Usmaíl's lover. By this time, Usmaíl approaches his sixteenth birthday, the rebellion never materializes, the US Navy stakes its land claim, and the island and its inhabitants are forced to reorder their lives and livelihood around maintaining the appearance of an amicable relationship with the imperial fleet. Usmaíl recognizes the complete futility of formal education that, upon graduation, will not help their financial condition when there are no sustainable jobs on the island. He becomes an apprentice of an old fisherman, Juan Solero, with whom he learns all about the "immense byways, the limitless warehouses, the savage raging and the most tender features of the friendly sea."[25] He also hears stories from the other fisherman about Narcisa Lomeña, the unmarried seamstress who is believed to be at least three times Usmaíl's age. They develop a friendship which evolves into a more romantic and intimate relationship that begins to move Usmail toward envisioning a future for himself beyond Vieques, beyond the clamor of the "prowling marines" who continue to wreak havoc on the island. As his relationship with Cisa intensifies, so does his anger against the colonial presence that is like a ravenous beast that will not be satisfied no matter how much it consumes:

> What more could they do to the island? Had it not already been debased enough? Hadn't they robbed and raped enough, and driven off part of the population that now cried from nostalgia in the Virgin Islands and Puerto Rico and New York?[26]

Usmail decides he cannot withstand the abuse any longer and, realizing he has no power to change the curse that has enveloped his land, he could change the curse that has enveloped his existence by changing his name. Leaving Vieques with no intention of returning, but telling Cisa otherwise, Usmaíl embarks on a journey to the main city (San Juan) on the blessed island, Puerto Rico, to create a new identity and future. Instead, he encounters what he has experienced his entire life—suffering, repression, and violence—which leads to another manifestation of the same existential captivity.

And so Soto's novel ends in the manner it begins: in the eye of a storm that is the cursed condition of Vieques and all of her inhabitants, made by God this way and summarily abandoned:

> The worst of all was memory, and to feel oneself so insignificant, hungry and scabby on one island of so many that God must have made on one of those nights He spent in confrontation with the Devil. God must have been disturbed that night, maybe more bothered than ever, before the malevolent stubbornness of Satan. Listening to him, as He entertained himself by kneading a fistful of clay, replying with words smooth, sweet and mild, not noticing that the desperation not permitted in His voice was dripping off His fingers onto the clay. Unaware that the failure foreseen by that hardheaded and misled angel, took form in that stony chunk of clay that He molded. And at the moment of farewell, the Devil, focusing on the handful of clay that God let fall from His hand, must have said: Bad piece of work, this one doesn't even have rivers for Your resident creature.

> And God, contemplating that proof of His desperation and sloppiness, must have responded with sorrow and shame: It's true.

> And the land is extremely rocky, the Devil must have insisted. Not even I could do better.

> And before God could ever recover his accursed handicraft, the Devil tossed it into the sea, taunting, "Let's see what Man can do with it."

> And there, the little piece of land fell, lost in the sea, far from the repentant hands of God. But He then leaned down to gather more clay to correct his error, this time with more love and caution, adding more earth and not forgetting about the rivers.

> And surely, He threw it also into the sea, not far from the first, and must have said: Man will know how to help himself.

> And so, while some found themselves here, in Vieques, in the midst of hopelessness and despair, the rest were on the other side of the channel, in

Puerto Rico, enjoying the rivers and the greenery, and the mountain peaks, forgetting the little island that God never meant to make.[27]

There seems to be an interesting shift in Soto's work from his writing of *Usmail* (1959) to *Hot Land, Cold Season* (1961) to *Spiks* (1970), that represents a subtle movement from complete resignation of one's economic, political, emotional, physical, or psychological circumstances, toward a recognition that the will to fight may be just enough to avoid succumbing to complete despair. While Usmail's deadly fight leads, most likely, to his own death, Nena (from "God in Harlem") desires to be born again into herself. Even when there seems to be no salvation from the anguish of their respective lives, salvation may be present in the moment of greatest pain. Soto's voice has shifted from "there is no God" through the words of Nana Luisa in *Usmail*, to the possibility of God located wherever we suffer. While God may have created the suffering of Vieques by a mistake of creation, God is in Harlem too, and everywhere we find the source and location of suffering in the Puerto Rican context.

PUERTO RICAN SUFFERING IN DIALOGUE WITH THE DOCTRINE OF SOTERIOLOGY

Pedro Juan Soto's literary works beg the question, "Why do we suffer?" All of his stories, regardless of setting and context, reflect the suffering in which the majority of Puerto Ricans find themselves. Each vignette in Soto's collection, *Spiks*, highlights the struggle for dignity and survival of Puerto Rican men and women, youth and elderly. We encounter men looking for sustainable employment with little success, leading to a host of substance abuse issues as well as physical abuse and violence. We encounter women forced into a life of prostitution, trying to be devoted mothers by day and objects of sexual pleasure by night, all the while making some kind of living to feed their children. We encounter young people swayed into a gambling life, a life of risk taking and wager making, without the guidance of a mentor who shows a different way. We encounter elderly people in desperation trying to make a living by selling their wares, only to be forced into confrontation with institutions that lack compassion and understanding, therefore making even the simplest tasks difficult.

Soto's works also reflect the emotional suffering endured by Puerto Rican people, particularly in relation to the migration experience from island to mainland and back again. In his novel *Hot Land, Cold Season*, Soto portrays in vivid detail the emotional trauma that is experienced when one is forced to leave one's homeland, learn a new language in an environment that is cold and unwelcoming, and make a new life for one's family without the communal support systems inherent to Puerto Rican social culture. The main character, Eduardo, returns to Puerto Rico in an effort to reconcile his father with his older brother; he discovers that he is the one in need of reconciliation with the splintered parts of himself that belong neither in New York nor Puerto Rico. Through his descent into the deepest and darkest parts of himself, symbolized by his journey into the nightlife of Nuyoricans, Eduardo emerges emotionally vulnerable, torn, and raw. He leaves Puerto Rico in the same state in which he arrived, yet at least knowing at the end of this journey what he did not realize upon its commencement: that he is in need of reconciliation between the two parts of himself which have yet to become one, the Puerto Rican and the US American.

Eduardo's quest for self-acceptance through the acceptance of others emphasizes the sense of alienation and isolation experienced by Puerto Rican people as a result of the migration experience and its aftermath. He is alone in New York, particularly after his best friend Lefty dies, and he is alone in his birthplace of Caramillo, Puerto Rico, not recognizing anyone from his childhood except a deaf mute. He has no spiritual or religious community from which to seek comfort. In fact, after a stormy night that led to an even more rainy morning, Eduardo's spiritual suffering is highlighted as he tries to resolve a dilemma while waiting for a taxi to take him back to his brother's house:

> Wait around in the rain or cross the street to the stores on the other side of the square, dodging the cars with wet brake drums, broken windshield wipers, and deafening horns. Because the only refuge on this side of the square was the church. And a church wasn't the best refuge, from the rain or anything else. Besides, he was sick and tired of seeking refuge.[28]

Eduardo's physical appearance—he is plagued by chronic acne—is referenced numerous times in the novel and is a symbol of his isolation as someone cast out, unwanted, without a place to belong because no one wants to look at him, much less be seen with him. He is like all the other Puerto Ricans who take a plane to New York:

> A Christ, Christ in person, with his face full of pimples and his thin blood. An outcast, an American, a Puerto Rican, a clown doing a tightrope act, a dweller in no-man's land, an elephant, a top, a propeller, and now a Christ…Nobody could make [Jacinto] come back to New York, where there were six hundred thousand Christ's. …Was it because he felt he had too many sins on his conscience, or because he wasn't strong enough to prevent that many thousands from being crucified?[29]

Soto leaves us at the end of this novel with a sense that the daily suffering of Puerto Ricans—physical, emotional and spiritual—is like a slow and steady torture, a crucifixion of sorts, of being left to die. At the same time, Soto's writing offers a glimmer of salvation in the midst of despair and suffering. Eduardo Marín is no longer the naïve boy stepping off the plane into the blinding Puerto Rican sun like an "athlete returning after triumphant victories abroad, as a soldier coming home from battle unharmed, as the prodigal son knocking once again at familiar doors."[30] Rather, he is now the tried and tested young man returning to New York, seeing things clearly without being blinded by "the sudden blaze of sunlight reflecting up from the pavement hit[ting] him right in the middle of the forehead."[31] This clear vision points toward renewal through continuous struggle in the midst of hardship; the nature of struggle implies a belief in the ability to overcome a hardship, and therein lies the promise of salvation.

Soto conveys this sense of salvation in the midst of tragedy most poignantly in his short story, "God in Harlem." The story's main character, Nena, experiences a moment of conversion into a believing community, while still carrying her dead child in the womb. Against a religious backdrop where the Madonna and Christ-child loom large within the Puerto Rican community, we are faced with the antithesis of this salvific motif. Nena does not deny the fact that her unborn child is dead. She does not deny the fact that she is essentially alone in her world. She does not deny the fact that it was the man who would have been her child's father who beat her so violently he caused the miscarriage and almost killed her. Yet, Nena becomes a woman who, as a result of her experience, finds a place to belong and a way to accept herself as she is. She recognizes that she need not do anything in particular to be saved, except believe in God's love, which precedes all penitential action. She feels God in response to her as a person; she feels God in the moment when she realizes all that she put her faith into is gone.

> Only she was losing her world: her hope. Because there was nothing more for her to do. Her child was lost, so she was lost. Tomorrow did not exist. Only the inferno of her loneliness, the continuation of an adventure begun five years before...
>
> She heard neither laughter nor comments. All she heard was the voice coming from afar: "I am the door: he who passes through me will be saved..."
>
> And feeling her belly, she murmured: "God-is-here God-is-here God-is-here..."
>
> She knew neither pain, nor hate, nor bitterness. She was being born.[32]

The possibility of encountering God only occurs when the characters of Soto's works are stripped of everything to which they have become accustomed; they are reduced to the bare minimum of existence, and live in a void where there is neither yesterday nor tomorrow. In that moment, Soto suggests, is where God can be found. While not so obvious on the surface, this is a radical message of compassion and hope for a community that feels it has been stripped of all hope for the future. It affirms the community's existential struggle in the face of efforts to erase all distinctive characteristics and traits, including language, art, and music; the artist in the vignette "Scribbles" continues to practice his art even when it is erased by his own wife, the one who should most understand his desire for a better life than the one they are living. This message is not explicit, however; Soto's skill as a writer confronts us with the agonizing details of Puerto Rican life in New York as a way of protesting those same conditions, leaving it in the hands of the reader to carry the message toward a different future reality, one of healing and joy.

WHY WE SUFFER: TOWARDS A PUERTO RICAN DECOLONIAL SOTERIOLOGY

The question of suffering is one that continues to challenge those who profess the Gospel of Jesus Christ. In Jesus' suffering and death on the cross, Christians are confronted with a horrific example of cruelty and suffering of the innocent. Jesus himself pleads with God on the cross when he asks, "Why have you forsaken me," echoing the words of the ancient Psalm of David.[33] How do we understand suffering in relation to our condition as human beings? More important for our purposes here, how do we anticipate God's intervention in our suffering as Puerto Ricans to bring about deliverance from it? Illustrating how suffering emerges from Puerto Rican literature as an important theme, I will now explore how this theme corresponds with the Christian theological definition of human suffering, as well as its overcoming through salvation.

Morse's analysis of the doctrine of salvation (soteriology) is helpful here in discerning the significance of human suffering in relation to salvation. If we discuss salvation, then it makes sense to talk about those things from which one must be saved. And for many Puerto Ricans living on and off the island, the daily suffering of their lives, as Soto has described so poignantly, is what they wished to be saved from. The voice that Nena hears as she rubs her pregnant belly is one which calls to her, "I am the door: he who passes through me will be *saved* [emphasis mine]..."

Morse makes the connection between the suffering of humanity, inflicted upon others and self, and the life of Jesus Christ as the foundation for the doctrine of salvation. Through the incarnation, resurrection, and parousia—or coming/presence—of Jesus, Morse affirms that God's grace through Jesus Christ "accomplishes the reconciliation of creation"[34]; that is, God puts all creation back into its rightful relationship, a relationship severed by the affliction and infliction of evil, of being wronged and doing wrong. In the words of the "Lord's Prayer," Jesus tells us that God offers salvation when we ask to be delivered from evil of both types: "forgive us our trespasses as we forgive those who trespass against us." Therefore, when we confess our Christian faith, we affirm our belief "that salvation as the reconciling work of the triune God is (1) by grace, (2) from sin, and (3) for righteousness."[35] I will illustrate how the experience of suffering illumines the doctrine of salvation within these three categories, through the lens of the Puerto Rican community.

Saved by grace: Salvation by grace means that God is for us infinitely and that God alone gives grace; grace is not given by anything or anyone within God's creation. Salvation by grace means, "human beings *are not* the source of their own salvation or of anyone else's."[36] We recognize that we are loved at all times and in all conditions, and not as a result of anything that we do ourselves; this love precipitates our freedom. When Christians affirm that God is for us infinitely, we affirm that our salvation by grace involves our human condition and that God is for us in the midst of our human condition. The life span of Jesus, inclusive of his incarnation, is testimony to God's love for humanity; "God so loved the world that he sent his only son." Therefore, our faith affirms that our bodies, in connection with our souls, are saved by God's grace. "Salvation, if accomplished through Christ's incarnation unto crucifixion, is by definition neither individual nor societal disembodiment."[37] Our physical as well as our spiritual suffering and pain is involved in God's saving grace, not disengaged from it. Physical and spiritual suffering are evidence of a severance of the right relationship of God's created order, a fallenness from Eden, a state of sin.

Christian faith also affirms that God's salvation by grace is not given to us because we want it, deserve it, need it, require it, or work for it; it is not the "product of our free choice."[38] At the same time, the gospel message as witnessed by the life span of Jesus demonstrates that salvation by grace has everything to do with God's love and freedom, by which we love and are free:

> God loves us into loving and frees us into freedom. Our receptivity to the gift of grace is all the while part of the gift as it comes to us. No creature can dispose the will of another without imposing upon the other's integrity and freedom of self-determination. The disposing of eternal love and freedom on our specific behalf, in contrast, by definition involves no such creaturely imposition. To be motivated by love and freedom is, in the history of Christian teaching, precisely what it means to be freely self-determining.[39]

This understanding of the doctrine of salvation by grace has much to say to and for the Puerto Rican community in relation to suffering. When a foundational element of the teaching states that all human beings are salvageable, not just those in the church or even those who profess faith as a precondition, a profound and incredible promise is made for all

Puerto Ricans. Our stories and our history tell us that our suffering is real, pronounced, and multi-layered; it has thwarted our ability to love others and ourselves fully. And yet, the Christian tradition tells us that our suffering, the opposition to our love and freedom, is no match for God's saving grace. Understood this way, the suffering we experience at the hands of others or, indeed, our own, is always and forever accessible to God's salvation; this is the consistent message of the gospel. This message tells us that regardless of our situation, we need not walk in fear. The light of God's saving grace is ever present regardless of whether we are aware of its existence.

Yet salvation by grace does not "bypass...worldly existence and its opposing powers of death, or that the limits of worldly existence with its opposing powers of death constitute the limits of grace."[40] This is significant for the Puerto Rican community because it affirms the belief that God's salvation is specific, in the here and now of our lives; God cares about our particular humanity, affirmed by the gift of Jesus on earth. At the same time, God's salvation cannot be equated with the eradication of the physical, concrete manifestations of suffering; there is a difference between God's salvation and the movements for justice and freedom on earth. As Puerto Ricans, we can gain enormously from an understanding that the God who saves is a God whose salvation is always within our reach; we need not wait for the cessation of suffering, physical and otherwise, to benefit from that grace. God's saving grace is not contingent upon our asking, waiting, or believing, nor is it contingent upon any worldly institution that promises to eradicate suffering.

Saved from sin: Salvation from sin, in Morse's interpretation, is twofold. The life span of Jesus, specifically his Incarnation and Resurrection, reveals sin in two similar but distinct ways. First, our Christian faith affirms that when we sin, we "attempt to look above or over the head of God who descends to the Cross (incarnation)," by considering ourselves better than God, by betraying God in refusing to accept God's grace as the source of salvation. Second, our Christian faith also affirms that when we sin, we also "look down upon ourselves and others, an under-valuation of the creaturely existence that is made new and raised with Jesus Christ (resurrection)," by considering ourselves unworthy of God, by demeaning the life of grace from which God alone saves us.[41] In short, our sinfulness entails either thinking so much of ourselves that we believe we need nothing or no one outside of ourselves for our own salvation, or thinking so little of ourselves that we consider ourselves unworthy of salvation from sin, in all its earthly manifestations, including but not limited to physical, spiritual, and societal suffering.

Neither is the exemption from physical, spiritual, and/or societal suffering a prerequisite for, or evidence of, salvation. We are cautioned, according to the gospel message, against any claim that makes the existence of suffering proof of the absence of God's saving grace, for any individual or community. Similarly, the gospel message affirms that there is no wrongdoing on this earth, no matter how unspeakable, that cannot be made right by the gift of salvation:

> We are not saved from the sound of Rachel's voice but from its unreconciled silencing...Christian faith, in not denying the ordeal of human existence, refuses to believe that there are any conditions inimical to the true taking place of life in love and freedom that are not overtaken by the apocalypse of rectifying grace.[42]

The truth of Christian faith in relation to salvation from sin also discloses a lie, a distortion of the truth that has served to maintain the suffering of Puerto Ricans and other oppressed communities. We have been seduced into believing that salvation is, in exclusive terms, otherworldly; therefore, the systems and institutions which contribute to our suffering are either beyond or unworthy of our critique. Those who would benefit from the detachment of salvation from its concrete, historical manifestations by perpetuating this lie have distorted the gospel message, which is the radical affirmation of humanity in the person of Jesus himself. "Systemic evils are institutionalized structures of dehumanization. They are the 'course of this world' insofar as its inhabitants are ensnared into a crowd mentality of complicity with the infliction of destruction and death (Ephesians 2:2)."[43] They are sinful; we contribute to their sinfulness by giving over our lives to them unquestioningly and uncritically. Salvation from sin, from a Puerto Rican perspective, also involves, but is not limited to, the uncovering of such distortions that have served to perpetuate our suffering in the opposition of love and freedom.

Another lie behind the truth of the doctrine of salvation is disclosed in relation to inflicted and afflicted suffering. That God's salvation is present in the midst of our suffering affirms that the existence of suffering does not disprove the eternal presence of God's saving grace. This point is critical for Puerto Ricans because it emphasizes our inherent goodness as a people, which confronts the "lie" that our people have fallen out of God's favor evidenced by the suffering we continue to experience. We must disclose the lie that states, in the name of Christianity, God has abandoned us, using our current suffering and sinfulness as proof. Similarly, we Puerto Ricans must uncover the distortion of this teaching which tells us that our suffering and sinfulness place us outside of God's favor and make us unworthy of salvation from sin. These distortions have been used against us, in the name of the gospel message, to perpetuate feelings of guilt, shame and unworthiness.

Saved for righteousness: Christian soteriological doctrine also has something to say about the state into which we are ushered through salvation. Central to this doctrine is the principle that, through Christ, we are situated in a space that makes room or "enables the working out of relationships of love and freedom."[44] Thus, being saved for righteousness means that God makes a place and a space for more good works to be done; our righteousness is not a result of good works performed. This new space and place does not change the superficial conditions of our humanly existence; the change is much deeper and more lasting than that. Being saved for righteousness can be likened to, perhaps, a change in the direction of our lives: we are not only on a new road, but are riding in a completely different vehicle altogether: "Sin is acknowledged to remain, although no longer to reign."[45] And there is some baggage we no longer need and have left behind completely: "Where righteousness is enacted...some things are not granted a place."[46]

Christian teaching on salvation for righteousness affirms that we are not easily made righteous. Something must die in order for us to live and be saved for righteousness; the gospel message attests to the overcoming of death itself as the matrix of salvation. Salvation is not cheap; there are certain "creature comforts" that must be discarded in order for us to truly live in Christ. Soto alludes to this in his telling of the story "God in Harlem" when he depicts Nena as a woman who was so invested in the false illusion of her life, a fantasy unraveled by the death of her child, her "nena" —a reflection of herself. This can be a prophetic call to our own people to reject the unrighteousness—anything obstructing our individual and communal well-being:

> What is eternally favored and destined for salvation, therefore, is the well-being of every creature; what is eternally disfavored and destined for rejection is all opposition, including self-opposition, to the creature's well-being....[A]ll captivity is eternally rejected, both in its affliction and infliction. [47]

If we, as Puerto Ricans, affirm our belief in salvation by grace, from sin, and for righteousness, then we must reject all forms of opposition to love and freedom, to our well-being, that come from outside or within our own community. In this opposition, we are suspicious of any lies beneath the truth of Christian teaching that tells us that we must wait passively for salvation to come in some undetermined future. Our freedom and self-determination, as well as our responsibility for acting in righteousness, avail us of the opportunity for grace, making a place and space for love and freedom in the world where it does not yet exist.

RACHEL'S SUFFERING IN JEREMIAH AND PUERTO RICAN SUFFERING

Once again, the example of Rachel's suffering, and God's response to it, offers a glimpse of how we can anticipate God's response to the suffering of Puerto Rican people. First in Genesis, Rachel is referenced again in the Hebrew Scriptures, only this time in the words of the prophet Jeremiah (31:15), as a mother weeping for her children and refusing to be comforted. In this text, Jeremiah is speaking to the exiled nation of Israel, descended from Rachel and Jacob. Jeremiah is speaking to and about a people in exile, suffering from captivity and needing salvation from their plight. Salvation, in this sense, means being restored to their sense of nationhood, which is intrinsically connected to the land. This text is part of a larger body of Jeremiah's prophecy called the "book of consolation."[48] Here, the prophet is concerned with the plight of a nation in exile. Their condition is not considered to be merely an external consequence of a more powerful nation; it is understood within the context of Yahweh's punishment of a disobedient and sinful people. Rachel is weeping for her lost children, the people of the northern kingdom of Israel who had been deported by the Assyrians at the end of King Josiah's reign. But Yahweh, who will restore the people to their land once they have repented for their sins, consoles her grief. God will reverse what the conquerors have done only after the people show a readiness to follow God's laws and abide by the covenant.[49]

Rachel's weeping for her people is significant in the book of Jeremiah because of her identity as a mother and a matriarch. Samuel Dresner suggests that the prophet of "doom and destruction," through whose words

God's rage can be heard, recalls Rachel's grief because of the type of mother she was in life and in death:

> It is the pain of the inconsolable mother that has the power to move God's pity. But Rachel is a special mother…Only Rachel named a first-born "Yosef" – *May the Lord add another son to me* (Gen 30:24) – and only Rachel died in the flower of life, giving birth to her second child. It is the total selflessness of the grieving mother, the single-minded zeal for her children that calls forth the divine compassion…Who could match her advocacy? Rachel's plea is unconditional…Hers is the spontaneous cry of a mother for a suffering child, and her weeping, the prophet affirms, is hearkened to on high (Jer 31:16-17).[50]

A God who loves and saves the people from their plight, Jeremiah affirms, will abate the suffering of the people. God hears the cries of even the silent ones; Rachel's words are not spoken here; we hear only her sobs. Her tears speak of sorrow; they also speak of Israel's repentance. Salvation is part of a covenant relationship, for God will only come to their aid once they have shown evidence of realigning themselves with God's word and law. Salvation comes ultimately from above, but begins from below through the concrete actions of a people ready to make good on their covenant with a God who loves them:

> Israel, punished with exile, repents, and God, whose love for them is as a mother for her children, forgives them. Compassion overcomes justice in the promise of eternal salvation. As everlasting as the laws of nature, so will be the people Israel. It is the final vindication of Rachel and her people, their eternal life in the love of God.[51]

THEOLOGICAL PERSPECTIVES ON SOTERIOLOGY

The theology of Gustavo Gutiérrez is particularly helpful for discerning a freedom-centered decolonial theology in terms of suffering and salvation. Gutiérrez's liberating theology is understood as critical reflection on historical praxis in light of the divine word of God received in faith. That is, theological reflection comes after direct praxis in the service of the poor. The Christian life, if it is true to the example and message of Jesus Christ as revealed in the gospel, is thus centered on a concrete and creative commitment of service to others.[52]

If the subject of theology is the relationship of God to God's creation, and one believes in the freedom and efficacy of the Creator, then it follows that freedom in every aspect should be the goal of our (at least temporal) lives. Gutiérrez, as one trained extensively in the classical Catholic tradition that stresses Augustinian and Thomistic theological categories, upheld the autonomy, freedom, and necessity of God. This affirmation led him to the conviction that if God's creation is good and longs for communion with God—as Aquinas held—then our goal is to participate in that divine freedom. Communion with God is thus related to our wholeness as human persons, a wholeness that cannot be achieved if we are not free.

Gutiérrez maintains the foundation of this classical Catholic theology of freedom while at the same time turning it upon itself by claiming that our discipleship with Jesus may in fact bind us in opposition to worldly standards of greed, injustice, and violence. That is, to walk with the poor in their struggle, to make that same struggle our own, is to walk on the path of liberation while being liberated to the will of God. Liberation is thus understood from three distinct levels, unified by the fact that they are all subject to the grace of God: liberation from social conditions of oppression, liberation from sin which is a separation from God and neighbor, and liberation to love God and others.[53]

The option for liberation and the path one takes to support this goal is "the obligatory and privileged locus for Christian life and reflection."[54] This is the locus for the Christian life because, in the midst of suffering and the hope of liberating struggle, one can encounter the living Christ. Following Jesus on such a path becomes the norm from which all theology emerges if it is to be faithful to the liberating message of the gospel and God's historical covenant with God's people.

After the publication of *A Theology of Liberation*, Catholic and Protestant theologians and church leaders alike heavily critiqued Gutiérrez for suggesting the relationship between Christian social ethics is akin to socialist (or even communist) revolutionary activity. He was thought to be twisting the Christian understanding of salvation to mean that we could bring about the kingdom of God on earth and enact our own salvation as a justification for socialist revolution.[55]

Gutiérrez's understanding of liberation theology is most certainly soteriological; that is, concrete historical and political conditions from which liberating activity emerges, including theological reflection in the cause of liberation, are part of the salvific process.[56]

> Salvation embraces all people and the whole [person]; the liberating action of Christ —made man in this history and not in a history marginal to the real life of [hu]man[ity] —is at the heart of the historical current of humanity; the struggle for a just society is in its own right very much a part of salvation history.[57]

But it would be a grave misunderstanding of both the work and faith of Gutiérrez to suggest that this affirmation denies the all-encompassing grace of God through the saving power of Jesus Christ as the matrix for salvation in history. God's salvific action underscores all human existence for Gutiérrez; this action is the catalyst for our actions of solidarity with the poor as a gift of and response to the gratuitous love of God.

Gutiérrez maintains that, according to the biblical tradition, creation and salvation are understood as one act in the Christian tradition, since both originated from God's love as illustrated in the creation story and the incarnation of God-self in Jesus. Likewise, creation and liberation are also affirmed in the Scripture (particularly Jeremiah and Second Isaiah) as one continuous act of God; the God who creates is the God who has let the captives free. And these acts, creation and liberation, can only be understood historically; they are evidence of God's power breaking into human history. Therefore, salvation and liberation are one and the same act.

While they are part of the historical process of humanity, salvation and liberation in history are not final for humanity. Gutiérrez is quite clear throughout all his works that communion with God and solidarity with others to transform history marks our authentic progress of salvation history.[58] However, the only way the kingdom of God as proclaimed by Jesus Christ can be made a reality is if Christians fulfill their part of the covenant with God to prepare a way for God's will to be done on earth.

> Without the liberating events in history, the kingdom does not grow, but the process of liberation only destroys the roots of oppression and of the exploitation of one human being by another; this is not the same thing as the coming of the kingdom, which is first and foremost a gift. It can even be said that historical, political, liberating actions mean the growth of the kingdom and are saving events; they are not however, the coming of the kingdom, they do not represent complete salvation. They are historical

embodiments of the kingdom and by that fact also pointers toward the fullness of the kingdom...[59]

For the most part, Gutiérrez asserts this relationship between ultimate salvation and temporal liberation for two reasons, both directed at the church. First, he is challenging the classical Catholic doctrine of salvation that places extraordinary emphasis on the institution of the sacraments. Through the receipt of the sacraments, one can attain that personal spiritual freedom that leads to the communion with God; it is only secondarily that this will lead to communion with others in such a way as to address social "sins." By contrast Gutiérrez claims that liberating action, personified by Jesus, is celebrated in the sacraments; this is an important point for Latin American people who have a "strong sense of the sacraments."[60] This sense is quite different from the classical one; namely, the poor of Latin America who experience the "shattering of human fellowship" through injustice on a social level has a profound communion with the suffering of Jesus on the cross. Likewise, the Easter hope brings sustenance to the poor to continue their struggle for justice. This is how the sacraments are understood in relation to salvation and liberation: in solidarity with Jesus' life, death, and resurrection and in community with those who suffer injustice daily. In the words of Gutiérrez as he defended his position on the sacrament of the Eucharist,

> [W]e do indeed celebrate the Eucharist in a history branded by sin, but we celebrate it in the hope of a true communion both within history and beyond it. The Eucharist is the celebration not of a finished human reality but of something being built; it brings a call to conversion, and indeed that is how we begin each Eucharist. For this reason, the proper celebration of the Eucharist with joy and thanksgiving for the Lord's gift must have consequences for the presence of Christians in history where they are to create a just and human world.[61]

Second, Gutiérrez is critiquing the church for its ethic of "neutrality" in relation to the political and social sphere, particularly in terms of human liberation from injustice. Gutiérrez offers a corrective based biblically in the messianic promise of God through Jesus and the actions of the disciples in faithfulness to that promise. In Gutiérrez's view, the church cannot hide behind a guise of neutrality for the sake of universal love while opting for the poor in our world; this guise is neither ethical nor Christian.[62] While some church officials[63] have considered the Christian requirement of universal love and a preferential option for the poor to be contradictory, Gutiérrez maintains that this supposed neutrality makes the church complicit by its unwillingness to act on behalf of those who suffer. By its silence in the face of a suffering body, the church has chosen to side with the oppressors while claiming that the choice is made on behalf of universal love without yielding to the pressure of a particular social situation. Gutiérrez confronts such a position head on when he states,

> We are not...confronting only the challenge of a 'social situation,' as if it were something that had nothing to do with the fundamental demands of the gospel. No: we are confronted here with something opposed to the reign of life that the Lord proclaimed; with something, therefore, that a Christian must reject.[64]

A PUERTO RICAN DECOLONIAL SOTERIOLOGY

The works of Pedro Juan Soto reflect the theme of suffering as a constitutive element of Puerto Rican life. What can Puerto Rican decolonial theology say about the suffering endured by our people when colonization is our existential starting point? Similarly, how does this suffering lead to a new understanding of salvation that is both particular to the Puerto Rican context and universal in its Christian foundations?

These are especially difficult questions for me to answer, on so many different levels. I have always been stumped by the question of salvation, posed personally from one too many inquisitors asking, "Are you saved?"; or collectively in its relationship to freedom and justice, "What constitutes salvation here on this earth?" What does it mean to be saved as a community of individuals in relation? How does the Puerto Rican community extract meaning from that definition that makes it relevant to a daily life of struggle?

In the history of Christian theology, theologians have attempted to formulate answers to such questions by focusing on the confessions of faith in the New Testament regarding salvation. We see from Paul's Letter to the Romans (10:9) that if "you confess with your lips that Jesus is Lord and believe in your heart that God raised him from the dead, you will be saved."[65] In the Gospel of Luke, we learn of the effect Jesus had on the tax collector, Zacchaeus, who, after being summoned down from the sycamore tree and deciding to give back all monies collected unjustly, is told, "Today salvation has come to this house, because he too is a son of Abraham. For the Son of Man came to seek out and to save the lost" (Luke 19:9–10).

In both scripture texts, the identity of Jesus as Lord and Christ is connected deeply and profoundly with the understanding of salvation: our belief and confession in Jesus as Lord and savior is what opens us up to the opportunity to be saved. Whether we speak first of Christian anthropology (identity) and then of soteriology (salvation), or vice versa,[66] the fact remains that Christian faith and its theological expressions affirm the intrinsic relationship between the life-span of Jesus and the salvation of the world.

We cannot get to the heart of the meaning of salvation for the Puerto Rican community without changing the terms of the question itself. If we accept the Christian doctrinal claim, as stated earlier, that the suffering and salvation of humanity is bound to the suffering of, and salvation afforded by, Jesus Christ, then the relevant soteriological question for Puerto Ricans is not, "Are you saved," but "What do you believe about Jesus Christ?" I can only approach an answer to this question by disclosing the ways Jesus has been presented to me that I, as a Puerto Rican woman, have refused to believe.

First, I refuse to believe in a Jesus whose maleness is normative for salvation. As a Roman Catholic Puerto Rican woman, I refuse to believe that Jesus' maleness made him more authentically divine and therefore more reflective of God's image. If I believed in Jesus on these terms, I would be, in essence, submitting myself as one needing salvation not only through Jesus but also through every male person with whom I am in relationship. In addition, to believe in Jesus' maleness as normative supports the perpetuation of maleness as normative for apostolic succession and the priesthood in Roman Catholicism. I refuse to believe in this type of Jesus as salvific.

Second, I refuse to believe in a Jesus whose whiteness is normative for salvation. While Jesus' ethnicity and color have been affirmed by numerous scholars as other than white, he is still projected as a white man on the consciousness of many people, including many Puerto Ricans who display icons and illustrations of the Sacred Heart of Jesus as a fair skinned/eyed/haired man. I do not reject the way in which Jesus is portrayed anthropologically—as a white, black, brown, red or yellow man. On the contrary, I simply refuse to believe that any one depiction and understanding of Jesus' particularity excludes any other from his saving grace.

Third, I refuse to believe in a Jesus whose salvation is ushered in on the heels of conquest. This refusal is, for me, the most difficult because it discloses my suspicion toward my own church in relation to the way Christianity, in its Roman Catholic and Protestant forms, came to Puerto Rico and Puerto Ricans. The gift came with a high price tag; I refuse to believe in a Jesus whose salvation comes at the expense of all other manifestations of divine love and freedom.

The Puerto Rican community has maintained a tradition during the Lenten season that communicates our understanding of salvation through Jesus, which is quite different from the refusals disclosed above. During Holy Week on both the island and in the Diaspora, we can witness a re-enactment of the Passion of Christ in all its detail and pageantry. These passion plays are taken very seriously: costumes are made, props designed, actors assigned their parts. The spectators are not passive by any means; they participate in the witness of the event through their response to it. And one cannot but respond to the suffering witnessed, even in its staged re-enactment. We see the flogging, the carrying of the cross, the falling and the beatings, the humiliation before all. We begin to see our own complicity in the suffering and it makes us tremble, to the point when we have to ask ourselves, "How did we let it come to this?" We want to stop the madness and cruelty, yet we feel powerless within ourselves to do so. We are powerless at the foot of the cross as we watch the son of humanity crucified to his death.

This is what we witness during these Passion plays: suffering at its very depth. To the outsider, it might look as if Puerto Ricans, in this case, experience a perverse pleasure in watching and participating in such a gruesome execution. Yet, the glorification of the suffering is not the emphasis in the passion play nor in our soteriological understanding as it relates to Jesus' suffering. While it is true that the death of Jesus makes soteriological sense only in relation to resurrection, as "Good Friday without Easter Sunday is senseless,"[67] the miracle and glory of the resurrection cannot be appreciated fully without comprehending, as best as humanly possible, the immense chasm that such a miracle has traversed. Not only is the sacrifice of unconditional love on display when we look at the crucifix; it also discloses the unjust systems of oppression and sin that permitted it. In the cross, we acknowledge "a very radical acceptance of life as it is, even in its most painful moments, [that] there is already the beginning of an experience of resurrection."[68] Our salvation is tied to our ability to accept our suffering insofar as we believe in its overcoming. The chasm of our suffering is deep and great; the miracle of our salvation by our belief in suffering's demise is greater and more profound. When we believe that God has the power to overcome all suffering, we are inspired to work as God's agents on earth toward that end.

Although we may have maintained the rituals such as the one described here, and perhaps we hang on to them when all else has failed, I believe that Puerto Rican Diaspora Christians have adopted an understanding of salvation as personal and pietistic, to our detriment. Hal Recinos, Puerto Rican Methodist pastor/theologian, suggests the same in both of his works.[69] Through his experience working with Puerto Ricans on the Lower East Side of Manhattan (Loisaida), Recinos witnessed a level of resignation regarding the experience of suffering, combined with an "otherworldly" understanding of salvation. At the onset of his ministry with a Lower East Side church, Recinos observed

> Many people thought the Church of all Nations was a place to get away from the frustrations of daily life. They believed spirituality had nothing to do with the dynamics of racism, classism and sexism. In their eyes, the pulpit was not to be used to promote an understanding of social, political, economic and cultural problems. Prayer and the devotional life were the marks of true discipleship.[70]

Esmeralda Santiago stated in one of her letters that our history has told us that the struggle for freedom is a "lost cause". The sentiment reflected by Recinos in relation to his congregants suggests the same with regard to the daily suffering of the Puerto Rican community. But I believe that the continuation of the ritual enactment of the passion, as well as other rituals in our communities, attests to the subterraneous hope that we are never a lost cause in the eyes of God. If God can overcome the most horrendous and scandalous suffering of Jesus on the cross, why not our own?

Thus, a Puerto Rican decolonial soteriology affirms that our salvation is contingent upon encountering and confronting the struggles of those who suffer in the here and now on earth. In fact, our turning toward the suffering is evidence of God's saving grace already at work within us: we love because God loves us first. Our salvation is not just about modeling Jesus' behavior, although this is an important point of departure. Our salvation is about walking in solidarity and compassion with those who suffer and addressing the suffering in all its forms, whether caused by physical ailment, emotional pain, economic strife, or political conditions, including colonialism. The enormity of the resurrection miracle makes sense to us, in all its mystery and glory, when we have first descended to the depths of despair. This is the meaning of the confession of faith articulated in Luke's Gospel and Paul's Letter to the Romans: "...you will be saved"... "[f]or the Son of Man came to seek out and to save the lost." In Jesus' cross and resurrection—in his suffering and salvation—there is always hope for the lost causes.

NOTES

1. Victoria Ortiz, "Introduction," in Pedro Juan Soto, *Spiks*. Translated by Victoria Ortiz (New York, NY: Monthly Review Press, 1973): 14.
2. Recently declassified FBI files have confirmed that this assassination was part of a larger plan to eliminate any pro-independence activity on the island and in the Puerto Rican community of the Diaspora; see Pedro Reina-Pérez, "Puerto Rico's imperial hangover," *The Boston Globe*, March 23, 2016; "Puerto Ricans Were Kneeling When Killed By Police, Officer Says," *The New York Times*. November 30, 1983. http://www.nytimes.com/1983/11/30/us/puerto-ricans-were-kneeling-when-killed-by-police-officer-says.html; Reginald Stuart, "Investigations and Indictments Harming Image of Puerto Rico Law; Officials," *The New York Times*, July 28, 1983, http://www.nytimes.com/1983/07/28/us/investigations-and-indictments-harming-image-of-puerto-rico-law-officials.html; Jim McGee, "Ex-Justice Offical Cites 'Coverup' by FBI in'78 Puerto Rico Shootings," *The Washington Post*, May 9, 1992, https://www.washingtonpost.com/archive/politics/1992/05/09/ex-justice-official-cites-coverup-by-fbi-in-78-puerto-rico-shootings/722ead3e-b875-461d-957e-9ef43f1c481b; the film "A Show of Force" (Paramount, 1990), was based on the book by Anne Nelson, *Murder Under Two Flags: The U.S., Puerto Rico, and the Cerro Maravilla Cover-Up* (Boston, MA: Ticknor and Fields, 1986).
3. Pedro Juan Soto, *Hot Land, Cold Season*, trans., Helen R. Lane (New York, NY: Dell Publishing Co., 1973) originally published in Spanish under the title *Ardiente Suelo, Fria Estación*, by Ficción Universidad Veracruzana, Mexico: 1961; Soto's *Spiks* was originally published in Spanish under the title *Spiks*, by Editorial Cultural, Rio Piedras, PR: 1970; Pedro Juan Soto *Usmail* (Rio Piedras, Puerto Rico: Editorial Cultural, 1959); Pedro Juan Soto, *Usmail* Trans., Charlie Connelly

and Myrna Pagan (St. John/US Virgin Islands: Sombrero Publishing Company, 2007).

4. Soto, *Hot Land, Cold Season*, 16, 17.
5. Ibid., 18.
6. Ibid., 24, 25.
7. Ibid., 97.
8. Ibid., 85–86.
9. Ibid., 94.
10. Ibid., 151.
11. Ibid., 177.
12. Ibid., 192.
13. This notion of the city as wilderness, seducer/seductress and trickster was originally developed in a 1979 paper presented by Anthony M. Stevens-Arroyo (unpublished) and presented by Ana María Díaz-Stevens in her class on Hispanic literature and religion at Union Theological Seminary (2003).
14. Soto, *Spiks*, 39.
15. Ibid., 47.
16. Ibid., 81.
17. Ibid., 92.
18. Soto, *Usmaíl*, trans. Charlie Connolly and Myrna Pagán, 242–243.
19. In Puerto Rico, a "morrocoyo" is a person who enters the pit of a latrine to clean it when filled with excrement, in the absence of a more modern sanitation system, but it can also be used as an insult.
20. James L. Dietz, *Economic History of Puerto Rico: Institutional Change and Capitalist Development* (Princeton, NJ: Princeton University Press, 1986), 146–147, 154–155.
21. Soto, *Usmaíl*, p. 5.
22. Ibid., 26.
23. Ibid., 66.
24. Ibid., 135.
25. Ibid., 161.
26. Ibid., 188.
27. Ibid., 2–3.
28. Soto, *Hot Land, Cold Season*, 191.
29. Ibid., 220, 222.
30. Ibid., 17.
31. Ibid, 224.
32. "God in Harlem," in Soto, *Spiks*, 91–92.
33. Matthew 27: 46; Mark 15: 34; Psalm 22: 1.
34. Christopher Morse, *Not Every Spirit: A Dogmatics of Christian Disbelief* (Valley, PA: Trinity Press International, 1994), 225–230.

35. Ibid., 227.
36. Ibid., 232. Even with this affirmation, we know that the salvific love of God is most often encountered through the gracious love extended from one to another as a human reflection of the love of God.
37. Ibid.
38. Ibid., 234.
39. Ibid., 234–235.
40. Ibid., 251.
41. Ibid., 240–241.
42. Ibid., 242.
43. Ibid., 242.
44. Ibid., 243.
45. Ibid., 244.
46. Ibid.
47. Ibid., 254–255.
48. Thomas W. Overholt, "Jeremiah," in *Harper's Bible Commentary*, James L. Mays, ed. with the Society of Biblical Literature (San Francisco, CA: Harper Collins, 1988), 634–637.
49. Ibid., 635.
50. Samuel H. Dresner, *Rachel* (Minneapolis, MN: Augsburg Fortress, 1994), 152–153.
51. Ibid., 173.
52. Gustavo Gutiérrez, *A Theology of Liberation: history, politics, and salvation*, revised edition, trans. Caridad Inda and John Eagleson eds. (London, UK: SCM, 2001), 11.
53. Gustavo Gutiérrez, *The Truth Shall Make You Free: confrontations*, trans. Matthew J. O'Connell (Maryknoll, NY: Orbis Books, 1990), 124–141; these categories are consistent with Morse's three-fold interpretation of the doctrine of soteriology as salvation (1) by grace [liberation to love God and others], (2) from sin [liberation from sin], and (3) for righteousness [liberation from social conditions of oppression], see Chapter Five, above.
54. Gutiérrez, *A Theology of Liberation*, 49.
55. This critique is implied in Gutiérrez's doctoral dissertation defense as recorded in *The Truth Shall Make You Free*, 34–41.
56. Gustavo Gutiérrez with Richard Shaull, *Liberation and Change* (Atlanta, GA: John Knox Press, 1977), 86.
57. Gutiérrez, *A Theology of Liberation*, 168.
58. Ibid., 149–187.
59. Gutiérrez, *The Truth Shall Make You Free*, 16.
60. Ibid., 45.
61. Ibid., 46.

62. Ibid., 75–81.
63. This does not include recently deceased Pope John Paul II who has spoken and acted in solidarity with the poor and, particularly as articulated in *Laborem Exercens,* has called "upon Christians and the entire church to commit themselves to movements in solidarity with workers," (no. 8); see Gutiérrez, *The Truth Shall Make You Free,* 76.
64. Ibid., 10.
65. I was drawn to this text after a conversation with David Asomaning (Union Ph.D. 2003), who dealt with the question of salvation in relation to his own dissertation on synchronicity and the miraculous. He helped me to identify the core issues at stake with regard to salvation, which allowed me to articulate more clearly my relationship to Jesus Christ, as an individual and for my Puerto Rican community.
66. The classic order of the doctrines has been to begin with Christology (who Christ is) and then proceed to soteriology (what Christ has done). Modern theology "has tended to reverse the classic order of the doctrines...[T]he modern temperament has been preoccupied with apologetics—depicting some human need or experience, then speaking of salvation in relation to that need or experience, and finally presenting Jesus Christ as the one through whom salvation comes," Walter Lowe in *Christian Theology: An Introduction to its Tasks and Traditions, Second Edition,* Peter C. Hodgson and Robert H. King, eds. (Philadelphia: Fortress Press, 1985), 222–223.
67. Virgilio Elizondo, *A God of Incredible Surprises: Jesus of Galilee* (Lanham, MD: Rowman and Littlefield Publishing Group, Inc., 2003), 101.
68. Ibid.
69. *Hear the Cry! A Latino Pastor Challenges the Church* (Louisville, KY: Westminster/John Knox Press, 1989) and *Jesus Weeps: Global Encounters on our Doorstep* (Nashville, TN: Abingdon Press, 1992), as well as in his article "Mission: A Latino Pastoral Theology," in *Mestizo Christianity: Theology from the Latino Perspective,* Arturo Bañuelas (Maryknoll, NY: Orbis Books, 1995).
70. Ibid., 111.

CHAPTER 6

The Works of Rosario Ferré: Puerto Rican Hope and Christian Eschatology

Rosario Ferré's growing literary corpus references themes of captivity and freedom. Her life and work are parabolic in the Crossanian sense: she and her literary creation embody contradiction, push us to the limits of language/comprehension, make us uncomfortable in the face of reality seen with new eyes, and make no apology for ambiguity. Born into the Puerto Rican bourgeois elite in 1938, Ferré witnessed and lived even in her own home the contradictions caused from the merging of two societies, two languages, two cultures, and a multitude of colors and influences. As is evident from her literary production for children and adults, Ferré was greatly influenced by Puerto Rican folkloric tradition—as passed on by her financier and later governor father[1] and her Black nanny—and the fairy tales of American/European culture (Grimm, Anderson, Carroll, etc.). Through these, as well as through her apprenticeship with Latin American literary notables such as Mario Vargas Llosa[2] and Margot Arce de Vásquez, and her exposure to the independence of thought in Puerto

---

This chapter is a more extensive development of my earlier work published as "Freedom is Our Own: Toward a Puerto Rican Emancipation Theology," in *Creating Ourselves: African Americans and Hispanic Americans on Popular Culture and Religious Expression,* Anthony B. Pinn and Benjamín Valentín, eds. (Durham and London: Duke University Press, 2009), 139–172.

© The Author(s) 2017
T. Delgado, *A Puerto Rican Decolonial Theology,* New Approaches to Religion and Power, DOI 10.1007/978-3-319-66068-4_6

143

Rican literature, Ferré developed a sophisticated literary style that has challenged and critiqued all levels of social injustice.[3]

Her position in society gave Ferré a particular kind of literary voice through which to expose society's ugliness. Her stories break open the dividing lines meant to bolster the status quo—between women, classes, racial distinctions—to reveal unexpected alliances and previously unmentioned antagonisms. She confesses secrets of the bourgeois elite, ones they would prefer to keep secret in order to preserve the illusion that all is well: incest, child molestation, adultery, racism, homophobia. By breaking the silence, Ferré does justice to those who are oppressed and silenced within the culture, a culture that she claims all of us perpetuate through our cultural complicity.

In a recent preface to her re-published collection of acclaimed short stories, *Sweet Diamond Dust*, Ferré reflects upon the metamorphosis of identity that has marked Puerto Rico and Puerto Ricans since our precarious relationship with the United States began. Her observations suggest that in order for Puerto Ricans to survive into the future, we must find a way to come to terms with and reconcile the often-conflicting aspects of our identity; the conflict itself creates an inner struggle that has become quite dangerous indeed. She states,

> The characters ask themselves the same questions that we have been asking ourselves for the past hundred years, and keep asking today: are we Latin Americans or North Americans? Should Spanish or English be our official language? Should we be a commonwealth, a state of the Union or an independent country? A nuclear base or a bridge between cultures?... A political puddle or linguistic poodle? A miniature macho cock, crowing defiance atop its weather vane, pointing toward the south when the north wind blows, and pointing toward the north when it gusts from the south? Hamlet is our secret patron saint. We define ourselves, as he did, by indecision, by constantly changing our minds. But we also know better than anyone how to bend the arrow without breaking it...
>
> ...The novel [*Sweet Diamond Dust*] is all gossip, lies, shameless slander – yet the story remains true.[4]

LITERARY ANALYSIS: "WHERE DO I GO FROM HERE?"

Like Santiago, Rosario Ferré's art cannot be separated from her politics of personal, relational, and national freedom. While I examine only one collection of short stories[5] and two novels[6] here, all of Ferré's stories convey desires for freedom and independence, for the assertion of self/ group identity and for self-determination. As a Puerto Rican woman, Ferré illustrates the quest for self-preservation that can leave the seeker feeling nihilistic and empty of true selfhood. Her work is consistent with the postmodern dilemma of acute literary self-consciousness. Robert Detweiler, in his article "Theological Trends of Postmodern Literature," states,

> Novelists are writing stories about novelists writing stories; characters watch themselves intently; images of mirrors, reflections, echoes, doubles abound. But they do so precisely because the concept of the self is fading. The eagerness to portray the self indicates a sense and fear of its immanent loss. This compulsive and anxious self-consciousness expresses itself in a vigorous "historicizing" effort, because if the self can identify itself historically, in factual time and space, it can reinforce its reality. At the same time, this...effort also encourages the self toward group-hood, for in locating oneself historically one also places oneself in the context of others.[7]

Ferré's novel *The House on the Lagoon* follows this description closely. It is the story of a woman, Isabel Monfort Antonsanti, writing the recollected family stories of her and her husband, Quintín Mendizabal, that they shared with each other before their marriage in order to

> examine carefully the origins of anger in each of our families as if it were a disease, and in this way avoid, during the life we were to share together, the mistakes our forebears had made. The rest of that summer, we spent many afternoons together, holding hands on the veranda and telling each other our family histories....
>
> Years later, when I was living in the house on the lagoon, I began to write down some of those stories. My original purpose was to interweave the woof of my memories with the warp of Quintín's recollections, but what I finally wrote was something very different.[8]

Ferré presents to us the finished product of Isabel's creation: an interweaving of her storytelling, her first person voice as commentary, and Quintín's third person commentary as notes on the margin. We are left to vacillate between fact (Quintín is an historian) and fiction (Isabel is a novelist), and wonder whether either distinction makes any difference to the true purpose of the story: to explore the freedom of the self, as individual and in relation to a community. For Ferré, the assertion of selfhood is a life or death mandate for women; through the story of a woman, she, like Santiago, makes that claim for Puerto Rico as well. The issue of the Puerto Rican woman's identity does not arise in opposition to that of national/cultural identity; rather, Ferré's novel illustrates that both must be integrated in order for Puerto Rican people to experience freedom.[9]

All of Ferré's stories, without exception, illustrate the need for our lives to be in balance; that is, we cannot live fully if we are split, cut off, from our own spirit. This split is particularly deadly, and more common-place, for women. In an oppressive environment that tries to maintain itself through the bifurcation of life and spirit, women who assert a bal-ance between the lives they lead on the surface and the journey of their inner spirit are usually severed, maimed, or tricked—physically and oth-erwise—into perpetuating the status quo of alienation.

Ferré's collection of short stories, *The Youngest Doll*, abounds with examples of such severance, maiming, and trickery associated with a lack of harmony/balance and a series of dichotomies. In the short story/fairy tale bearing the same name, the leg of an unnamed aunt is infected by, and now the permanent habitat of, an angry river prawn. The doc-tor betrays her healing trust by leaving the prawn in place so that he can garnish fees from her weekly visits and send his son to medical school "up north." The youngest niece marries the doctor's son and receives a beautiful doll made by the aunt as a wedding gift; the doll takes on the persona of its maker and enacts revenge against the doctor for his mis-treatment of the aunt, as well as for his insatiable greed.

In "Sleeping Beauty," Ferré brings us another fairy tale, Puerto Rican style: we meet the daughter of an aristocratic family, María de los Angeles (Mary of the Angels), whose dream of pursuing her heart's desire as a dancer is shattered by the expectations of living the caged life of a high society daughter/wife/mother. Her parents, her husband, and the church conspire to repress her spirit; her unwanted pregnancy and status as a mother crush her inner desire but satisfy the social expectations of a proper heir.

In "Mercedes Benz 220 SL," the sexy allure of the luxury car speed-ing along the island roads in the pre-dawn mist of a sleepy Sunday masks the lingering anguish over the disappearance of the son, an anguish felt only by his mother (the perennial passenger) and not his father (the driver), for whom the Benz is like a drug.

It's always been like this, since we got married twenty years ago he buys me everything, he's a good provider, but always the same deafness, I'm always at his side and always alone, eating alone, sleeping alone, once I looked myself in the mirror, I opened my mouth, touched my palate with my finger to see if any sound came out, testing,.. but nothing came out, it was clogged up in there as if the opening were too small or the words too large.... I forced the words upward from the back of my throat but to no avail.... Then my son was born and I could speak again.[10]

The birth of her son and the resurrection of her voice merge the outer and inner life, only to be estranged again by the father/son antagonism, by the son's disappearance, and finally by the son's unrecognized/unmourned death. We are left to wonder whether she will ever know of her son's death, and if her knowledge of his passing will bring her inner voice back.

Ferré's novel, *The House on the Lagoon*, is replete with cases of severance, maiming and trickery as well. Early in the story, told within the context of Puerto Rican slave history, we meet Barnabé, whose name means "son of prophecy"; he had been a chieftain of his tribe when stolen from the territory now known as Angola, "a spiritual leader whose duty was to look out for [his] people."[11] He maintained his native language and, by virtue of it, was able to organize a rebellion with other slaves without dutiful and docile *criollo* (mixed) slaves discovering the plans. After the insurrection was aborted, Barnabé was sentenced to a special punishment: his tongue was cut off. "One's tongue," Isabel tells us when speaking of Barnabé's language, Bantu,

was so deeply ingrained, more so even than one's religion or tribal pride; it was like a root that went deep into one's body and no one knew exactly where it ended. It was attached to one's throat, to one's neck, to one's stomach, even to one's heart.[12]

Isabel's mother, Carmita, suffers a loss of similar magnitude at the hands of her well-meaning mother Gabriela who had made her six daughters, all born within her first six years of marriage, promise they would have only one child every five years. After breaking that pledge, intended to maintain a woman's inner peace, her mother forced Carmita to drink a concoction to terminate the pregnancy. It did just that and more: Carmita hemorrhaged and, after complications set in due to the advanced stage of pregnancy, was unable to have any more children. The blood of her loss, signified even in her name (Carmita = Carmen = crimson) was the blood of death, not creative life. Gabriela did what she believed was in the best interests of Carmita; so hemmed in was she by her own ideology that she was unable to see her daughter's inner desire to carry the child to term. Unlike the Angel Gabriel announcing the life to be born to the Virgin Mary, Gabriela is an angel of death to her own daughter's desire to bear a child outside the imposed restrictions.

Margarita, a nineteen-year old who came to live with the Mendizabals from the mountains of Puerto Rico, is entrusted to the care of Isabel, her second cousin, only to be transported back to the countryside in a coffin. It had been decided that her birthmark, an oval shaped hairy mole above her right eyebrow, should be removed in order to make it easier for Margarita to find a good husband. While originally Quentín's idea, Isabel also considered the operation to be a necessary investment in Margarita's future: she was able to convince her cousin of its benefits, even though Margarita saw the birthmark as a good luck charm, a third eye that "made her aware of other people's needs, made her more compassionate and sympathetic."[13] Although Isabel suspects the operation may cause harm, especially after hearing the prayers of the elder domestic, Petra (Barnabé's granddaughter, who, as a medicine woman/healer, believed the mole protected Margarita from evil), they went ahead with the procedure. Within hours of the magic birthmark being removed, Margarita was dead.

William Mendizabal, son of Quintín and Carmelina (Petra's granddaughter) and adopted by Isabel, survives the loss of vision in his left eye but lives to tell about it. In a violent clash between police and *independentistas* in front of the house on the lagoon, led by Quentín and Isabel's eldest son Manuel, Willie is brutally beaten by police in a case of mistaken identity. His maiming causes justifiable anguish; as a painter, Willie questions whether he will ever be able to practice his craft again. But as one who had often met the face of death in life as a result of epileptic fits, Willie learns to see the loss of sight in a different way: as a pathway to a renewed life.

"The repressed in Ferré's stories always return with violence."[14] The physical and psychological severance, maiming, and trickery against the spirit which chooses to live out in the open is thus forced into a subterraneous and subversive life; it, too, can re-emerge violently in an attempt to free (or seek revenge for) itself, as these examples from the stories show. But freedom from injustice means something more here. Ferré fiercely critiques the upper classes of Puerto Rican society who, in the unfair privilege of class usually reserved for the lightest skinned and purest bred (Spanish) Puerto Ricans, fail to do justice for/with the working-class poor Puerto Ricans of more obvious African descent.[15] Her stories, and their attention to the history and current reality of Black/mulatto Puerto Ricans, break the silence and invisibility that has characterized the official history of the island.[16] Ferré suggests that those on the margins of society, in this case Afro-Puerto Ricans, understand deeply the question, "Is the outward living of your life in harmony with your spirit?" This is not to say that Afro-Puerto Ricans automatically live the balanced life that Ferré seems to advocate. Rather, overt and covert societal racism has not afforded Afro-Puerto Ricans the same "opportunities" as Spanish Puerto Rican descendants to be lured into the seduction of a split life in a socio-economic sense. The alienation has come via other means—substance abuse, gang violence, and disease—which plague the poorest communities on the island and mainland.

Still, Ferré's work continues to hold those of African descent in high esteem; they constitute the spiritual foundation of her stories. This is nowhere more obvious than in *The House on the Lagoon*, where Petra Avilés (the *santera/curandera*) is truly the rock upon which the story is built, as her name conveys. She lives in the dirt-floored cellar with the other domestic laborers who access the lower level of the house via the lagoon. Ferré's attention to the character of Petra, her function in the family and her spirituality, reflect how Ferré's authorship is prophetic: She is questioning and challenging the validity and the assumed security upon which the house, as the archetype of the condition of one's psyche/relationships/nation, has been built.[17] This formidable piece of architectural mastery that is the Mendizabal home is built on a swamp, but only those who enter via the swamp (the servants) are fully aware of this. The water is the true foundation, for it remains long after the house is gone. It is no mere postscript that the house was built originally over an underground spring; this fact is central to understanding that what is on the surface is illusory and what is closer to the water is more authentic for humanity. Petra lives at the same level as the spring; her subterraneous existence is closer to the original life source of water. Those who avail themselves of her wisdom, who enter the underground cellar where the spring resides, come closer to mending the wounds of life-long maiming/scarring. Those who pay attention to their healing processes can then bring that wisdom to the surface; the wisdom cannot remain underground if it is to change the world order.

Rosario Ferré's *Eccentric Neighborhoods*[18] is somewhat of an autobiographical novel that draws from her personal experiences with her father, an industrialist turned governor of Puerto Rico. Though both vacillate between fact and fiction, in *Eccentric Neighborhoods* the facts lose their credibility and what is fictional becomes convincingly true and what is believed.

Similar to the way Soto romanticizes the natural world, connecting it with freedom and self-determination, Ferré employs a more nuanced understanding of *la naturaleza*. The industrial overrides the natural but the natural remains in some way in spite of the industrialization. For example, the first half of the book is about the Rivas de Santillana family that owns a sugar plantation and maintains their ties to the land at all costs. They are a family deeply connected to *la naturaleza* and have a keen sense of the aesthetic and beautiful, a sensitivity that is influenced by the lush and breathtaking environment of Emajaguas.

> Emajaguas was a place where one could find peace simply by admiring the geometric perfection of a red poinsettia or by glorying in the bougainvillea vines that hung from the palm trees like purple mantles. At Emajaguas, nature gave you back the guilelessness of innocence in spite of the fact that a sugarcane worker's life expectancy was forty years, that his salary was less than a hundred and fifty dollars a year, and that during the *tiempo muerte* – between harvests – he often starved to death. The human misery that raged outside Emajaguas' ten–foot wall had no relevance within. Justice and beauty were never at odds with each other there.[19]

For all of its sensuality, privilege, and beauty, the people of Emajaguas, children and adults alike, take great pride in the simplicity, austerity, and frugality of their lives. Skylights were installed in every room of the Rivas de Santillana house in order to conserve electricity; the only room without a skylight was the toilet, so that "one relieved oneself in total darkness…so as not to offend the aesthetic sensibilities that prevailed in the Rivas de Santillana family."[20] Abuela Valeria, the matriarch of the Rivas de Santillana clan, never threw anything away for fear of needing it one day if the family fell into dire financial straits; "the squeezed grapefruits were boiled with sugar and made into compote, the water from the boiled grapefruits was made into *refresco de toronja*, the beef bones were dropped into the bean stew, and the chickens were cooked whole."[21] Amid the frugality, the family was still able to eat beef and chicken at a time when this was a mark of privilege. Still, food platters were presented at the table only half full, though more was waiting in the kitchen to be served; water was conserved during the rainy season by everyone bathing outdoors under the gutter spout.

Miña, the wet nurse, is an important character to the story for a number of reasons. Like Petra Avilés in *The House on the Lagoon*, Miña is a stabilizing presence in the family, one who protects and defends, who nurtures with her body by virtue of her breast milk, and with her soul by virtue of her spirituality. She knew things about the family that each individual person desperately kept from the others; all of their secrets were collected in one magnificent ball of soap which "smelled of every single person in the house...And above all, Miña's smell, which held all the scraps of soap together in one marvelous perfumed globe."[22]

The second half of the book about the Vernet family chronicles the rise of industrialization (through the example of their cement factory), and creates a link with the economic structures of the USA. Star Cement is the company that the four Vernet brothers and their father, Santiago, own in the town of La Concordia. The company began to flourish during the Second World War, when equipment and military products were desperately needed, as well as after the inauguration of Operation Bootstrap. The brothers were sophisticated in their dealings with the USA in part because of their university education in the States. The brothers rejected their Catholic roots and embraced Free Masonry as their religion. Theirs was a life of practicality and decisiveness, unhampered by concerns with nature or beauty and focused on the transformation and industrial growth of the island. The inland town of La Concordia was a "town of entrepreneurs...Concordians were a practical, down-to-earth people who liked to call things like they saw them. The town hospital was found on Calle Salud; the school stood on Calle Educación; the butcher's street was Calle Matadero."[23]

Freemasonry was a strong presence and influence in La Concordia; its values of humanity, fraternity, and harmony were also names of streets in the town. As such, Freemasons such as the Vernets aligned themselves with the position of statehood for Puerto Rico, believing that the connection with the US American way of democracy—"with liberty and justice for all"—would be of great benefit to Puerto Rico. This perspective was very different from that of the Rivas de Santillana family; the spirit of Emajaguas was a spirit of self-sufficiency, strong nationalism, and independence. Anyone who espoused other political opinions, including those who advocated statehood, was not fully welcomed into the Rivas de Santillana fold. This would prove to be quite a challenge for Clarissa Rivas de Santillana and Aurelio Vernet, whose daughter Elvira connects the tales of both families as she is heir to both.

In spite of all the practical entrepreneurial spirit, there was yet room for some artistic expression in the Vernet family through Aurelio and his love of the piano, which was as much a release for him as an expression of creativity. His mother Adela considered Aurelio Vernet to be the "chosen one." On her deathbed, she imparted a special blessing to him, letting the family know who was to be in charge of all family business.

At the helm of the family cement business, Aurelio was the negotiator and deal maker, the one who maintained the connections with US businesses and governmental agencies, a role which would serve him well later as he ran for, and won, the governorship of Puerto Rico in 1968. For Aurelio, politics and particularly the quest for statehood, was a primary motivation in his life. This motivation often placed him at odds with his wife, Clarissa who, as a Rivas de Santillana, had less confidence in the dealings of men (politics) and more confidence in the dealings of the natural order (God). Still, Aurelio was the patriarch of the family and, as such, Clarissa stood by her husband on his journey into business and politics. Their two children, Elvira and Alvaro, were afforded all the luxuries of the day as heirs of an industrialist. But their wealth and access did not change this one fact in Elvira's mind, which she finally realized after nine years of her own marriage to a man who wanted to keep her in a cage:

> First I had belonged to Father and now I was Ricardo's. That's why women understood the politics of colonialism so well: if you treat them well, feed them, clothe them, and buy them a nice house, they won't rebel. Except that hatred keeps smoldering inside them.[24]

Unlike her daughter, Clarissa subordinated herself to her husband's dreams and aspirations, putting the needs and desires of her children and husband over her own. She was a Rivas de Santillana through and through, with a keen sense of aesthetics without the pretense of a nuevo riche. She was the product of the sugar plantation, an agricultural way of life that was steadily on the decline with the ascendancy of industry.

Clarissa experienced the stark cultural shock of moving from the coastal richness of Emajaguas (a name that evokes the Taíno language) to La Concordia (a name that is firmly grounded in Spanish tradition).

Although her own personal dreams of working outside the home, attending a university, and maintaining financial independence were thwarted by the patriarchal culture upheld by her husband and supported in the society, Clarissa would never imagine divorcing her husband Aurelio. Her strong Catholic roots combined with a sense that all things tend toward unity and harmony precluded any attempt of severing that connection. In her final conversation with Elvira before her death, Clarissa confirms this belief:

> Nature, the positive current of the universe where everything is interconnected, is what really matters. Our duty is to partake of that unity, not of its differences. To try to understand ourselves and, by the way, to find God. That's why getting a divorce from Ricardo in order to live like an independent woman won't do you any good. You have to be independent in your own soul.[25]

Clarissa's death is a reflection of her life: a sacrifice from within that is not visible from the outside until something is stirred. While her deathbed seems almost pristine, Clarissa is able to put forth one last act in death that speaks volumes of her life: After Clarissa breathes her last breath, an assistant turns her on her side to bathe her in preparation for burial; when she does, fresh blood spills from Clarissa's mouth. "The sacrifice had taken place after all."[26]

Elvira is the narrator of the story which spans over one hundred years of her maternal Rivas de Santillana and paternal Vernet ancestry. She weaves the stories of her family in and out of each other, overlapping some and distinguishing others; in every case, she tells the stories of their lives in the context of the environment around them. The setting of the stories is essential to understanding the inner meaning of the story itself; Ferré, after all, intentionally quotes Octavio Paz at the beginning of the novel: "Geographies can be symbolic: physical spaces determine the archetype and become forms that emit symbols."[27]

Ferré opens the autobiographical novel with a description of *el Río Loco* (the crazy river) that the family had to cross by car without a bridge in order to get from La Concordia to Emajaguas. In the voice of Elvira, we are told that the river reminds Elvira of her own mother, that they share the same temperament, and could never be fully understood, controlled, or dammed:

> *Río Loco* got its name because it was so temperamental. When it rained in the valley and other rivers stampeded toward the sea like runaway horses, *Río Loco* was dry. But when the sun was nailed to the sky like a hot coal, charring the cane fields and forcing the scorpions out of their burrows to look for water, it reared up like a muddy demon and tumbled this way and that over the dusty plain, enraged at everything that stood in its way. The river's source was far away in the mountains, and when it rained the floods rose, even when there was fair weather in the valley.[28]

Elvira grows up believing that she and her mother are in stiff competition with each other for her father's love, not understanding until she is a wife herself that, in her father's eyes, she and her mother were two parts of the same entity, both to be managed and protected. As a result of such competition, Elvira believes her mother is unnecessarily harsh and strict with her; she runs to her father on every possible occasion for sympathy and refuge. Underneath the surface, Elvira is trying to reconcile herself to her separate yet intricately connected family histories; through the telling of her story, Elvira is trying to come to a conclusion about loyalty to either, or neither, side.

The reconciliation that Elvira tries to negotiate within herself parallels the dualisms in the conflict in and around her: cement versus roses, statehood versus independence, father versus mother, Protestant versus Catholic, US American versus Puerto Rican, etc. She desperately wishes to be an independent person and is faced with the reality that such independence must come at a high price, namely her mother's life.

Elvira's last dream of her mother is a telling one: it describes not only the struggles of the many women who had lived before her, but tells the story of women of privilege and status. It demonstrates the difficulty of giving up the benefits of patriarchy, or colonialism for that matter, when the only alternative to such a coddled life is to swim against the current. It is a choice that comes with a price, significantly higher than the dollar Clarissa waves from the safety of the car:

> I dreamed about Mother one last time. We were crossing *Río Loco* and the family's temperamental Pontiac had stalled on us again. The river was

rushing past, but instead of dogs, pigs, and goats being pulled along the murky rapids I saw Abuela Valeria, Abuela Adela, Tía Lakhme, Tía Dido, Tía Artemisa, Tía Amparo, all swimming desperately against the current. Clarissa and I sat safely inside the Pontiac, dressed in our Sunday best. She took a dollar out of her purse, rolled down the window just enough so she could wave the bill at the men on the riverbank, who soon came and pulled us out. And as we drove away I could hear through the open window the voices of those I could no longer see, but whose stories I could not have dreamed.[29]

Understood allegorically, Ferré challenges the foundations of our national identity as Puerto Rican; in a sense, she is questioning the political and economic foundations of our colonial relationship to the USA as if to say, "What is really at the core of who we are as a people and how do we restore that?" Her prophetic call forces us to determine whether we have the will to do justice to that core identity by destroying what has been a false construction, a theft and plagiarism from the start.[30] The storyteller within the story of the *House on the Lagoon*, Isabel, comes closer to restoring her own identity and voice as her relationship with Petra blossoms; the same could be said of Elvira in relation to Miña. As the migrant—vehicle and translator between both worlds—Isabel and Elvira try to integrate the two by giving voice to their tension, interplay, and interdependence. Only then can the story be told.

Ferré's work is also prophetic in its challenge to the "set-in-stone" ideologies which have bolstered the construction of a false identity, including nationalism, capitalism, racism, sexism and even feminism: ideologies which, if not accepting of the flux of history and the changing needs of people, become destructive of the very spirit they intend to reflect. Gabriela's insistence on a child only every five years may have been noble in intent, and quite progressive for her time; but its destructive result, through Carmita, carried over to future generations in ways she never could have imagined.

Amidst these constructions, Ferré's stories reflect a prophetic hope for the future in a number of ways. First, the main characters of her works demonstrate that we must understand our past and history in order to reconstruct the silences and create a new voice. Second, they demonstrate that, when we are attentive to the wisdom of those who have suffered most, we are able to move into a future with the tools to face such suffering. Third, the stories themselves illustrate the necessity of reconciliation with the conflicting parts of one's own being to move into a future with hope. Finally, the stories articulate the dialectic of death and life; something must die in order for hope to be made new and a new future to be restored in the present moment.

PUERTO RICAN HOPE IN DIALOGUE WITH THE DOCTRINE OF ESCHATOLOGY

Rosario Ferré's writing, in both style and function, engages in the hopeful revision of what does not yet exist, in relation to the island landscape of Puerto Rico, and by extension, the Puerto Rican community. The author presents us with a view of the physical locale of the island of Puerto Rico in vivid detail and history; the titles of both novels, *The House on the Lagoon* and *Eccentric Neighborhoods*, each suggest physical places situated in geographical space and time. But they do more than that. In *The House on the Lagoon*, the house itself is situated in an unstable environment, with the currents of water flowing underneath, suggesting a shifting and changing of the very foundations upon which the house is built. In fact, this shifting of foundations mirrors the shifting that takes place in the story itself; Isabel and Quintín vacillate between versions of their respective stories, only to have the more elusive and imaginative version win out in the end. In this story, the movement and unsteadiness of the house, seen as a solid immovable entity from without, mirrors the movement and unsteadiness of the characters' feelings, sensibilities, priorities, decisions and even their politics; what could be taken as fact one moment can easily become fiction in the next.

By situating the house and the story on water, Ferré creates a vision of a new reality, one that shifts and moves, is fluid and flowing. Like water, the landscape navigates around obstacles and, with enough momentum and force, can easily force its way through any barrier. Over time, this same flowing water can carve out a new path in the most impermeable rock solid surface. Within the story, we see that the water is both boundary and access, that which limits and frees at the same time. And in the end, the house itself, the outward manifestation of all that is secure and safe, succumbs to fire that rages until all that is left is the bare remnant of a foundation built on water. Reminiscent of the demise of Manderley in Daphne du Maurier's *Rebecca*, the house on the lagoon is razed; this is the only way those who called it home can move into a new future in hope, free from the chokehold of the past. In the absence of the house, in the space where nothing remains, we visualize a new terrain where the water is primary.

Likewise, *Eccentric Neighborhoods* suggests a community of family relationships living together in one general area and sharing not only their physical space but also a characteristic peculiarity. Both the space and the people who reside in it are defined by unconventional behavior; both the river (*Río Loco*) and the women who cross it are most definitely unconventional by Puerto Rican standards.

Two seemingly incompatible "neighborhoods"—the sugar plantation *haciendado* and the cement industrial monoplex—come together in the person of Elvira, the narrator of the story and the one who is left to carry the legacy of both. The question is whether she can reconcile the two polarities within herself in order to live into the future and create a new landscape that values both, in different measures. We are offered a hint of that future landscape at the end of the story in the form of Elvira's dream after her mother's death. In the dream, she is a young girl again crossing the crazy river in the family Pontiac with her mother. She sees her aunts and other women in the family being taken by the river's current, unable to cross or reach safety because of its strength. But she is able to cross with her mother who opens the window just enough to enlist the help of men on the shore by offering them a dollar. Elvira embodies both the culture of industry and agrarian life, not knowing which to call upon in any given situation, but feeling the conflict of values, community, and relationships in the interaction of both. We are left not knowing how or whether such reconciliation can ever happen; the vision of the new landscape is unclear and daunting, like crossing a river without knowing its depth.

In *The House on the Lagoon*, the one who truly understands that everything begins and ends in water is Willie, the epileptic with use of only one eye:

Maybe I had to become partially blind to understand what she meant. When I realized I might never be able to paint again, I cried so much I couldn't believe the body could hold so much water. Tears, saliva, semen, blood - our bodies are mostly water.

Petra knew that water is love....Every time we wet our feet or wade into the sea, we touch other people, we share in their sadness and their joys.

> Because we live on an island there is no mass of mountains, no solid dyke of matter to keep us from flowing out to others. Through water, we can reach out and love our neighbors, try to understand them…
>
> Water permitted the Avilés family to travel from Morass to Alamares Lagoon in the first place….After all, I was conceived in the swamp, isn't that right, Mother? And it was in the mangroves that Carmelina Avilés fell into Father's arms.[31]

The image of water as the medium of creation (beginnings/birth) is also the medium of destruction (endings/death). The water is always changing that which comes into contact with it. The house on the lagoon did not require a final inferno to ensure its demise; the water would have eroded it over time. Likewise, our personal and cultural identity as Puerto Rican women/people has been changed via the water: Spanish and US American ships which have introduced five hundred years of colonization were brought to us by water, over which our newest migrations patterns have also traversed. The water that now divides Puerto Ricans on the island and mainland will help us forge a new identity, even with the knowledge that this definition will always be elusive. The water is both boundary and access.

In Ferré's novels, water is feared as a destructive force that washes away everything in its path; tears blind rather than enhance spiritual vision. Water is seen through the lens of death in tension with life. Her works do not negate death but illustrate the tension between life and death that we must face directly and honestly to ensure a future beyond death. Ferré suggests that our hope in the future is not primarily a political question—about statehood, independence, or commonwealth— although we must face this issue directly as well. But if we are a faithful people who treasure those things that have not been defeated through our history—the gifts of life and love, our freedom of will, our voice, our ability to face death and survive—then we will live in dignity in whatever political structure we determine is best for us to maintain those aspects of our identity. That is, the political decision will not lead to harmony in itself; the balance, and our will to maintain it, must be sought first from within. This balance is based on love and freedom, reflected in our ability to embrace the contradictions and ambiguities we embody. The water instructs us to wash away those aspects of ourselves that are in opposition to love and freedom. This understanding echoes the image of water in Christian tradition: the waters of the flood and baptism are evidence of both justice and righteousness.

Ferré's writing reflects Puerto Rican hope because it leaves the story in the hands of those who will carry on, from Isabel in *The House on the Lagoon*, to Elvira in *Eccentric Neighborhoods*, as well as countless other characters from her short stories. These characters embody Puerto Rican hope because they are left with the task of reconciling the conflict of two or more competing allegiances, as if to say that our future hope is dependent upon the process of reconciliation. The move toward freedom, in Ferré's style, is reconciliation: mending wounds, creating balance, and restoring unity. Her work also suggests that, as part of the move toward freedom, some things must die in order for others to move on into a renewed future of hope.

WHERE OUR HOPE IS FOUND: TOWARDS A PUERTO RICAN DECOLONIAL ESCHATOLOGY

The hope of the gospel message is perhaps one of its most compelling characteristics that continues to animate those who believe in its promise of peace, love and life eternal. While Jesus' death on the cross confronts the Christian with torturous suffering, the resurrection miracle attests to the affirmation that suffering and death do not have the final word. "He is risen," claims the Easter narrative, and with that pronouncement a community is held together by a belief that "neither death, nor life, nor angels, nor rulers, nor things present, nor things to come, nor powers, nor height, nor depth, nor anything else in all creation, will be able to separate us from the love of God in Christ Jesus our Lord."[32] How do we embrace a message of hope and promise when our human condition seems to reflect anything but hope? More directly, how can Puerto Ricans maintain and sustain hope in God in the midst of suffering and despair? Along with identity and suffering, hope emerges from Puerto Rican literature as an important theme; I will now explore how this theme corresponds with the Christian theological definition of human hope for a future that is yet to come.

Morse outlines four areas of the Christian doctrine of eschatology that are worth mentioning here in relation to the theme of hope in Ferré's writing. He categorizes these areas as (1) "on trial for hope"; (2) "the coming cloud"; (3) "hellfire and damnation," and (4) "looking forward: resurrection of body and world." Guiding his assessment of these doctrinal categories is the belief that eschatology has as much to do with this world as with the world to come. "To confess that the...dominion of heaven is 'at hand' is to characterize, not the way the sky is, but the way the earth is from the perspective of the gospel's frame of reference. Earth is not simply what is overarched by the sky; earth is what is overarched by an unimpeded dominion of love and freedom, that is 'heaven.'"[33] I will use these categories to summarize the main principles of the doctrine of eschatology as well as to reflect upon how they influence the Puerto Rican community's hope for the future.

On trial for hope: Morse uses this phrase of Paul from the Acts of the Apostles[34] as a means of connecting the self-understanding of the church (ecclesiology) with eschatology within Christian faith. The statement by Paul affirms the belief in the promise made by God, which supersedes all potential in the present moment; whereas the current situation may seem devoid of hope, God promises that hope reigns eternal. As believers in the promise and covenant made by God through Jesus, we can also trust more in the promise of the life that is to come than we can trust in tomorrow's coming. "Faith that is based upon this testimony thus entails a refusal to believe that there is no trustworthy future facing us in coming events wherever and whenever we are."[35]

The biblical witness illustrates that as a function of our eschatological faith we are called upon to act in the present moment based on the promise of the future; in the process of acting in the present, we are, in effect, bringing the future into the present. We are not disengaged from the moment by any means; the eschatological promise mandates that we engage ourselves in the world fully, energized by the hope in what God has in store for us and for the world.

This understanding of an eschatological hope grounded in the here and now proscribes an overdependence on otherworldliness, of waiting passively for the time when God will make all things right. At the same time, an eschatological hope that is grounded in the work of love on earth also cautions us from placing too much value on the earthly tomorrow, rather than working for its renewal. Ferré's writing, from the perspective of the Puerto Rican elite class, illustrates that all the money, status, and prestige in the world cannot eradicate death. The Christian theological tradition affirms that only God can promise a tomorrow that is certain and eternal. Houses may succumb to fire or water; God's promise for life never fades and that promise is given to all.

Being "on trial for hope" also uncovers a deception about placing all hope in the life that is to come. The proof of our belief in the life to come does not entail disengagement in the life that is. Our communities are plagued with those who will try to convince us that true believers do not participate in the mundane workings of the world. This belief is a distortion of the gospel message, which says, "Whatsoever you do for the least of these, you do to me." (Matthew 25: 40) Puerto Ricans must know and act upon an understanding of eschatological hope that does not yield to our struggles, our trials, of today. In fact, our belief in God's promise of a truly new tomorrow is the light that illumines today's struggle.

The coming cloud: The notion of the "end times," or the apocalypse, weighs heavily in the Christian teaching on eschatology; it has gained increased currency in an age of nuclear warfare, environmental destruction and economic collapse across the globe. The "end of the world" is envisioned through the biblical accounts as a moment of tremendous upheaval in which "people will faint with fear and foreboding of what is coming upon the world, for the powers of heavens will be shaken. Then they will see the Son of Man coming in a cloud with power and great glory." (Luke 21: 26–27) Morse details the various interpretations of both the text and its application in the modern age; the majority of these seem to focus on the text as a prediction of what is to come, and how we are to discern its approach by the "signs of the times." Others who do not wish to use the text as a fortune-teller have often discarded it as either outmoded thinking or promoting irresponsibility in the present moment.[36]

Yet, there is another interpretation of the text that seems to address both its purported outdatedness and lack of ethical inspiration. If we understand our present existence as a life "on trial for hope" in terms of God's covenant with us in the future, then the words of Luke take on an entirely different meaning, one that is less about "doom and gloom" predictions that instill fear and more about a promise about overcoming fear. Believing in the eschatological hope of "the Son of Man coming in a cloud" is to believe that amidst the fear and trembling provoked by the present day, God's promise to overcome the fear and trembling is ever present.

This is an incredible promise for Puerto Ricans because it affirms the belief in eternal community and communion: no matter how much isolation or alienation we experience, we know that we can look ahead to find Jesus with us in solidarity. This same truth uncovers a deception that tries to seduce us into thinking that our fear is evidence of a weak faith. And the conditions in which so many of our people live breed an even greater sense of fear: fear of violence, of each other, of the unknown. What if we were told instead that our God, through whom all fear fades, meets our fear head on?

Sometimes, we have to be fearful, as our fear can be an early warning system that danger looms near. For many of us who live under the threat of violence, or on Vieques for that matter, this fear is necessary and valuable because it keeps us from dangerous situations. The same fear can also awaken in us a desire to eradicate those injustices that create environments of fear. In our struggle against that which instills fear, in opposition to our life, we look to "Son of Man coming in a cloud" to remind us that Jesus walks with us so that we can walk through the fear unscathed.

Hellfire and damnation: Christian teaching regarding the future eschaton, the end of times, implies a day of judgment when God will make some choices about who will enter the kingdom of heaven and who will be refused entry. On this point, much disagreement has taken place; surely, the number of Christian denominations at present attests to the difficulty of coming to a consensus about this and other touchy doctrinal issues. What is at stake in the conviction that some will be chosen is the assertion that some have the unique ability to define who enters and who does not. Despite disagreements on the details, Christian teaching affirms the existence of two groups, the elect and the rejected, at the moment of judgment.

Morse cautions us to consider a message that the gospel repeats over and over: those who love God and those who deny God's love have access to God's grace in equal measure. That is, in terms of God's love for humanity, there is no difference since "all have sinned and fall short of the glory of God." (Romans 3: 23) Therefore, the sinfulness that is common to all humanity is matched by the grace that is available to all humanity: "human solidarity in sin is also.... solidarity in grace."[37] When eschatological doctrine affirms that God will judge and make choices, it affirms that God will not choose certain groups of humanity over others.

Like many other communities, Puerto Ricans have fallen for the tactic of "divide and conquer" in the area of God's judgment on the last day. There are some among us, truth be told, who are certain of their place among the elect, and equally certain of others' place among the rejected, based on the salvation criteria of their own particular church. I'll never forget the day many years ago when I was literally cornered by a Puerto Rican college classmate, demanding that I justify my Roman Catholic beliefs in Mary and the saints, since she was convinced, from her

Pentecostal perspective, that these amounted to idol worship. Although I do not recall how I slithered out of that situation then, I know how I would handle it now: I would assert that God's judgment has less to do with *who* we are than what we are *for or against* in relation to God and neighbor. Therefore, all of us, regardless of status, have the potential to stand among the elect; similarly, all of us bear the risk of rejection when we oppose the love and freedom of God. This is precisely the function of Petra and Miña in Ferré's novels (*House on the Lagoon* and *Eccentric Neighborhoods*, respectively). They are not women of status by economic, political, racial, or social standards. But they are part of the elect in that their every word and action is circumscribed by God's love and freedom made manifest.

The truth of this eschatological promise uncovers the lie that the Puerto Rican, and every other, community will be judged based on adherence to some US American standard of Christianity. Perhaps we should consider our reaction in learning that even those who practice Santeria, *espiritismo*, or vodun may be taking their place among the elect. The truth uncovers the lie that election is based on superiority of any definition, whether islander to mainlander, light-skinned to dark-skinned, Protestant to Catholic, or English to Spanish. These false divisions will make no difference in God's final judgment, which will care less about the "who" and more about who and what opposes or promotes love and freedom.

Looking forward: the resurrection of body and world: The gospel, in general, and Jesus' life, death, resurrection, and ascension specifically, send a clear message: God promises life after death. This promise extends to both the individual and the community, to our bodies as well as our souls. While the Scriptures offer no clarity on the specifics of such life to come, Christian eschatological teaching is firm in its conviction that (1) death is never bypassed; (2) "the communal and the individual are never separated in the hope of the gospel's promise of a kingdom"[38]; and (3) the promise initiated will be fulfilled in the end. This understanding of the "life to come" may seem obscure and mysterious; there are no blueprints for what this "life everlasting" looks like to us. The core principle affirmed by this teaching is that we, as individuals in community, can rest in the promise that what the world leaves unfinished, God will complete fully and perfectly.

This interpretation of the doctrine is important for Puerto Ricans for a number of reasons. First, it affirms the experience of our bodies, holistically and in relationship to the communal body of Puerto Rican people. The individual and the community are part of the same entity. Therefore, in a society that degrades our bodies by telling us they are bad—too sensual, sexual, expressive, for example—or by exploiting them for others' benefit, we know that God values our bodies as much as our souls and will ensure our resurrection in the flesh in the life to come. This does not mean that we can bypass the trial, struggle, and eventual death of our bodies, literally and figuratively; we must descend before we ascend. Yet the doctrine of the eschatological hope in the resurrection of the body and world asserts that the trial, struggle, and eventual death of our bodies is not the final act.

Because God so values our bodies, as individuals and community, enough to ensure their resurrection, then why would we think God requires us to deny our bodies here on earth? While our fullest becoming will happen in God's time and not our own, our own time calls for the appreciation and attention to our bodies making way for their perfection in God. Our own time calls for a different way of being in relation to our physical bodies; the health prognosis for the Puerto Rican community is frightening on so many levels, from infant mortality rates, and diabetes to substance abuse, cancer, and high blood pressure. Surely many of these ailments have a great deal to do with the oppressive and sub-standard environment in which we live. Still, the neglect of our bodies reflects a resignation to those oppressive forces that devalue our humanity. Such neglect says that our bodies do not matter to others or to ourselves. Yet, this doctrine affirms that God, who created us in the image and likeness of God-self, values our bodies in all their beauty and sensuality. We know this instinctively as Puerto Ricans; the environmental damage on Vieques would not mean as much to us if we did not understand the land as part of our communal body in suffering and pain.

The Story of Rachel in the Gospel of Matthew

The reference to Rachel in the Gospel of Matthew relates significantly to the theme of hope and the doctrine of eschatology. This segment of the Gospel (Matthew 2: 16–18) is commonly referred to as the "slaughter of the innocents" in which King Herod, anxious about the Magi's prophecy of an Israelite redeemer, murders all boys age two and under in and around the vicinity of Bethlehem. In Matthew's Gospel, this massacre is related to the prophecy of Jeremiah where Rachel is heard weeping in Ramah, "for her children are no more." Her life of suffering and rejection is juxtaposed with the story of the coming of Messianic hope and restoration. In the course of Matthew's text, Jesus is like the new Israel, the birth of a new nation and identity, in the same way Rachel's husband Jacob was given a new identity, Israel, after he wrestled with the angel in the twilight before dawn. Rachel is connected with the first "installation" of a new nation through Jacob/Israel; she is connected with the second coming of a new nation through Jesus.[39]

The purpose of Matthew's Gospel, in the context of the Synoptic Gospels, was to convey a connection with the history of the Jewish people and how God has fulfilled the prophecies of the past by breaking into history through the life, death and resurrection of Jesus. God's fulfillment is connected to the salvation history of the world, relating further to the notion of identity: God initiates God's activity through a particular people in a particular time and place.

In Matthew's narrative of the Nativity, that particular time and place belonged to the Romans, and particularly to King Herod. If we were to get into the mind of Herod, as the symbol of absolute political power at the time, we can surmise that he very much feared the loss of his power through the birth of one who was prophesied to overturn the existing power structure. He was afraid of the "light of the world" embodied in Jesus: the light emitted by the star of Bethlehem that led the Magi from the far corners of the earth to witness and pay homage to the savior of the world. The two powers are in fierce conflict: the powers of the light surrounding Jesus and the powers of the shadow of death surrounding Herod. Despite his efforts, Herod is unable to secure victory in his attempt to annihilate all hope; there are many forces of light working to protect the Christ child from harm, including the visions received by Joseph (to go to Egypt for safety) and the Magi themselves (to return to their land by a different route). In spite of all the efforts to extinguish the light, the Son of God is born and lives.

We can say that the story emphasizes the belief that God alone gives the hope that can console the type of suffering experienced by Rachel, or by the mothers of Bethlehem on that murderous night. Their suffering is too deep and broad to be consoled by human empathy. Jewish midrash speaks of this deep suffering in relation to Jacob as he mourns the passing of his beloved wife; Dresner tells us of this midrash:

> The death of Rachel is the watershed in the life of Jacob...We read no more of power and wealth or encounters with angels, no more heroic tales

to add to the record of his life. Only sorrow, sorrow so unremitting that it carries him all the way to the grave. Overnight he falls into depression, hardly recognizable, a solitary, morose figure, given over to mourning his beloved Rachel, concerned only that what she left be preserved.[40]

Rachel left her sons, Joseph and Benjamin, given to her by God as it was God who opened her womb. Through Rachel's children, God's covenant with God's people is restored. Thus, the suffering is mitigated only through the hope for the future embodied in the children to whom Rachel gave birth. The same rabbis whose midrash recount Jacob's sorrow also "ascribe to [Rachel] a vicarious joy," by applying to her the title "a happy mother of children."

Only God can bring joy in the midst of this incredible pain; only God can bring life in the midst of death. And God does just that, we are told by this story; in the Gospel of Matthew, God does the same in the birth of Christ. Here we see God once again taking the side of the powerless and the lowly. We see God bringing joy, life, and hope as only God can, that point toward the future when the present holds suffering, death, and despair.

THEOLOGICAL PERSPECTIVES ON ESCHATOLOGY

On the question of eschatology, a necessary element of all Christian systematic theology, James Cone states,

> If God is truly the God of and for the oppressed for the purpose of their liberation, then the future must mean that our fight for freedom has not been for naught. Our journey in the world cannot be a meaningless thrust toward an unrealizable future, but a certainty grounded in the past and present reality of God. To grasp for the future of God is to know that those who die for freedom have not died in vain; they will see the kingdom of God. This is precisely the meaning of our Lord's resurrection, and why we can fight against overwhelming odds. We believe in the future of God, a future that must become present.[41]

Black theology refuses to hand the oppressor the victory of the present by resting all the hopes of the eradication of oppression on the distant, unseen future. On the contrary, Cone asserts that the efficacy of an eschatology of hope rests squarely on the shoulders of the present, and is informed by nothing less than Jesus' resurrection, which asserts boldly that death need not have the final word. The eschatological perspective put forth by Cone on behalf of the black community is no "sweet potato pie in the sky" perspective that endures uncritically immediate suffering because of the promise of heaven to those who await its coming obediently. His theological perspective shares more with those who espouse a "theology of hope" such as Moltmann, by claiming that eschatology is "related to action and change" in the present moment.[42]

> Hope must be related to the present, and it must serve as a means of transforming an oppressed community into a liberated - and liberating - community. Black theology does not scorn Christian hope; it affirms it. It believes that, when Christians really believe in the resurrection of Christ and take seriously the promise revealed through him, they cannot be satisfied with the present world as it is...Christian eschatology is bound up with the resurrection of Christ. He is the eschatological hope. He is the future of God who stands in judgment upon the world and forces us to give an account of the present.[43]

Justo González echoes Cone's eschatology from a Hispanic perspective. Clearly articulated in his book *Mañana: Christian Theology from a Hispanic Perspective*, González suggests that the spirituality of Hispanic peoples is like that of the early Christian community by its foundation in the gift of the Holy Spirit. His understanding of spirituality is not based on individual piety or meditation; rather,

> 'spiritual' means living out of the future we have been promised, precisely because that promise has been sealed and guaranteed by the Holy Spirit... Christian spirituality...is eschatological in nature. It is future oriented. It is life lived out of expectation, out of a hope and a goal. And that goal is the coming Reign of God. To have the Spirit is to have a foot up on the stirrup of the eschatological future and to live now as those who expect a new reality, the coming of the Reign of God.[44]

The coming Reign of God of which González speaks is a vision of that which does not yet exist in the present but which can come to be through the Spirit. The vision of a different future orients the action that is taken today. In this sense, González claims that *mañana* represents an overturning of the way in which Hispanics have been depicted as lazy people who put off everything and anything they can until tomorrow. *Mañana* is a time that is unlike the present, a sentiment affirmed by Cone as well.[45] The vision of *mañana* affirmed by Scripture is a new creation both in the making and already in existence, which is also a "word of judgment on today,"[46] because it suggests that we need to envision a reality different from the present because the present falls short. We see again that the eschatological emphasis of liberation from oppression has much to do with action and change, with how we align our lives in relation to the vision of *mañana*, with an ethic of liberation, guided by the Holy Spirit.

The action and change evoked by a liberation ethic[47] in the present is fueled by joy and thanksgiving. "Every prophetic proclamation of total liberation is accompanied by an invitation to participate in eschatological joy....Our joy is paschal, guaranteed by the Spirit."[48] The joy of which Gutiérrez speaks here, and which he develops further in both *We Drink From Our Own Wells* and *The God of Life*, is by no means superficial. It stems from the realization of God's gratuitous gift of love toward us and God's preferential option for the poor. It is celebrated in the Eucharist, amidst the pain and suffering of everyday life, in such a way as to sustain and give meaning to the struggle for liberation.

The joy that is part of a spirituality of liberation brings hope, Gutiérrez claims. Such joy goes beyond the kind of celebration that is commonplace among poor and oppressed people; in Latin America, the poor have no shortage of celebrations as temporary escape from oppressive daily life. But the joy of which Gutiérrez speaks here is much more than this because, out of the faith that God walks with them in their struggle for justice, the poor have hope that justice will be done in history. The joy emerges from an unfaltering belief that God is a God of life, that the violence and injustice are not from God, and that God's love compels the believer to stand for life even in the face of death. Believers in a God of life affirm the conviction that death, in all its cruelty, cannot be forgotten when we continue to struggle against that which causes the poor to die before their time. This struggle continues with a profound sense of joy and thanksgiving because of the belief in the resurrection promise:

> There is no affirmation of life that does not entail passing through death, confronting death. This is the witness that so many in Latin America have given us in our time. The message of the resurrection of Jesus and of our resurrection in union with his is clear: life, not death, has the final word in history.[49]

The joy and thanksgiving of which Gutiérrez speaks allows the poor to understand the resurrection promise in celebration, in *fiesta*, which Arturo Bañuelas notes

> is more than simply a party. It is a celebration of eschatological hope. It proclaims who we are as *mestizos* and offers the possibility of a new universalism already beginning in a people who through rejection and struggles continue to proclaim *que la vida es lucha, pero con victoria* (that life is struggle, but with victory). *Fiesta* prophetically announces in festive form the table being readied for the day all peoples can be as one.[50]

Elizondo echoes this sentiment and adds that *fiesta*, as a celebration of eschatological hope, has a prophetic purpose, calling a people to commitment and action through shared struggle that is energized by joy and love:

> *Fiestas* without prophetic action easily denigrate into empty parties, drunken brawls, or the opium to keep the people in their misery. But prophetic action without festive celebration is equally reduced to dehumanizing hardness. Prophecy is the basis of *fiesta*, but the *fiesta* is the spirit of prophecy. It is in the combination of the two that the tradition of faith is both kept alive and transmitted to newcomers. It is through the two of them that the God of history who acts on...behalf of the poor and the lowly, continues to be present among us bringing the project of history to completion....[*Fiestas*] are the lifeline of our tradition and the life sources of our new existence.[51]

As the life source of a new existence, a new identity, the *fiesta* is an intrinsic part of who we are and who we are becoming. Roberto Goizueta makes the explicit connection of *fiesta* as the link between theological anthropology—who we are in relation to God—and theological eschatology—who we are becoming in relation to God. By demonstrating fiesta's challenge to the modern notion of the subject who "makes history," Goizueta argues that fiesta is a liturgical expression, "a communal act of worship...an act of praise and thanksgiving which commemorates the saving love of God as this has been manifest in the remembered past, is experienced in the celebrated present, and is anticipated in the promised future."[52] The saving love of God is made, experienced, and anticipated within life itself; God's gift is the gift of life that we receive in trust. We respond to God's gift by celebrating, often defiantly, the life we have in the present and the life that is to come in the future.

A Puerto Rican Decolonial Eschatology

Puerto Rican theology can look to the story of Rachel in Matthew's Gospel as a source that confirms the emphasis on eschatological hope found in our own life stories, as also reflected in the literature. Emphasized in this gospel narrative of the nativity is that hope radically confronts the despair of the moment, then and now; despair that goes beyond all human consolation is met with hope that transcends all human suffering.

Where is such hope and promise found for Puerto Ricans and for Puerto Rico? Where can we catch a glimpse of a new tomorrow that is but a faint glimmer today? Our stories and our histories demonstrate that the hope and promise of a renewed future is not often found in the churches, in the places of worship of our respective traditions. Our stories and histories illustrate that we have had to use lots of creativity to maintain the life-giving and life-sustaining aspects of our identity. These same stories and histories have reminded us that some things must die in order for others to grow, making way for a new creation.

I believe that the *fiesta*, as an embodiment of the renewal of relationships among family, friends, community, is one place where hope can be found for Puerto Rican people. I affirm all that has been said regarding the profound significance of the fiesta for the Latinx community in general. The Puerto Rican experience tells me that our understanding of *la tierra*, the earth, our homeland, is connected to the celebration of life, in a particularly Puerto Rican way; it is manifested in what has been called the "revolving door migration"[53] pattern attributed to the Puerto Rican community since 1964.

For many Puerto Ricans, going back and forth from island to mainland is, at the very least, an annual event. In the course of the event, family and friends are reunited, meals and laughter are shared, memories exchanged, relationships renewed, plans are made. These *visitas* are not a matter of luxury but a necessity of maintaining a connection to the people and the country, in defiance of a dominant culture of assimilation, which seeks to break it down. The revolving door is nothing less than a sacred portal of hope and promise, where the scenery is the same upon return but the travelers are not. In other words, the journey into the sacred space of communion with the other side transforms and renews. The revolving door is an eschatological bridge of hope and promise that one day the journey between the two worlds will not be so long and arduous, so expensive and difficult; it will be as effortless and joyful as the *fiesta*.

Such an effortless and joyful journey presumes a foundation of reconciliation. Forgiveness and peacemaking are the supports which maintain the bridge's strength and function. It can be quite an effort and less than joyful to journey back to the places and people of the past when one has not made peace with one's story. It seems much easier to block out the harsh memories and difficult experiences associated with a life's journey. Yet, we can reconcile these painful elements of our past, and indeed our present, in the promise that there is no pain so great that it will undo God's love for us; the face of Jesus in the "coming cloud" affirms this. Therefore, the revolving door of Puerto Rican migration is evidence, in the present, of our eschatological hope in the future made manifest. It is evidence that, amidst suffering and despair, we can journey into joy with hope. While we may not feel secure in who we are or who we are becoming, we explore the possibilities of a new identity that goes back and forth, in wholeness. The water, over which the JFK to San Juan jetliner crosses, is boundary and access once again.

This notion of reconciliation is quite different from that articulated by other US liberation theologians, particularly James Cone, in relation to oppressed communities. Speaking from the African-American experience of oppression, in its many forms, Cone warns that we must not fall too quickly into a desire for reconciliation between whites and blacks before the full implications of such reconciliation are expressed and exposed freely. His concern for his people compels him to be wary of any efforts to "make nice" with whites at the expense of the liberation of his, or any, oppressed community. He insists that "liberation *must* be expressed in uncompromising language and actions, for only then can the conditions be created for reconciliation.[54]

Cone continues by stating that the liberation struggle must be focused less on the process of superficial reconciliation with white people, and more on the gift of reconciliation among and within oppressed communities themselves. With the emphasis on the latter,

> We find that reconciliation is not a theological idea but a human struggle,
> a fight to create dignity in an inhumane situation. Reconciliation is not

sitting down with white liberals and radicals, assuring them that we don't have any hard feelings toward them. Rather, it is a vision of God's presence in our lives that lets us know that the world will be changed only through our blood, sweat and tears…From the experience of divine truth in our social existence, we now know that reconciliation must start *first* with black brothers and sisters who have suffered the pain of a broken community…. Reconciliation, like love, must begin at home before it can spread abroad.[55]

I am deeply indebted to Cone's theological interpretation of reconciliation, particularly his unapologetic stance for the primacy of liberation on behalf of the African-American community, which was in many ways the prophetic voice that called me to question the conditions of my own Puerto Rican community. His analysis of reconciliation in relation to liberation also helped me to understand more clearly the dynamics of both at work for Puerto Ricans, and their significance for a Puerto Rican eschatology. Cone positions "black" and "white" on two opposite poles, and addresses the meaning of reconciliation/liberation in two distinct ways. Cone asserts that reconciliation within the black community is a priority and a precondition for lasting liberation. Achieving reconciliation between black and white people, while an important task, should never be attempted at the expense of the hopes and dreams of liberation for black people. While Cone is not against black and white solidarity, particularly when that solidarity is created on black terms, he still articulates his vision of reconciliation in "us/black" and "them/white" categories.

This is where the uniqueness of the Puerto Rican experience diverges from that of the African-American theological analysis of reconciliation and liberation. While we share many common experiences of oppression in the USA, our relationship to the "other" is less distinct; it is not an "us/them" relationship. The "other" is within ourselves; as Puerto Ricans, we are both self and other simultaneously. Therefore, the process of reconciliation in relation to freedom cannot occur "at home before it can spread abroad"; the process is authentic only when it addresses the multiple, intersectional, and often conflicting, relationships we embody at once: island/mainland, Puerto Rican/American, Spanish/English, Catholic/Protestant, modernity/coloniality, etc. Again, Anzaldúa reminds us of the open wound that is created at the place of boundary/*la frontera*.

Thus, the eschatological vision of hope and promise in a future presupposes a foundation of reconciliation embodied in the process of the revolving door. This door is not a one-way exit or entrance; it is a constant process of change and transformation that connects the past with the present, and both with the future. It demonstrates that, as Puerto Ricans, we are no longer afraid to travel in the blurred boundaries of "either/or" but consider that space to be sacred in itself. The revolving door marks the fluid passage between the *mañana* we work toward achieving and the today in which we live with hope.

Even with the categories of Latinx theology, the Puerto Rican experience demonstrates greater complexity and possibilities with regard to racial/ethnic understanding and reconciliation. As demonstrated earlier, Elizondo speaks of "mestizaje" as a theological category which parallels the life-span of Jesus of Galilee, thereby creating an opportunity for Mexican Americans to understand their own *mestizaje*, the racial/cultural encounter between Spaniard and Indian, as a place of reconciliation. Other Latinx theologians have spoken of *mulataje* in similar fashion, which recognizes the racial/cultural encounter between Spaniard and African, as a source and locus of theologizing. The Puerto Rican experience demonstrates that neither one of these categories adequately captures our unique cultural makeup, nor do they offer an authentically Puerto Rican opportunity for reconciliation and decoloniality. We need to speak a new word that captures the multi-dimensional quality of our racial/ethnic/cultural identity and reflects it honestly while pointing beyond it prophetically. The hope and promise for a renewed Puerto Rican tomorrow is embodied in the resurrection of our body and the world—our transformed *mulatizaje*[56]—that rejects all that denies the love and freedom of our collective body that embodies Blackness as much as any other category of our racialized identity.

But to understand such hope in a way that helps to bring it to bear upon a suffering reality, Puerto Rican theology seeks to bring forth a radical conversion of our very community: a radical conversion to the message of the gospel in order to respond to the call of living into a true and full identity, of participating in the work of salvation, and of ushering into the present the vision of an eschatological future of hope. This means that Puerto Ricans need to start questioning critically those powers that undermine our quest for identity, that undermine our efforts to end suffering and that cloud our vision of a future lived in freedom, even if those powers exist from within our own community and within ourselves.

Puerto Rican decolonial theology requires that we experience a deep and radical conversion within our community and within our community in relationships of solidarity. This is the task of true Christian discipleship in relation to the poor. When Jesus said, "leave all that you own and follow me," he is mandating our conversion, of leaving our comfort zone, so to speak, to take on his way of life dedicated to the oppressed. His mandate is all about getting our hearts rightly aligned to a way of life that focuses less on what J. Lo's latest love interest is, as the emblem of Puerto Rican importance, or whether Ms. Puerto Rico will win the Ms. Universe pageant, or whether salsa is better than merengue and reggaeton better than both. A Puerto Rican theological perspective on eschatology, the "end of things" offers a way of living into a state of decolonial freedom, not waiting for that honor to be bestowed by others but claiming it in the now for ourselves because it is already promised by God. Our hearts will only be free if we begin with the internal task of reconciliation between the oppressors and oppressed—our *mulatizaje*—which we embody within ourselves.

NOTES

1. Her father, Luís A. Ferré, held the highest political/social position in Puerto Rico as its governor from 1968–1972, advocating statehood through the New Progressive Party.
2. Ferré studied with Llosa at the University of Puerto Rico; she also studied at Manhattanville College and the University of Maryland.
3. Julia M. Gallardo Colón, "Rosario Ferré," *Biographical Dictionary of Hispanic Literature in the United States*, Nicolás Kanellos, ed. (New York, NY: Greenwood Press, 1989), 99–105.
4. Rosario Ferré, *Sweet Diamond Dust and other stories, with a new preface by the author* (New York, NY: Plume/Penguin Books, 1996), x.
5. Rosario Ferré, *The Youngest Doll [Papeles de Pandora]* (Lincoln, NE: University of Nebraska Press, 1991).
6. Rosario Ferré, *The House on the Lagoon* (New York, NY: Farrar, Straus and Giroux, 1995) and Rosario Ferré, *Eccentric Neighborhoods* (New York, NY: Farrar, Straus and Giroux, 1998).
7. Robert Detweiler, "Theological Trends of Postmodern Fiction," *Journal of the American Academy of Religion* 44.2 (1976): 225–237.
8. Ferré, *The House on the Lagoon*, 5–6.
9. René Marqués, in *The Docile Puerto Rican* (Philadelphia, PA: Temple University Press, 1976) claimed that machismo was the last, and a necessary, cultural bulwark to resist US imperialism and Puerto Rican docility. These authors challenge assumptions that the self-determination of women and Puerto Rico are mutually exclusive; and that to critique Puerto Rican sexism is to negate Puerto Rican culture. See Diana L. Vélez, "Cultural Constructions of Women by Contemporary Puerto

Rican Women Authors," *The Psychosocial Development of Puerto Rican Women*, 31–59; This is interestingly the same position the women of the Young Lords Party took regarding the connection between Puerto Rican women's freedom and Puerto Rican political freedom (see writings on "the revolution within the revolution" in The Young Lords Party, *Palante* [Chicago, IL: Haymarket Books, 2011]).

10. Ferré, *The Youngest Doll*, 122–123.
11. Ferré, *The House on the Lagoon*, 59.
12. Ibid., 60; the word "Bantu", in the Tshiluba language of the Luba peoples of Angola and the Congo, means "people," where the term "Bantu bafika" means "black people".
13. Ibid., 305.
14. Jean Franco, "Forward," in Rosario Ferré, *The Youngest Doll [Papeles de Pandora]* (Lincoln, NE: University of Nebraska Press, 1991), xiii.
15. I say "more obvious" here because I believe that all Puerto Ricans have African blood running through our veins, regardless of whether our physical features reflect this fact in lesser degree. Puerto Rico's slave history, as well as the forced and consensual interrelationships which have marked our history since, bears witness to this reality.
16. Ileana Rodríguez-Silva, *Silencing Race: Disentangling Blackness, Colonialism, and National Identities in Puerto Rico* (New York, NY: Palgrave Macmillan, 2012); and Isar P. Godreau, *Scripts of Blackness: Race, Cultural Nationalism, and US Colonialism in Puerto Rico* [Global Studies of the United States] (Urbana, Chicago, IL and Springfield, MA: University of Illinois Press, 2015).
17. See Chap. 3 for a complete description of the meaning and function of archetypal symbols.
18. The author's use of the term "neighborhoods" suggests a community, a terrain, that has the ability to transform or shift with the comings and goings of successive generations. Neighborhoods do not always remain the same; they can experience their own process of life, deterioration, restoration, etc., just as those who inhabit it. The neighborhood can be a transitional place, in the realm of archetypal symbols; in fact, Ferré quotes Octavio Paz from *Postdata* at the onset of her novel: "Geographies can be symbolic; physical spaces determine the archetype and become forms that emit symbols," 1. Walter D. Mignolo also speaks of the decolonial option as an epistemological delinking from the "hubris of the zero point," a geography of reason that relegates the colonial subject to spaces outside of that center; "The democratization of epistemology is under way…and 'I am where I think' is one basic epistemic principle that legitimizes all ways of thinking and de-legitimizes the pretense of a singular and particular epistemology, geo-historical and bio-graphically located,

to be universal." *The Darker Side of Western Modernity: Global Futures, Decolonial Options* (Durham, NC: Duke University Press, 2011), 80–81.

19. Ferré, *Eccentric Neighborhoods*, 30.
20. Ibid., 16.
21. Ibid., 19–20.
22. Ibid., 99.
23. Ibid., 148–149.
24. Ibid., 331.
25. Ibid., 334.
26. Ibid., 338.
27. From *Postdata*, in Ibid., 1.
28. Ibid., 3.
29. Ibid., 340.
30. In the novel, an architect apprentice of Frank Lloyd Wright, who stole some of his designs and recreated them in Puerto Rico where no one would recognize his theft, designed the house.
31. Ferré, *The House on the Lagoon*, 389.
32. Romans 8: 38–39.
33. Christopher Morse, *Not Every Spirit: A Dogmatics of Christian Disbelief* (Valley, PA: Trinity Press International, 1994), 318–319.
34. Acts 26: 6, "And now I stand here on trial for hope in the promise made by God to our ancestors."
35. Morse, *Not Every Spirit*, 327–328.
36. Ibid., 329–333.
37. Ibid., 339.
38. Ibid., 342.
39. Robert A. Spivey and D. Moody Smith, *Anatomy of the New Testament: A Guide to its Structure and Meaning* (New York: Macmillan Publishing Co., 1982), 102–105; "The Hebrew male children were killed at the birth of Moses; the Bethlehem male children were killed at the birth of Jesus (Matthew 2: 16–19; cf. Exodus 1: 15–2: 10). Yet the text seems to imply something more than a Moses-Jesus topology. Jesus is not a new Moses, but a new Israel" (102).
40. Samuel H. Dresner, *Rachel* (Minneapolis, MN: Augsburg Fortress, 1994), 102–103.
41. James Cone, *A Black Theology of Liberation* (Maryknoll, NY: Orbis, 1986), 141.
42. Ibid., 139.
43. Ibid., 140.
44. Justo L. González, *Mañana: Christian Theology from a Hispanic Perspective* (Nashville, TN: Abingdon Press, 1990), 163.
45. Cone, *A Black Theology of Liberation*, 142.

46. González, *Mañana*, 164.
47. Enrique Dussel asserts that 21st century context of globalization is one in which an ethic of liberation must be understood simultaneously as an ethic of life: "The threatened destruction of the majority of humanity demands an *ethics of life* in response, and it is their suffering on such a global scale which moves me to reflection, and to seek to justify the necessity of their liberation from the chains in which they are shackled;" *Ethics of Liberation: In the Age of Globalization and Exclusion* (Durham, NC and London, UK: Duke University Press, 2013), xxii.
48. Gustavo Gutiérrez, *A Theology of Liberation: history, politics, and salvation, revised edition*, trans. Caridad Inda and John Eagleson eds. (London, UK: SCM, 2001), 207.
49. Gustavo Gutiérrez, *The God of Life*, trans. Matthew J. O'Connell (Maryknoll, NY: Orbis Books, 1991), 14–15.
50. Arturo Bañuelas, "U.S. Hispanic Theology: An Initial Assessment," in *Mestizo Christianity: Theology from the Latino Perspective*, Arturo Bañuelas ed. (Maryknoll, NY: Orbis Books, 1995), 77.
51. Virgilio Elizondo, "*Mestizaje* as a Locus of Theological Reflection," in *Mestizo Christianity: Theology from the Latino Perspective*, Arturo Bañuelas ed. (Maryknoll, NY: Orbis Books, 1995), 25–26.
52. Roberto S. Goizueta, "Fiesta: Life in the Subjunctive," in *From the Heart of Our People: Latino/a Explorations in Catholic Systematic Theology*, Orlando O. Espín and Miguel H. Díaz, eds. (Maryknoll: Orbis Books, 1999), 95.
53. See Ana María Díaz-Stevens, *Oxcart Catholicism on Fifth Avenue: The Impact of the Puerto Rican Migration upon the Archdiocese of New York* (Notre Dame: University of Notre Dame Press, 1993).
54. James H. Cone, *God of the Oppressed* (San Francisco, CA: Harper and Row Publishers, 1975), 243.
55. Ibid., 245.
56. I recognize that this word—*mulatizaje*—is not a "real" word in Spanish. I am coining it here to make the point that reconciliation for us means, in part, that we mend the parts of ourselves that have served to split our identity, and our allegiances, into parts without embracing the fullness of our multi-dimensional humanity, inclusive of the African, Taíno, Spanish cultures, as well as a myriad of other heritages which have become a unique mixture in contemporary Puerto Rican life. It also serves as a corrective to ways in which Blackness has been minimized and undermined among our own Puerto Rican people, who have also ascribed to racialized categories of white supremacy.

CHAPTER 7

Conclusion: The Best of Witnesses Among the Dry Bones

As I have tried to bring together all of the stories I have told—Santiago's, Soto's, Ferré's, my own and those of my people—to make some sense of them theologically, I feel as though I am standing in the middle of nowhere, in a wilderness of sorts. In that interstitial place, I was drawn back to the words of Albert Memmi, in his influential work *The Colonizer and the Colonized*. Written originally in 1957, Memmi uses his own experience as a Tunisian Jew educated in Paris with all the contradictions and ambiguities such an identity presented to him. Neither fully accepted in the world of the Sorbonne elite, nor among the Algerian Muslim majority, he chose to highlight the ills of colonization for both colonizer and colonized because he embodied and rejected the dehumanizing aspects of both. In a candid preface to the 1965 American edition (which he dedicated to "colonized" African Americans, just 5 years before James Cone would publish *A Black Theology of Liberation*), Memmi makes a startling admission: "My portrait of the colonized, which is very much my own, is preceded by a portrait of the colonizer. How could I have permitted myself, with all my concern about personal experience, to draw a portrait of the adversary? Here is a confession I have never made before: I know the colonizer from the inside almost as well as I know the colonized."[1]

Jean Paul Sartre[2] offers yet another insight into Memmi's perspective that is informed by such a precarious identity:

© The Author(s) 2017
T. Delgado, *A Puerto Rican Decolonial Theology*, New Approaches to Religion and Power, DOI 10.1007/978-3-319-66068-4_7

Memmi himself has experienced a twofold liability, a twofold rejection, in the process that sets colonizers against colonized, and "self-rejecting colonizers" against "self-accepting colonizers." He has understood the system so well because he felt it first as his own contradiction. He explains it very clearly in the book that such rendings of the spirit, plainly introjections of social conflicts, do not dispose the individual to action. But the man who suffers them, if he becomes aware of himself, can enlighten others through his self-examination: a "negligible force in the confrontation," he *represents* no one, but since he *is* everyone at once, he will prove to be the best of witnesses.[3]

As a Diaspora Puerto Rican woman in the USA, I see myself as a "negligible force in the confrontation," standing in the same place of contradiction articulated by Memmi out of his particular context almost half a century ago. I am a citizen of the USA by virtue of my birthplace; I am an heir of Puerto Rican nationality by virtue of my parentage. I live within a supposedly democratic governmental system; I acknowledge that the reality of my Puerto Rican colonial status falls far short of the democratic ideals espoused by that same system. I claim my heritage as Puerto Rican; I am rejected as such by many on the island who believe that I have lost the right to assert such ethnicity when my dominant language is English and I am privileged by all the benefits of life on the mainland. All the while, I am rejected, or at the very least held in suspicion, by the dominant white culture of the US as a Hispanic who is trying to take over the country with bilingualism and other such unmentionables. I am a Catholic Christian for whom the notion of freedom under God is more than just a notion; yet, I am troubled by the feeling of living in the "now" of oppression and the "not yet" of freedom. All of these contradictions are in tension within my very being; I straddle these multiple identities constantly, hoping to find a place to ground my footing.

And yet, the place of straddling is once again affirmed, by Memmi and Sartre and others, as a place of "incredible surprises," to use a term of Virgilio Elizondo's. This place is the home of Puerto Ricans in the United States; it is the space that resonates with the story of Rachel, for she too is a character of liminality, of inbetweenness. Perhaps that is why her name is invoked in the exilic prophecy of Jeremiah, who speaks of a God who hears the cries of a mother's anguish and offers the only type of comfort that can be offered when the children of a nation are no more. Perhaps that is why her name is invoked in the Gospel of Matthew on the occasion of the slaying of the innocent children at the hands of Herod, when the children of a nation are murdered and the one who survives is none other than the Son of God. Rachel *represents* no one, but since she *is* everyone at once, she will prove to be the best of witnesses.

I am not suggesting that the political climate in which Puerto Ricans live mirrors that of Memmi's Algeria, or Rachel's Judah. In fact, there is less of a distinction between the colonizer and the colonized, the oppressor and the oppressed, in the case of the Puerto Rican nation. However, I am suggesting that precisely because the lines are blurred and indistinctive, we are offered a unique opportunity to move toward self-acceptance and forgiveness, toward bridge building and solidarity. That is, we as Puerto Ricans cannot exactly expel the colonizer from our land in a revolutionary attempt to assert national sovereignty and begin to build anew, any more than we can expel the colonizer from within ourselves. We would be left with no one for all Puerto Ricans embody the colonizer in one way or the other, truth be told. It is not as simple as that; Puerto Rican opinion on both the island and mainland has neither confirmed the desire to maintain cultural sovereignty nor affirmed political colonialism via the perpetuation of the status quo. But delving deeper, perhaps we can imagine a day when, as Memmi envisions, the "liquidation of colonization is nothing but a prelude to complete liberation, to self-recovery." In this sense, the political arena is but a backdrop to the true and lasting work, which is the liberative transformation of the self into a full humanity. "The colonized must start with his own oppression, the deficiencies of his group. In order that his liberation may be complete, he must free himself from those inevitable conditions of his struggle... What will he then become?...Having reconquered all his dimensions, the former colonized will have become a man like any other...a whole and free man."[4]

What does this have to do with theology, one might ask? What makes this quest for freedom more than simply a changing of the guards at the gate? I believe it is a theological quest because it is one embarked upon with a vision of humanity that was bestowed upon us by our Creator, that we are fashioned in the image of God, whole and free. This covenant has been confirmed and affirmed over and over again through history where we see miracles happening on behalf of those who were rejected by society, who were turned away by the powerful and the mighty, yet who were favored by a God of the oppressed. I believe we, as Puerto Ricans, are among those who are looked upon with favor in the eyes of God, particularly when we are relegated to the margins of insignificance by the world. This is particularly true now as the trials of other nations and people across the globe—from Syria, to North Korea, to Afghanistan—take immediate precedence, and attract greater media attention, than the social, economic and political status of Puerto Ricans. Yet, I believe that God has a particular message to tell through the lives of our people, which is that even though we walk through the valley of death, we shall fear no evil because God is with us. I believe that God walks with us even when, in our ambiguous and precarious identity crisis, we have no ground upon which to walk. That is the story of God's preferential option for the lowly, which is the message repeated time and again by Jesus. And because we, as Puerto Ricans, represent no one, we are, in fact, everyone at once and may prove to be the best of witnesses.

The nature of a Puerto Rican decolonial theology, informed by identity, suffering and hope, and grounded in the life/death/resurrection of Christ is a powerful theology because it says that we, as Puerto Ricans, dare to live, right now, as a people who are called by name; we know who we are and what our purpose is. It is a powerful theology because it says that we, as Puerto Ricans, dare to experience our suffering as salvific in itself, not for the purpose of glorifying that suffering but to say that we need not wait for the suffering to diminish to experience salvation. We are saved because God has saved us here and now through God's free and unconditional love for us. It is a powerful theology because it says that we, as Puerto Ricans, can, will and do hope, not just in the future but in the present even in the midst of despairing situations; our hope is freeing because it says that we refuse to believe that despair is our lot in life. There is a promise that has been made to us already and we have yet to claim it. There is a promise that has been made to us already and we have yet to claim it by prophesying to our freedom.

The words of the prophet Ezekiel remind us that prophesying into the abyss of death can and does bring about life:

> They say, 'Our bones are dried up and our hope is gone; we are cut off.' Therefore, prophesy and say to them: 'This is what the Sovereign Lord says: My people, I am going to open your graves and bring you up from them; I will bring you back to the land of Israel. Then you, my people, will know that I am the Lord, when I open your graves and bring you up from them. I will put my Spirit in you and you will live, and I will settle you in

your own land. Then you will know that I the Lord have spoken, and I have done it, declares the Lord.'[5]

The project of a Puerto Rican decolonial theology, then, is a project of hearing the voices of our own people who, in subaltern and subversive ways, have been prophesying our freedom all along. We have been deafened, however, by the shrill of coloniality which tunes our ears toward a center that is beyond our subjectivity. Our voices call us back to ourselves, to a place that is not centered on the discourses of political status but rather on the interstices, small as they may be, between "torture and resistance."[6] If the thirty plus years of incarceration of Oscar López Rivera has taught us anything, it is that "spiritcide" is the objective of those who refuse our freedom, and an objective unsuccessfully attempted on Lopez Rivera as evidenced by his persistent efforts to write, paint, and communicate his subjectivity:

> I use the word "spiritcide" to describe the dehumanizing and pernicious existence that I have suffered since I have been a prisoner, particularly the years that I have been in this dungeon (labyrinth). It is spiritcide because the death and annihilation of the spirit are what the jailers are seeking by keeping me in such deleterious conditions. I face, on the one hand, an environment that is a sensory deprivation laboratory, and on the other hand, a regimen replete with obstacles to deny, destroy or paralyze my creativity. We know that sensory deprivation and the denial of creative activity causes the spirit to wither and die. That is exactly what the jailers are seeking by keeping me here."[7]

Oscar López Rivera embodies the colonial condition of the Puerto Rican community; while in no way minimizing the brutality of torture he experienced while incarcerated, what has been done to him via his imprisonment is a microcosm of what has been done to our people over the past 120 years of colonial subjugation by the USA. As a people, we must recognize the spiritcide that has been attempted on all fronts, not the least of which is a resignation that theology has nothing to say about coloniality. A Puerto Rican decolonial theology is not an exercise in the abstract; rather, it is

> ...a historical process of the liberation of socio-historical subjects, who have memory of their past, of their already past liberation battles (forgetting is part of falling into an entropic self-regulation), who have projects

and programs for a future fulfillment...who define strategy, tactics and methods of struggle to *transform* (at any level of practical complexity: from the norm to the ethical system) the social reality and subjectivity of each living human subject....[8]

The resistance to colonial oppression, to spiritcide, has been prophesied by our own stories, by our own experience, by our own people. Our Puerto Rican identity, our Puerto Rican suffering and our Puerto Rican hope have been woven through our stories, our embodied expressions of our creativity, not as colonial subjects, but as decolonized selves, standing on our feet in a vast multitude, in freedom and self-determination, not as a lost cause but transformed as the children of God.

NOTES

1. Albert Memmi, "Preface," in *The Colonizer and the Colonized*, (Boston: Beacon Press, 1965), xiii.
2. It is interesting to note that James Cone utilizes the work of Sartre significantly in *A Black Theology of Liberation* ([Maryknoll, NY: Orbis, 1986] 84–85), particularly in Chapter Five, "The Human Being in Black Theology," as a means of debunking the Christian understanding of humanity as it reflects a God that is aligned with the oppressor. "Although we see no need to deny the existence of God, we are glad for the presence of Camus and Sartre to remind theologians that the God-problem must never be permitted to detract from the concern for real human beings."
3. John Paul Sartre, "Introduction," in Memmi, *The Colonizer and the Colonized*, xxii.
4. Memmi, *The Colonizer and the Colonized*, 151–153.
5. Ezekiel 37: 1–14
6. Oscar López Rivera, *Between Torture and Resistance*, Luis Nieves Falcón ed. (Oakland, CA: PMPress, 2013).
7. Ibid., 47.
8. Enrique Dussel, *Ethics of Liberation: In the Age of Globalization and Exclusion* (Durham, NC and London, UK: Duke University Press, 2013), 398.

BIBLIOGRAPHY

(1) Socio-Historical Sources (Inc. Puerto Rican Religious/Missionary History)

a. General

Acosta-Belen, Edna. *The Puerto Rican Woman: perspectives on culture, history and society.* New York, NY: Praeger, 1986.

Barreto, Amilcar Antonio. *Language, Elites and the State: nationalism in Puerto Rico and Quebec.* Westport, CT: Praeger, 1998.

Bean, Frank D. *The Hispanic Population of the United States.* National Committee for Research on the 1980 Census: Russell Sage Foundation, 1987.

Benítez, José Antonio. *Puerto Rico and the Political Destiny of America.* Birmingham, AL: Southern University Press, 1958.

Bloomfield, Richard J., ed. *Puerto Rico: The Search for a National Policy.* Boulder, CO: Westview Press, 1985.

Bolioli, Oscar, ed. *The Caribbean: Culture of Resistance, Spirit of Hope.* New York, NY: Friendship Press, 1993.

Briggs, Laura. *Reproducing Empire: Race, Sex, Science, and U.S. Imperialism in Puerto Rico.* Berkley and Los Angeles, CA: University of California Press, 2002.

Burnett, Christina Duffy and Marshall, Burke, eds. *Foreign in a Domestic Sense: Puerto Rico, American Expansion and the Constitution.* Durham, NC and London, UK: Duke University Press, 2001.

© The Editor(s) (if applicable) and The Author(s) 2017
T. Delgado, *A Puerto Rican Decolonial Theology*, New Approaches to Religion and Power, DOI 10.1007/978-3-319-66068-4

Carr, Raymond. "Puerto Rico: a colonial experiment." *America* 152 (June 1985): 477.

Chávez, Linda. *Out of the Barrio: Toward a New Politics of Hispanic Assimilation.* New York, NY: HarperCollins Publishers, 1991.

"Children and the Households They Live In: 2000." Census 2000 Special Reports [Censr-14].

"Church leaders rally against U.S. Navy base [Vieques, Puerto Rico]." *Christian Century* 117. 8 (Mar 2000): 268–269.

Collazo, Sonia G., Camille L Ryan, Kurt J. Bauman. "Profile of the Puerto Rican Population in United States and Puerto Rico: 2008." Presentation. Annual Meeting of the Population Association of America, Dallas, TX. April 15–17, 2010.

Cordasco, Francesco and Bucchioni, Eugene, eds. *The Puerto Rican Experience.* Totowa, NJ: Littlefield, Adams and Co., 1973.

Denis, Nelson A. *War Against All Puerto Ricans: Revolution and Terror in America's Colony.* New York: Nation Books, 2015.

Díaz–Stevens, Ana María and Stevens-Arroyo, Anthony. *Oxcart Catholicism on Fifth Avenue: The Impact of the Puerto Rican Migration Upon the Archdiocese of New York.* Notre Dame, IN: University of Notre Dame Press, 1993.

———. *Recognizing the Latino resurgence in U.S. religion: the Emmaus paradigm.* Boulder, CO: Westview Press, 1998.

Dietz, James L. *Economic History of Puerto Rico: Institutional Change and Capitalist Development.* Princeton, NJ: Princeton University Press, 1986.

Diffie, Bailey Wallys and Justine Whitfield. *Puerto Rico: a Broken Pledge.* New York, NY: Vanguard Press, 1931.

Dolan, Jay P. and Vidal, Jaime R. *Puerto Rican and Cuban Catholics in the United States, 1900–1965.* South Bend, IN: University of Notre Dame Press, 1994.

Duany, Jorge. *Puerto Rican Nation on the Move: Identities on the Island and in the United States.* Chapel Hill, NC: University of North Carolina Press, 2002.

Duggan, Janie Prichard. *Child of the Sea: a Chronicle of Puerto Rico.* Philadelphia, PA: Judson Press, 1920.

Enck-Wanzer, Darrel. *The Young Lords: A Reader.* New York: New York University Press, 2010.

Ennis, Sharon R., Merarys Ríos-Vargas, and Nora G. Albert. *The Hispanic Population: 2010.* United States: U.S. Census Bureau, 2011.

EPICA Task Force. *Puerto Rico: A People Challenging Colonialism.* Washington, DC: EPICA Task Force, 1976.

del C. Fernández, Johanna L. "Radicals in the Late 1960s: A History of the Young Lords Party in New York City, 1969–1974." Dissertation. Columbia University, 2004.

Fitzpatrick, Joseph P. *Puerto Rican Americans: The meaning of migration to the mainland.* Englewood Cliffs, NJ: Prentice Hall, 1987.

———. *The Stranger is Our Own: Reflections on the journey of Puerto Rican migrants.* Kansas City, KS: Sheed and Ward, 1996.

Flores, Juan. *Divided Borders: Essays on Puerto Rican Identity.* Houston, TX: Arte Público Press, 1993.

Franks, Angela. *Margaret Sanger's Eugenic Legacy: The Control of Female Fertility.* Jefferson, NC: McFarland & Company, Inc. Publishers, 2005.

Garcia Coll, Cynthia T. and Mattei, Maria de Lourdes, eds. *The Psychosocial Development of Puerto Rican Women.* New York, NY: Praeger, 1989.

Godreau, Isar P. *Scripts of Blackness: Race, Cultural Nationalism, and U.S. Colonialism in Puerto Rico.* Urbana, Chicago, IL and Springfield, MA: University of Illinois Press, 2015.

Grosfoguel, Ramón. *Colonial Subjects: Puerto Ricans in Global Perspective.* Berkeley, CA: University of California Press, 2003.

Guerra, Lillian. *Popular Expression and National Identity in Puerto Rico: the struggle for self, community and nation.* Gainesville, FL: University Press of Florida, 1998.

Hanson, Earl Parker. *Transformation: the Story of Modern Puerto Rico.* New York, NY: Simon and Schuster, 1955.

Haslip-Viera, Gabriel and Baver, Sherrie L., eds. *Latinos in New York: Communities in Transition.* Notre Dame, IN: University of Notre Dame Press, 1996.

Howell, Leon. "Puerto Rico: Colony or country?" *Christianity and Crisis* 38 (May 1978): 120–123.

———. "For those in peril on Vieques." *One World* 55 (Apr 1980): 10–11.

Humphrey, Marj. "Vieques—invasions of privacy." *Catholic Worker* 48 (Apr 1982): 3–4.

Jackson, John P. and Nadine M. Weidman. *Race, Racism and Science: Social Impact and Interaction.* New Brunswick, NJ: Rutgers University Press, 2006.

James, Arthur. *Thirty Years in Puerto Rico: a Record of the Progress Since American Occupation.* San Juan, PR: Porto Rico Progress, 1927.

Jeffrey, Paul. "Vieques vs. the U.S. Navy: Island struggle rekindled." *Christian Century* 116: 767–769.

Latin American Perspectives. *Puerto Rico: Class Struggle and National Liberation.* Volume III, Number 3. Summer 1976. Riverside, CA: Latin American Perspectives, 1976.

Lewis, Gordon K. *Puerto Rico: Freedom and Power in the Caribbean.* New York, NY: Monthly Review Press, 1963.

López, Adalberto, ed. *The Puerto Ricans: their history, culture and society.* Rochester, VT: Schenkman Books, Inc., 1980.

López, Alfredo. *The Puerto Rican Papers: Notes on the Re-emergence of a Nation.* Indianapolis, IN: The Bobbs-Merrill Company, Inc., 1973.

López, Iris. *Matters of Choice: Puerto Rican Women's Struggle for Reproductive Freedom.* New Brunswick, NJ: Rutgers University Press, 2008.

López Rivera, Oscar. *Between Torture and Resistance.* Edited by Luis Nieves Falcón. Oakland: PM Press, 2013.

Macartney, Suzanne, Alemayehu Bishaw, and Kayla Fontenot, "Poverty Rates for Selected Detailed Race and Hispanic Groups by State and Place: 2007–2011." *American Community Survey Briefs.* Washington, D.C.: United States Census Bureau, 2013.

Machado, Daisy L. "The Historical Imagination and Latina/o Rights." *Union Seminary Quarterly Review* Vol. 56. Nos. 1–2 (2002): 162–165.

Maldonado–Denis, Manuel. *Puerto Rico y los Estados Unidos, emigración y colonialismo: un análisis sociohistórico de la emigración puertorriqueña.* Historia Imediata, 2nda edición. Mexico: Siglo Veintiuno Editores, 1978.

Manrique Cabrera, F. *Historia de la literatura puertorriqueña.* Rio Piedras, PR: Editorial Cultural, 1982.

Meléndez, Sara E. "American Democracy: A Puerto Rican perspective," in *A Voice of Our Own: leading American women celebrate the right to vote.* Nancy M. Neuman, ed. San Francisco, CA: Jossey-Bass Publishers, 1996.

Memmi, Albert. *The Colonizer and the Colonized.* Boston, MA: Beacon Press, 1965.

Mignolo, Walter. *The Darker Side of Western Modernity: Global Futures, Decolonial Options.* Durham, NC: Duke University Press, 2011.

Mintz, Sidney Wilfred. *Worker in the Cane: a Puerto Rican Life History.* New Haven, CT: Yale University Press, 1964.

Moore, Joan and Pinderhughes, Raquel, eds. *In the Barrios: Latinos and the Underclass Debate.* New York, NY: Russell Sage Foundation, 1993.

Morales Carrión, Arturo, ed. *Puerto Rico: A Political and Cultural History.* New York, NY: W. W. Norton and Company, Inc., 1983.

Morris, Nancy. *Puerto Rico: culture, politics and identity.* Westport, CT: Praeger, 1995.

Negron-Muntaner, Frances and Grosfoquel, Ramon, eds. *Puerto Rican Jam: rethinking colonialism and nationalism.* Minneapolis, MN: University of Minneapolis Press, 1997.

Nelson, Anne. *Murder Under Two Flags: The U.S., Puerto Rico, and the Cerro Maravilla Cover-Up.* Boston, MA: Ticknor and Fields, 1986.

Nelson, Jennifer A. "Abortions under Community Control." *Journal of Women's History* 13.1 (2001): 157–180.

Noonan, Daniel P. "Puerto Rico: a land and a people in search of an identity." *Our Sunday Visitor* 69: 3 (Dec 1980).

Pérez y González, María E. *Puerto Ricans in the United States.* Westport, CT: Greenwood Press, 2000.

Picó, Fernando. "Let Puerto Rico Decide [editorial]." *America* 178 (May 1998): 3–5.

Ramirez, Roberto and G. Patricia de la Cruz. *The Hispanic Population in the United States: March 2002.* Washington, D.C.: Current Population Reports U.S. Census Bureau, 2002.

Rand, Christopher. *The Puerto Ricans.* New York, NY: Oxford University Press, 1958.

Rivera-Batíz, Francisco L. and Santiago, Carlos E. *Island Paradox: Puerto Rico in the 1990's.* New York, NY: Russell Sage Foundation, 1996.

Rivera Pagán, Luís N. "Discovery and Conquest of America: Myth and Reality" *Apuntes* 9.4: 75–92.

Rodríguez, Clara E. *Puerto Ricans: Born in the U.S.A.* Boston, MA: Unwin Hyman, Inc., 1989.

———, Sánchez Korrol, Virginia and Alers, José Oscar, eds. *The Puerto Rican Struggle: Essays on Survival in the U.S.* New York, NY: Puerto Rican Migration Research Consortium, Inc., 1980.

Rodríguez-Silva, Ileana. *Silencing Race: Disentangling Blackness, Colonialism, and National Identities in Puerto Rico.* New York, NY: Palgrave Macmillan, 2012.

Rothenberg, Paula and Kelly Mayhew. *Race, Class and Gender in the United States.* 9th Edition. New York, NY: Worth Publishers, 2013.

Rowe, Lee Stanton. *The United States and Puerto Rico, with Special Reference to the Problems Arising Out of Our Contact with the Spanish American Civilization.* New York, NY: Longmans, Green and Co., 1904.

Saenz, Lydia Martínez. "The Pain of Racism: an Hispanic Perspective." *Engage/ Social Action* 9.10: 17–22.

Saenz, Michael. *Economic Aspects of Church Development in Puerto Rico: a Study of the Financial Policies and Procedures of the Major Protestant Church Groups in Puerto Rico from 1898 to 1957.* Dissertation. Philadelphia, PA: University of Pennsylvania, 1961.

Saez, Florencio. *Entre Cristo y Ché Guevara: historia de la subversion política en las iglesias evangélicas de Puerto Rico.* San Juan, PR: Editorial Palma Real, 1972.

Sandoval, Moises. *On the Move: a History of the Hispanic Church in the United States.* Maryknoll, NY: Orbis Books, 1990.

Schleicher, Andrew. "Bombs Away." *Sojourners* 28: 17 (Sept–Oct 1999).

Senior, Clarence Ollson. *The Puerto Ricans: Strangers—Then Neighbors.* Chicago, IL: Quadrangle Books, 1965.

———. *Puerto Rican Emigration.* Rio Piedras, PR: Social Science Research Center, University of Puerto Rico, 1974.

Silen, Juan Angel. *We, the Puerto Rican People: a story of oppression and resistance.* Trans. Cedric Belfrage. New York, NY: Monthly Review Press, 1971.

Silva Gotay, Samuel. "El Partido Acción Cristiana: trasfondo histórico y significado sociologico...en Puerto Rico." *Cristianismo y Sociedad* 29. 2(1991): 95–116.

———. *Protestantism y política en Puerto Rico, 1898-1930: hacia una historia del protestantismo en Puerto Rico [2nd edition].* San Juan, PR: Editorial de la Universidad de Puerto Rico, 1997.

Stevens-Arroyo, Anthony M. *Cave of the Jagua: The Mythological World of the Taínos.* Albuquerque, NM: University of New Mexico Press, 1988.

——— and Sánchez, María E., eds. *Toward a renaissance of Puerto Rican studies: ethnic and area studies in university education.* Boulder, CO: Social Science Monographs; Highland Lakes, N.J.: Atlantic Research and Publications; New York: Distributed by Columbia University Press, 1987.

——— and Pérez y Mena, Andrés I., eds. *Enigmatic powers : syncretism with African and indigenous peoples' religions among Latinos.* New York, NY: Bildner Center for Western Hemisphere Studies, 1995.

——— and Cadena, Gilbert R., eds. *Old masks, new faces : religion and Latino identities, first edition.* New York, NY: Bildner Center for Western Hemisphere Studies, 1995.

——— with Segundo Pantoja. *Discovering Latino religion: a comprehensive social science bibliography.* New York, NY: Bildner Center for Western Hemisphere Studies, 1995.

Suhor, Mary. "On the redemption of Puerto Rico." *Witness* 64 (1981): 14–16.

Talbot, John F. "The Oldest Colony is Growing Older." *America* 178(1998): 15–17.

The Young Lords Party. *Palante.* Chicago, IL: Haymarket Books, 2011.

Torres, Andrés and Velásquez, José E., eds. *The Puerto Rican Movement: Voices from the Diaspora.* Philadelphia, PA: Temple University Press, 1998.

Tumin, Melvin Marvin, and Feldman, Arnold S. *Social Class and Social Change in Puerto Rico.* Princeton, NJ: Princeton University Press, 1961.

United States War Department. *Annual Report of the Chief of the Bureau of Insular Affairs.* Washington, D.C.: United States War Department, 1924.

Wagenheim, Kal. *Puerto Rico: A Profile.* New York, NY: Praeger, 1970.

——— and the United States Commission on Civil Rights. *Puerto Ricans in the Continental U.S.: an Uncertain Future.* A report of the U.S. Commission on Civil Rights. Washington, DC: United States Commission on Civil Rights, 1976.

Walsh, Catherine E. *Pedagogy and the Struggle for Voice: Issues of Language, Power and Schooling for Puerto Ricans.* New York, NY: Bergin and Garvey, 1991.

Wanzer-Serrano, Darrel. *The New York Young Lords and the Struggle for Liberation.* Philadelphia, PA: Temple University Press, 2015.

Wiley Zwickel, Jean. *Voices for independence: in the spirit of honor and sacrifice.* Pittsburg, CA: White Star Press, 1988.

Weber, Max. *The Protestant Ethic and the Spirit of Capitalism.* Translated by Peter Baehr and Gordon C. Wells. New York, NY: Penguin Books, 2002.

Williams, Eric. *From Columbus to Castro: The History of the Caribbean, 1492–1969.* New York, NY: Vintage Books, 1970.

Zavala, Iris M. *Colonialism and Culture: Hispanic modernism and the social imaginary.* Bloomington, IN: Indiana University Press, 1992.

────── and Rodríguez, Rafael, eds. *The Intellectual Roots of Independence: An Anthology of Puerto Rican Political Essays.* New York, NY: Monthly Review Press, 1980.

b. Missionary Activity in Puerto Rico: 1898–1955

Davis, J. Merle. *The Church in Puerto Rico's Dilemma.* New York, NY and London, UK: International Missionary Council, 1942.

Dinwiddie, William. *Puerto Rico: Its Conditions and Possibilities.* New York, NY and London, UK: Harper and Brothers, 1899.

Douglass, H.P. *Congregational Missionary Work in Puerto Rico Conducted by the American Missionary Association.* New York, NY: American Missionary Association, n.d.

Drury, Marion R. *Mission Triumphs in Puerto Rico and Santo Domingo: a Story of Progress and Achievement in the West Indies.* Ponce, PR: Puerto Rico Evangélico Press, 1924.

Grose, Howard Benjamin. *Advance in the Antilles: the New Era in Cuba and Puerto Rico.* New York, NY: Presbyterian Home Missions, 1910.

Guernsey, Alice Margaret. *Lands of Sunshine.* New York: Women's Home Missionary Society of the Methodist Episcopal Church, 1916.

Hanson, Earl Parker. *Transformation: the Story of Modern Puerto Rico.* New York, NY: Simon and Schuster, 1955.

Inman, Samuel Guy. *Twenty-five Years of Mission Work in Puerto Rico.* Reprint from The Christian Work. 1925.

International Missionary Council. *The Church in Puerto Rico's Dilemma: a Study of the Economic and Social Basis of the Evangelical Church in Puerto Rico.* New York, NY: Department of social and economic research and counsel, International Missionary Council, 1942.

James, Arthur. *Progress and Promise in Puerto Rico.* Pamphlet. New York, NY: Board of National Missions, 1924.

Morehouse, Henry L. *Puerto Rico: a Narrative Sketch of Baptist Missions in the Island.* New York, NY: The American Baptist Home Mission Society, n.d.

Morton, Clement Manly. *Kingdom Building in Puerto Rico: a Story of Fifty Years of Christian Service.* Indianapolis, IN: United Christian Missionary Society, 1949.

Mount, Graeme S. "The Presbyterian Church in the USA and American rule in Puerto Rico, 1898—1917." *Journal of Presbyterian History* 57.1(1979): 51–64.

———. "Presbyterianism in Puerto Rico: Formative Years, 1899–1914." *Journal of Presbyterian History* 55 (3): 241–254, 1977.

Presbyterian Church in the USA. *Puerto Rico Calls.* A report of the Presbyterian Church. New York, NY: Polytechnic Institute of Puerto Rico, 1954.

(2) Literary Sources

a. Primary

Ferré, Rosario. "The Writing Kitchen," *Feminist Studies* 2 (Summer 1986): 243–249.

———. *Sweet Diamond Dust and other stories.* New York, NY: Ballantine Books, 1989.

———. *The Youngest Doll.* Lincoln, NE: University of Nebraska Press, 1991.

———. *The House on the Lagoon.* New York, NY: Ferrar, Straus, Giroux, 1995.

———. *Eccentric Neighborhoods.* New York, NY: Ferrar, Straus, Giroux, 1998.

———. *The Flight of the Swan.* New York, NY: Penguin Putnam, 2001.

Santiago, Esmeralda. *When I Was Puerto Rican.* New York, NY: Vintage/ Random House, 1993.

———. *América's Dream.* New York, NY: HarperCollins, 1996.

———. *Almost A Woman.* New York, NY: Vintage/Random House, 1999.

——— and Davidow, Joie, eds. *Las Christmas: Favorite Latino Authors Share their Holiday Memories.* New York, NY: Vintage/Random House, 1999.

Soto, Pedro Juan. *Usmaíl.* Trans., Charlie Connelly and Myrna Pagán. St. John/ US Virgin Islands: Sombrero Publishing Company, 2007. Originally published in Spanish under the title *Usmaíl* by Editorial Cultural, Rio Piedras, PR: 1959.

———. *Hot Land, Cold Season.* Trans., Helen R. Lane. New York, NY: Dell Publishing Co., 1973. Originally published in Spanish under the title *Ardiente Suelo, Fria Estación,* by Ficción Universidad Veracruzana, Mexico: 1961.

———. *Spiks.* Trans., Victoria Ortíz. New York, NY: Monthly Review Press, 1973. Originally published in Spanish under the title *Spiks,* by Editorial Cultural, Rio Piedras, PR: 1970.

b. Secondary (Inc. Literature/Theology Dialogue)

Acevedo, Ramon L. *Del Silencio al Estallido: narrativa femenina puertorriqueña.* Rio Piedras, PR: Cultural, 1991.

Acosta-Belén, Edna. *Literature and Ideology in the Works of the Puerto Rican Generation of 1950.* Dissertation. New York, NY: Columbia University, 1977.

Alves, Rubem. *The Poet, The Warrior, The Prophet.* London, UK and Philadelphia, PA: SCM and Trinity Press, 1990.

Anzaldúa, Gloria. *Borderlands/La Frontera: The New Mestiza.* Fourth Edition. San Francisco, CA: Aunt Lute Books, 2012.

Brown, Robert MacAfee. *Persuade Us to Rejoice: The Liberating Power of Fiction.* Louisville, KY: Westminster/John Knox Press, 1992.

—— and Salyer, George, eds. *Literature and Theology at Century's End.* Atlanta, GA: Scholars Press, 1995.

Detweiler, Robert and Jasper, David, eds. *Religion and Literature: A Reader.* Louisville, KY: Westminster John Knox Press, 2000.

Fiddes, Paul S. *Freedom and Limit: A Dialogue between Literature and Christian Doctrine.* Macon, GA: Mercer University Press, 1999.

Gallagher, Susan VanZanten, ed. *Postcolonial Literature and the Biblical Call for Justice.* Jackson, MS: University Press of Mississippi, 1994.

Gómez, Alma, Moraga, Cherríe and Romo-Carmona, Mariana, eds. *Cuentos: Stories by Latinas.* New York, NY: Kitchen Table: Women of Color Press, 1983.

Gonzáles-Berry, Erlinda and Tatum, Chuck, eds. *Recovering the U.S. Hispanic Literary Heritage.* Volume 2. Houston, TX: Arte Público Press, 1996.

Jasper, David, ed. *The Study of Literature and Religion.* Minneapolis, MN: Fortress Press, 1989.

Jens, Walter and Küng, Hans, *Literature and Religion.* Trans., Peter Heinegg. New York, NY: Paragon House, 1991.

Kanellos, Nicolás, ed. *Biographical Dictionary of Hispanic Literature in the United States.* New York, NY: Greenwood Press, 1989.

Mahoney, John L., ed. *Seeing into the Life of Things: Essays on Religion and Literature.* New York, NY: Fordham University Press, 1998.

Marqués, René. *The Docile Puerto Rican.* Philadelphia, PA: Temple University Press, 1976.

Middleton, Darren J. N., ed. *God, Literature and Process Thought.* Burlington, VT: Ashgate Publishing Co., 2002.

Mohr, Eugene. *The Nuyorican Experience: Literature of the Puerto Rican Minority.* Westport, CT: Greenwood Press, 1982.

Morales, Rosario and Levins Morales, Aurora. *Getting Home Alive.* Ithaca, NY: Firebrand Books, 1986.

Pérez, Emma. *The Decolonial Imaginary: Writing Chicanas into History.* Bloomington and Indianapolis, IN: Indiana University Press, 1999.

Reagan, Charles E. and Stewart, David, eds. *The Philosophy of Paul Ricoeur.* Boston, MA: Beacon, 1978.

Ricoeur, Paul. *The Symbolism of Evil.* Emerson Buchanan, trans. Boston, MA: Beacon, 1967.

——. *The Conflict of Interpretations: essays in hermeneutics.* Don Ihde, ed. Evanston, IL: Northwestern University Press, 1974.

————. *Figuring the Sacred: religion, narrative and imagination*. David Pellauer, trans. Minneapolis, MN: Fortress Press, 1995.

————. *Memory, History, Forgetting*. Kathleen Blamey and David Pellauer, trans. Chicago, IL: University of Chicago Press, 2004.

Ryan-Ranson, Helen, ed. *Imagination, Emblems and Expressions: Essays on Latin American, Caribbean, and continental culture and identity*. Bowling Green, OH: Bowling Green State University Popular Press, 1993.

Sánchez-González, Lisa. *Boricua Literature: A Literary History of the Puerto Rican Diaspora*. New York, NY: New York University Press, 2001.

Santiago, Roberto, ed. *Boricuas: Influential Puerto Rican Writings—An Anthology*. New York, NY: Ballantine Books, 1995.

Scott, Nathan. *The Broken Center*. New Haven, CT: Yale University Press, 1966.

Walton, Heather and Hass, Andrew W., eds. *Self/Same/Other: Re-visioning the Subject in Literature and Theology*. Sheffield, UK: Sheffield Academic Press, 2000.

Wright, T. R. *Theology and Literature*. Oxford, UK: Basil Blackwell, 1988.

(3) Archetypal Psychology Sources

Estés, Clarissa Pinkola. *Women Who Run with the Wolves: Myths and Stories of the Wild Woman Archetype*. New York, NY: Ballantine Books, 1992.

Hall, Calvin S. and Nordby, Vernon J. *A Primer of Jungian Psychology*. New York, NY: Penguin Books USA, Inc., 1973.

Ulanov, Ann and Barry. *Religion and the Unconscious*. Philadelphia, PA: The Westminster Press, 1975.

————. *The Healing Imagination*. Mahwah, NJ: Paulist Press, 1991.

Winquist, Charles. *Homecoming: Interpretation, Transformation and Individuation*. Ann Arbor, MI: Scholars Press, 1978.

(4) Theology/Ethics/Religion Sources

a. Latinx Theology/Ethics/Religion (Inc. Caribbean and Latin American)

Ábalos, David T. *Latinos in the United States: the Sacred and the Political*. Notre Dame, IN: University of Notre Dame Press, 1986.

Aquino, María Pilar. "Directions and Foundations of Hispanic/Latino Theology: Toward a Mestiza Theology of Liberation." *Journal of Hispanic/Latino Theology* 1.1: 5–21.

———— and Goizueta, Roberto S., eds. *Theology: Expanding the Borders*. Mystic, CT: Twenty-third Publications, 1998.

Álvarez, Carmelo. "Theology from the Margins: A Caribbean Response..." in *Theology: Expanding the Borders*. María Pilar Aquino and Roberto S. Goizueta, eds. Mystic, CT: Twenty-third Publications, 1998.

Alves, Rubem. *A Theology of Human Hope*. Cleveland, OH: Corpus Books, 1969.

Bañuelas, Arturo, ed. *Mestizo Christianity: Theology from the Latino Perspective*. Maryknoll, NY: Orbis Books, 1995.

Barrios, Luís. *Josconiando: Dimensiones Sociales y Políticas de la Espiritualidad*. Santo Domingo, DR: Editora Aquiar, 2000.

Bradford, William Penn. "Puerto Rican Spiritism: Contrasts in the Sacred and the Profane." *Caribbean Quarterly* 24.3–4: 48–55.

Carmona, Juan A. *The Liberation of Puerto Rico: a theological perspective*. D. Min. Thesis. Rochester, NY: Colgate-Rochester Divinity School/Crozer Theological Seminary, 1982.

Cortés, Carlos E. ed. *Protestantism and Latinos in the United States*. New York, NY: Arno Press, 1990.

Costas, Orlando E. *Christ Outside the Gate: Mission beyond Christendom*. Maryknoll, NY: Orbis Books, 1982.

Davis, Kortright. *Emancipation Still Comin': Explorations in Caribbean Emancipatory Theology*. Maryknoll, NY: Orbis Books, 1990.

Deck, Allan Figueroa. *Frontiers of Hispanic Theology in the United States*. Maryknoll, NY: Orbis Books, 1992.

———. "Latino Theology: the Year of the 'Boom'." *Journal of Hispanic/Latino Theology* 1.2: 51–63.

Díaz, Rey. "La Liberación Hispana En USA." *Apuntes* 9.1: 13–15.

Díaz-Stevens, Ana María and Stevens-Arroyo, Anthony M., eds. *An Enduring Flame: Studies on Latino Popular Religiosity*. New York, NY: Bildner Center of Western Hemisphere Studies, 1994.

———. *Galilean Journey: the Mexican-American Promise*. Maryknoll, NY: Orbis Books, 1983.

———. *Guadalupe: Mother of the New Creation*. Maryknoll, NY: Orbis Books, 1997.

———. *The Future is Mestizo: Life Where Cultures Meet, revised edition*. Boulder, CO: University Press of Colorado, 2000.

Elizondo, Virgilio. *A God of Incredible Surprises: Jesus of Galilee*. Lanham, MD: Rowman and Littlefield Publishing Group, Inc., 2003.

Erskine, Noel Leo. *Decolonizing Theology: A Caribbean Perspective*. Maryknoll, NY: Orbis Books, 1981.

Espín Orlando O. and Díaz, Miguel H., eds. *From the Heart of our People: Latino/a explorations in Catholic systematic theology*. Maryknoll, NY: Orbis Books, 1999.

Fenton, Jerry Floyd. *Understanding the Religious Background of the Puerto Rican*. B.D. Thesis. New York, NY: Union Theological Seminary, 1964.

Fernández, Eduardo C. *La Cosecha: Harvesting Contemporary United States Hispanic Theology, 1972–1998)*. Collegeville, MN: Liturgical Press, 2000.

García, Sixto J. "Sources and Loci of Hispanic Theology." *Journal of Hispanic/ Latino Theology* 1.1: 22–43.

Gómez, José Ramos. *The Santos: Symbol of Puerto Rico's Identity Conflict.* Dissertation. Berkeley, CA: Graduate Theological Union, 1981.

González, Justo L. "Prophets in the King's Sanctuary [Introduction to First Issue of Apuntes; Amos 7:13]." *Apuntes* 1.1: 3–6.

Gutierrez, Gustavo. *Mañana: Christian Theology from a Hispanic Perspective.* Nashville, TN: Abingdon Press, 1990.

———. "The Christ of Colonialism." *Church and Society* 1(Jan-Feb 1992): 21–23.

———, ed. *Voces: Voices from the Hispanic Church.* Nashville, TN: Abingdon Press, 1992.

———. *The Power of the Poor in History: selected writings.* Translated by Robert R. Barr. Maryknoll, NY: Orbis Books, 1983.

———. *On Job: God-talk and the suffering of the innocent.* Translated by Matthew J. O'Connell. Maryknoll, NY: Orbis Books, 1987.

———. *The Truth Shall Make You Free: confrontations.* Translated by Matthew J. O'Connell. Maryknoll, NY: Orbis Books, 1990.

———. *The God of Life.* Translated by Matthew J. O'Connell. Maryknoll, NY: Orbis Books, 1991.

———. *A Theology of Liberation: history, politics and salvation, revised edition.* Translated and edited by Caridad Inda and John Eagleson. London, UK: SCM, 2001.

———. *We drink from our own wells: the spiritual journey of a people, 20th anniversary edition.* Translated by Matthew J. O'Connell. Maryknoll, NY: Orbis Books, 2003.

——— with Shaull, Richard. *Liberation and Change.* Atlanta, GA: John Knox Press, 1977.

Isasi–Díaz, Ada María. "Apuntes for a Hispanic Women's Theology of Liberation." *Apuntes* 6.3: 61–71.

———. "Praxis: the Heart of Mujerista Theology." *Journal of Hispanic/Latino Theology* 1.1: 44–55.

——— and Tarango, Yolanda. *Hispanic Women: Prophetic Voice in the Church.* San Francisco, CA: Harper and Row Publishers, 1988.

Lara–Braud, Jorge. "Reflexiones Teológicas Sobre La Migración." *Apuntes* 2.1: 3–7.

López, Hugo L. "Toward a Theology of Migration." *Apuntes* 2.3: 68–71.

———. "El Divino Migrante." *Apuntes* 4.1: 14–19.

Orsini Luiggi, Sadi. *Canto al cemí: leyendas y mitos taínos.* San Juan, PR: Instituto de Cultura Puertorriqueña, 1974.

Recinos, Harold J. *Hear the Cry! a Latino Pastor Challenges the Church.* Louisville, KY: Westminster/John Knox Press, 1989.

———. *Jesus Weeps: Global Encounters on Our Doorstep.* Nashville, TN: Abingdon Press, 1992.

Rembao, Alberto. "Hispanic Culture and Christian Faith." *Theology Today* 16.3: 338–344.

Rivera Pagán, Luís N. *Liberación y Paz: Reflexiones Teológicas desde América Latina.* Guaynabo, PR: Editorial Sonador, 1988.

———. *A La Sombra Del Armagedón.* Rio Piedras, PR: Editorial Edil, 1989.

———. *A Violent Evangelism.* Louisville, KY: Westminster John Knox Press, 1992.

Rodríguez, Jeanette. "Experience as a Resource for Feminist Thought." *Journal of Hispanic/Latino Theology* 1.1: 68–76.

Rosado, Caleb. "Thoughts on a Puerto Rican Theology of Community." *Apuntes* 9.1: 10–12.

Sandín–Fremaint, Pedro A. "Hacia Una Teología Feminista Puertorriqueña." *Apuntes* 4.2: 27–37.

Silva Gotay, Samuel. *El Cristiano Revolucionario en América Latina y el Caribe.* Salamanca, ES: Sígueme, 1982.

———. *La Teología de la Liberación: implicaciones para la iglesia y para el marxismo: implicaciones de la teología de la liberación para la sociología de la religión.* Santo Domingo, DR: Ediciones de CEPAE, 1985.

———. "La iglesia católica en el proceso político." *Cristianismo y Sociedad* 23. 4 (1985): 7–34.

Sobrino, Jon. *Spirituality of Liberation* [English translation]. Maryknoll, NY: Orbis Books, 1988.

Solivan, Samuel. *Orthopathos: prolegomenon for a North American Hispanic theology.* Dissertation. New York, NY: Union Theological Seminary, 1993.

Stevens–Arroyo, Anthony. *Prophets Denied Honor: an Anthology of the Hispano Church of the United States.* Maryknoll, NY: Orbis Books, 1980.

Traverzo, David. "Towards a Theology of Mission in the U.S. Puerto Rican Migrant Community: from Captivity to Liberation." *Apuntes* 9.3: 51–59.

Villafañe, Eldín. *The Liberating Spirit: Toward an Hispanic American Pentecostal Social Ethic.* 1992 University Press of America. Grand Rapids, MI: William B. Eerdmans Publishing Co., 1992.

b. General Theology/Ethics (Inc. Biblical Sources)

Adams, James Luther. *Paul Tillich's Philosophy of Culture, Science and Religion.* New York, NY: Harper and Row, 1965.

Barnes, Michael Horace, ed. *Theology and the Social Sciences.* College Theology Society 2000 Volume 46. Maryknoll, NY: Orbis Books, 2001.

Brown, Delwin. *To Set at Liberty: Christian Faith and Human Freedom.* Maryknoll, NY: Orbis Books, 1981.

Brueggeman, Walter. *The Prophetic Imagination.* Philadelphia, PA: Fortress Press, 1978.

Cone, James H. *God of the Oppressed*. San Francisco, CA: Harper and Row, 1975.
———. *A Black Theology of Liberation, second edition*. Maryknoll, NY: Orbis Books, 1986.
———. *Black Theology and Black Power, 20ᵗʰ anniversary edition*. San Francisco, CA: HarperCollins Publishers, 1989.

Crossan, John Dominic. *The Dark Interval: Towards a Theology of Story*. Sonoma, CA: Polebridge Press, 1988.

Dresner, Samuel H. *Rachel*. Minneapolis, MN: Augsburg Fortress, 1994.

Dussel, Enrique. *Ethics of Liberation: In the Age of Globalization and Exclusion*. Durham, NC and London, UK: Duke University Press, 2013.

Gorringe, Timothy J. *Discerning Spirit: A Theology of Revelation*. London, UK: SCM Press; Philadelphia: Trinity Press International, 1990.

Hodgson, Peter C. and King, Robert H, eds. *Christian Theology: An Introduction to its Tasks and Traditions, second edition*. Philadelphia, PA: Fortress Press, 1985.

Kaspar, Walter. *The Christian Understanding of Freedom and the History of Freedom in the Modern Era*. Milwaukee, WI: Marquette University Press, 1988.

Kelly, Geffrey B., ed. *Karl Rahner: theologian of the graced search for meaning*. Minneapolis, MN: Augsburg Fortress Press, 1992.

Law, David R. *Inspiration*. London, UK and New York, NY: Continuum Books, 2001.

Mays, James L., ed., with the Society of Biblical Literature. *Harper's Bible Commentary*. San Francisco, CA: HarperCollins, 1988.

McKelway, Alexander J. *The Freedom of God and Human Liberation*. London, UK: SCM Press, 1990.

Migliore, Daniel. *Called to Freedom: liberation theology and the future of Christian doctrine*. Philadelphia, PA: Westminster, 1980.

Morse, Christopher. *Not Every Spirit: A Dogmatics of Christian Disbelief*. Valley Forge, PA: Trinity Press International, 1994.

Newsom, Carol A. and Sharon H. Ringe. *The Women's Bible Commentary*. Louisville, KY: Westminster/John Knox Press, 1992.

Nolan, Edward Peter. *Cry Out and Write: A Feminine Poetics of Revelation*. New York, NY: Continuum, 1994.

Novak, Michael. *Freedom with Justice: Catholic social thought and liberal institutions*. San Francisco, CA: Harper and Row, 1984.

Ortega-Aponte, Elias. "Young Lords Party." In *Hispanic American Religious Culture, Encyclopedia*. Edited by Miguel De La Torre. Pages 583–585. United States: ABC-CLIO, 2009.

Rahner, Karl. *Nature and Grace*. Trans., Dinah Livingstone and G. Richard Dimler. London, UK: Sheed and Ward, 1963.

———. *Meditations on Freedom and the Spirit*. Translated from the German by Rosaleen Ockenden, David Smith, and Cecily Bennett. New York, NY: Seabury Press, 1978.

———. *Theological Investigations: Vol. XVIII, God and Revelation*. New York, NY: Crossroad, 1983.

Reeves, Donald. *The Church and the State*. London, UK: Hodder and Stoughton, 1984.

Song, Choan-Seng. *Tell us our names: story theology from an Asian perspective*. Maryknoll, NY: Orbis Books, 1984.

Spivey, Robert A. and Smith, D. Moody. *Anatomy of the New Testament: A Guide to its Structure and Meaning*. New York, NY: Macmillan Publishing Co., 1982.

Tillich, Paul. *Theology of Culture*. New York, NY: Oxford University Press, 1959.

———. *Political Expectation*. New York, NY: Harper and Row, 1971.

Walsh, David. *After Ideology: recovering the spiritual foundations of freedom*. San Francisco, CA: Harper, 1990.

Wartenberg, Thomas E., ed. *Rethinking Power*. Albany, NY: State University of New York Press, 1992.

Weaver, Jace. *That the people might live: Native American literatures and Native American community*. New York, NY: Oxford University Press, 1997.

Weigel, George, ed. *A New Worldly Order: John Paul II and human freedom*. Washington, D.C.: Ethics and Public Policy Center, 1992.

West, Cornel. *Prophesy Deliverance!: An Afro-American Revolutionary Christianity*. Philadelphia, PA: Westminster Press, 1982.

Wink, Walter. *Unmasking the Powers: The Invisible Forces That Determine Human Existence*. Minneapolis, MN: Augsburg Fortress Press, 1986.

———. *Engaging the Powers: Discernment and Resistance in a World of Domination*. Minneapolis, MN: Augsburg Fortress Press, 1992.

Worsley, Richard. *Human Freedom and the Logic of Evil*. Bassingstoke, UK: Macmillan Press; New York: St. Martin's Press, 1996.

Wozniak, Kenneth W. M. and Grenz, Stanley J., eds. *Christian Freedom: Essays in Honor of Vernon C. Grounds*. Lanham, MD: University Press of America, 1988.

(5) Print/Online News Sources

Fritz, Sonia. *América*. Puerto Rico: Isla Films, 2011. Film.

Gibney, James. "As Cuba rises, Puerto Rico keeps on slipping: Caribbean U.S. Policies Raise Questions." *Bloomberg View*. March 27, 2016.

Letter from Admiral V.E. Clark, Chief of Naval Operations, to Gordon England, Secretary of the Navy, on December 10, 2002. *Vieques Libre*. 2002. www.viequeslibre.com.

McGee, Jim. "Ex-Justice Offical Cites 'Coverup' by FBI in '78 Puerto Rico Shootings." *The Washington Post.* May 9, 1992. https://www.washington-post.com/archive/politics/1992/05/09/ex-justice-official-cites-coverup-by-fbi-in-78-puerto-rico-shootings/722ead3e-b875-461d-957e-9ef43f1c481b.

Melendez, Josue. "Clearing Out without Cleaning Up: The U.S. and Vieques Island." Council on Hemispheric Affairs (COHA) Forum, May 19, 2011.

Pew Research Center. "Puerto Rican Population By County." August 11, 2014. http://www.pewhispanic.org/2014/08/11/puerto-rican-population-by-county/

"Puerto Ricans Were Kneeling When Killed By Police, Officer Says." *The New York Times.* November 30, 1983. http://www.nytimes.com/1983/11/30/us/puerto-ricans-were-kneeling-when-killed-by-police-officer-says.html;

Reina-Pérez, Pedro. "Puerto Rico's imperial hangover." *The Boston Globe.* March 23, 2016.

Rubin, A. "Records No Longer for Doctors' Eye Only." *Los Angeles Times.* September 1, 1998.

Stuart, Reginald. "Investigations and Indictments Harming Image of Puerto Rico Law; Officials." *The New York Times.* July 28, 1983. http://www.nytimes.com/1983/07/28/us/investigations-and-indictments-harming-image-of-puerto-rico-law-officials.html;

(6) Legal Sources

H.R. 1645 Vieques Recovery and Development Act of 2011. https://www.congress.gov/bill/112th-congress/house-bill/1645.

Submission to the United Nations Universal Periodic Review. Ninth Session of the Working Group on the UPR Human Rights Council. "THE NEGATIVE IMPACT OF U.S. FOREIGN POLICY ON HUMAN RIGHTS IN COLOMBIA, HAITI AND PUERTO RICO." November 2010.

INDEX

A

African, 23, 24, 29–31, 35, 48
Alienation, 146, 149, 161
Almost a Woman, 74, 78, 84, 95, 102, 103
América's Dream, 74, 75, 84, 95, 101
Anthropology, 62, 84, 86, 89, 94, 96–99, 105
Anzaldúa, Gloria, 90, 103
Archetype, 149, 153, 175
Autonomy, 2, 5, 27–29, 32, 37, 38, 49, 51, 131

B

Bañuelas, Arturo, 169, 177
Barbosa, José Celso, 28
Barrio, 41–46
Betances, Ramón Emeterio, 28
Bush, 4

C

Calle 13, 46
Catholic, 24, 25, 27, 30, 31, 35, 36, 42, 44, 48, 50, 53, 131, 133, 135, 136, 151, 153, 154, 162, 163, 172, 177
Campos, Pedro Albizu, 33, 34, 39
de Castro, Román Baldorioty, 28
Catholicism, 25, 30, 33, 35, 53, 54, 56
Center for Puerto Rican Studies, 9
Cerro Marrovilla Massacre, 108
Christian, 25, 30, 48, 50, 86–94, 103, 108, 124–132, 134, 135, 139, 141, 158–163, 166, 167, 173, 176
Christianity, 24, 30, 35, 48, 128, 136, 141, 163, 177
Church, 146, 160, 162
Cintrón, Rosendo Matienzo, 28, 34
Clinton, 3, 4
Coffee, 23, 26, 27, 31, 34
Colonial, 4, 6, 8, 11, 13, 15, 25–28, 30, 32, 33, 35, 39, 42, 45, 46, 49, 54, 155, 175, 180, 183, 184
Colonialism, 138, 152, 154, 181
Colonization, 8, 12, 21, 25–27, 47, 56, 134, 158, 179, 181
Colonized, 9
Commonwealth, 5, 9, 16

© The Editor(s) (if applicable) and The Author(s) 2017
T. Delgado, *A Puerto Rican Decolonial Theology*, New Approaches to
Religion and Power, DOI 10.1007/978-3-319-66068-4

Community, 73, 77, 78, 81, 83, 85, 86, 88, 89, 91, 93, 94, 97, 98, 102, 103, 121–127, 129, 133–138, 141, 145, 156, 157, 159–161, 163, 164, 167, 170–173, 175
Cone, James, 97, 166, 171, 176, 179, 184
Cotidiano, 11
Creation, 143, 145, 158, 159, 168, 170
Cuba, 26, 28, 29, 59

D
Debt, 38, 46
Decolonial, 6, 11, 12, 14, 21, 130, 134, 137, 182, 183
Democracy, 151
Democratic, 180
Depression, 31, 33
Detweiler, Robert, 145, 174
Diaspora, 63, 65, 68, 180
Díaz-Stevens, Ana María, 9, 20
de Diego, José, 28, 33, 61, 70

E
El Grito de Lares, 29
Elizondo, Virgilio, 180
Emancipation, 29, 50
Empire, 26, 27, 33, 49
Eschatological, 160–164, 166–173
Eschatology, 62, 159–161, 164, 166, 167, 169, 172, 174
Esperanza, 5
Espín, 10

F
FALN, 40, 44
Ferré, Luís, 39, 40

Ferré, Rosario, 24, 47, 143, 144, 150, 156, 174, 175
Fiesta, 169–171
Foracker Act, 32
Freedom, 4, 6, 9–15, 74–79, 86–90, 92, 93, 95, 98, 101, 105, 109, 125–131, 133, 134, 136, 137, 143–145, 149, 150, 158–160, 163, 166, 172–175, 180–184

G
Garbage Offensive, 45, 58
Generation of 1940, 107, 108
Genesis, 90, 93, 94
Goizueta, Roberto, 169
González, Jose Luís, 107
González, Justo, 167
Gospel, 124, 134, 138
Grace, 124–127, 129, 131, 132, 136, 137, 140
Great Migration, 12, 14
Great Puerto Rican Migration, 36
Grosfoguel, Ramón, 100, 105
Gutiérrez, Gustavo, 21, 130, 140

H
Hope, 4, 7, 9, 12, 16, 62–66, 69–71, 155, 157–161, 163–173, 176
de Hostos, Eugenio Maria, 28
The House on the Lagoon, 145, 147, 149, 151, 156, 157, 159, 174–176

I
Identity, 2, 7, 9, 12, 16, 62, 65–67, 69–71, 77, 79, 81–87, 89–101, 103–105, 119, 129, 135, 144–146, 148, 155, 158, 159, 165, 169–171, 173, 177

Independence, 5, 9, 11, 14, 26, 28, 29, 32–35, 39, 40, 46, 49, 52, 59, 143, 145, 152–154, 158
Industrialization, 150, 151
Industry, 152, 157
Injustice, 144, 149, 168
Isasi-Díaz, 7, 8, 10

J
Jasper, David, 62, 71
Jeremiah, 93, 94, 99, 129, 130, 132, 140, 164, 180
Justice, 10, 15, 21, 45, 65, 66, 72

K
Kingdom, 162, 163, 166
Kingdom of God, 131, 132

L
La naturaleza, 150
Lares, 28
La tierra, 170
Latinx theology, 6–8, 11
Lebrón, Lolita, 40
Liberation, 131–133, 140, 166, 168, 171, 172, 177
Lincoln Hospital, 45, 58
Llosa, Mario Vargas, 143
Love, 86–89, 91–93, 98, 100, 103, 110, 114, 115, 119, 123, 125–132, 134, 136, 137, 140

M
Marín, Luís Muñoz, 35, 37, 109
Marqués, René, 11, 20, 107
Matthew, 93, 94, 103, 161, 164–166, 170, 176, 177, 181
Memmi, Albert, 179, 184

Mestizaje, 96, 97, 173
Migration, 35–37, 39, 40, 43, 54, 55
Morales, Rosario, 68, 72
Morse, Christopher, 87, 93, 103
Movement for National Liberation, 44
Mujerista, 7
Mulataje, 173
Museo del Barrio, 45
Myth, 74–76, 78, 101

N
Nationalism, 152, 155
Nationalist Party, 33, 35, 39, 44
Nationality, 180
Navy, 2–5, 16–18
Nuevo Despertar, 46
Nuyorican, 45

O
Operation Bootstrap, 15, 20, 36–39, 54, 55, 151
Oppression, 131, 132, 136, 140

P
Parable, 75, 76, 78, 84, 86, 101
Patriarchy, 154
Pentecostal, 30, 36, 47, 163
PIP, 40, 44
Political, 108, 120, 131–133, 137, 138, 181–183
Ponce massacre, 34
Postmodern, 145
PPD, 37, 39, 40
Prophecy, 129, 180
Prophetic, 6, 9, 10, 12, 74, 76, 93, 94, 99, 149, 155, 168, 169, 172
Protestant, 30, 31, 35, 36, 44, 50, 51, 53
Puerto Rican Socialist Party, 44

Puerto Rican Student Union, 44

R
Rachel, 93–96, 100, 104, 127, 129, 130, 140, 164–166, 170, 176, 180, 181
Reconciliation, 154, 156, 157, 159, 171–174, 177
Revolution, 131
Revolving door, 170–172
Rivera, Luís Muñoz, 28
Rivera, Oscar López, 46, 59, 183, 184
Rodríguez, David Sanes, 1–3
Rodríguez, Sanes, 2, 6

S
Salvation, 7, 16, 108, 117, 120, 122, 124–137, 140, 141
Sánchez, Luís Rafael, 107
Santiago, Esmeralda, 24, 47, 62, 73, 74, 84, 101, 137
Santiago, Roberto, 63, 71
Sartre, Jean Paul, 179
Segovia, 7, 8, 10
Self-determination, 145, 150, 174
Silence, 63, 66–70
Sobrino, Jon, 64, 71
Socialist, 131
Solidarity, 1, 3–5, 9, 14, 22, 46, 47, 132, 133, 138, 141, 161, 162, 172, 173, 181
Soteriology, 62, 108, 120, 124, 130, 134, 135, 137, 140, 141
Soto, Pedro Juan, 24, 47, 62, 107, 120, 134, 138
Spirituality, 149, 151, 167, 168
Statehood, 5
Stevens-Arroyo, Anthony, 9

Suffering, 12, 16, 62, 64, 66, 69–71, 108, 117, 119–122, 124–127, 129–131, 133–137, 155, 159, 164–168, 170, 171, 173, 177
Sugar, 26, 27, 29, 31, 34, 37, 52, 150, 152, 157
Sweet Diamond Dust, 144, 174

T
Taíno, 24, 25, 30, 35, 48
Traverzo, David, 10, 19

U
U.S. military, 2, 3
U.S. Navy, 2–5
United States, 21, 22, 27, 28, 30–32, 34–37, 39–41, 45–47, 50–52, 54–59
Usmaíl, 108, 116–120, 138, 139

V
Valcarcel, Emilio Díaz, 107
de Vásquez, Margot Arce, 143
Velázquez, Nydia, 42
Vieques, 1–6, 13–19, 74, 102, 116–120, 162, 164
Villafañe, Eldin, 22, 47, 50

W
Water, 149, 150, 154, 156–158, 160, 171

Y
Young Lords, 42, 44, 45, 48, 55, 57, 58

CPSIA information can be obtained
at www.ICGtesting.com
Printed in the USA
LVOW05*1048260917
550110LV00009B/19/P